SECRETS OF

The Pie Place Café

RECIPES & STORIES THROUGH THE SEASONS

BY KATHY RICE

Lake Superior
Port Cities Inc.

First Edition: June 2016

Lake Superior Port Cities Inc.
P.O. Box 16417
Duluth, Minnesota 55816-0417 USA
888-BIG LAKE (888-244-5253)

5 4 3 2 1

Library of Congress Cataloging-in-Publication Data

Rice, Kathy, 1951-
    Secrets of the Pie Place Café : recipes & stories through the seasons /
    by Kathy Rice. – First edition.
         pages cm
    Includes index
    ISBN 978-1-938229-32-9
    1. Cooking, American – Midwestern style. 2. Dinners and dining – Minnesota – Grand Marais.
    3. Seasonal cooking – Minnesota – Grand Marais. 4. Pie Place Café (Grand Marais, Minn.)
    I. Title.
    TX715.2.M53 R5323 2016
    641.5977 – dc23   2016009609

Editors: Konnie LeMay, Ann Possis, Barb LeMasurier
Design: Tanya Bäck
Cover images: Mary Beams, Kathy Rice and Karin Holen.
Printer: Friesens, printed in Canada

For Cheryl …

Still here.

The Journey Continues

What a joy to return to the creative process of publishing another cookbook for The Pie Place Café with people whom we've come to think of as friends.

When I called Paul and Cindy Hayden at *Lake Superior Magazine* and Lake Superior Port Cities Inc. to see if they would be interested in publishing our second cookbook, I was met with Cindy's warm and enthusiastic response: "Can you meet with us sometime in the next couple of weeks?"

I was delighted!

Our friends at *Lake Superior Magazine* have become such an important part of our life. They are people who have believed in me, encouraging me to continue writing the stories of restaurant life and about the guests we've had the privilege to serve and love. They've taken my vision and made it more than I could have imagined.

It seems that I learn something from my editor, Konnie LeMay, every day. She's a wellspring of creativity and inspiration, gently guiding me to bring my words to life on the page. "We want the folks reading your stories to feel included in the narrative," she once advised. I knew then that we spoke the same language.

The staff, Siiri Branstrom, Barb LeMasurier, Amy Larsen and all the rest, lend their professionalism and creative expertise to the publishing process. In addition, they are warm, friendly folks that we can't wait to sit down to share a cup of coffee and a scone with and catch up on what's happening in their (and our) lives.

Then, of course, there are our guests at The Pie Place Café, a continued source of inspiration. They are the voices within my stories. As I've always told them, "Without you, there wouldn't be a cookbook."

Me enjoying a farmers' market bounty, like the bushels of apples, facing page. (photos by Karin Holen)

I am ever grateful, too, for my family. We've traveled far together, our life a shared vision of serving others and creating a world in which the most important thing is love. Each person brings all that they are to the creative process of our culinary life as a restaurant family. Like a homemade pie, each slice is critical to the whole.

A special "Thank You" goes to Clare Shaw. As with our first cookbook, Clare has stood by me, steadfast in typing recipes and deciphering my many notations to make the recipes clear, concise and easy to follow. It's an arduous task, one that has freed me to focus on the creative aspect of writing. She is yet another person without whom I couldn't have done this book.

It hardly seems possible that it's been six years since our beloved Cheryl Polson passed on – perhaps because we feel her presence with us every day. Cheryl's vision and inspiration for regional home-cooked food with a gourmet flair lives on in the pages of this cookbook. She believed that sharing good food brings people together, nourishing them body and soul. She believed that food made with love has the power to heal.

This is the essence of our experience as a restaurant family.

And so I felt Cheryl often by my side, guiding me as she always has, while this cookbook was written. Her final words remain forever my inspiration and philosophy: "The only way through this is love."

Every day that simple, essential truth reminds me of what's truly important. Those who walk with us make this journey called Life so much richer.

Thank you all for taking this journey with me.

Summer's day at Artists' Point. (photo by Phil Bencomo)

Contents

Introduction: Seasons

"To everything there is a season . . ."

Outside my window, the brilliant leaves of autumn rain from the trees, piles swirling around the ground that far too soon will be covered with newly fallen snow. Until then, I savor this season, one of my favorites.

Cheryl always teased me about my "autumnal vignettes" as I eagerly gathered crab apples, lustrously colored fall leaves, pumpkins and assorted squashes to adorn our tables in the restaurant and at home. Add a few beeswax candles, and a mood was created. I just can't seem to help myself; it makes me happy!

Another summer is behind us with its memories of lupines adorning the roadsides, of adults and children strolling the rocky shore of Lake Superior or skipping stones over its glassy surface, of hiking trails that weave their magic throughout the boreal forest and of picnic baskets filled to the brim with summer fare. Summer, after all, isn't summer without homemade blueberry pie (for me at least). Add a dollop of homemade ice cream and life really is good.

Some folks grow sad with the quietus ending of another summer, but for me, the passing of one season brings anticipation of all the next one has to offer – especially of its flavors and foods. It's probably

Lupines along Devil Track Road. (photo by SteveOrtmann.com)

no accident that each "season" adds its own "seasoning" to what's on the table.

Spring gifts us with wild mushrooms sprouting from moist earth, perfect to flavor homemade pasta or simply to sauté in a cast-iron skillet with lots of fresh sweet butter. It brings memories of a home-raised chicken, roasted until crispy and golden brown and surrounded with new potatoes and early vegetables. If you're lucky enough to have a rhubarb patch, a flaky pie can delight eager guests.

Summer yields fresh garden produce, tender salad greens, ruby red tomatoes. If there is a fisherman in your family, a fresh catch likely will grace your summer table. For those willing to endure the pollinating blackflies, the forest provides buckets of wild blueberries, perfect for a pie or scones.

Late summer most places – or early fall here – heralds the harvest of potatoes, squash, onions, beans and root vegetables for stews and cassoulets – the perfect dish to savor in front of the fire on those first frosty nights. And who can imagine autumn days without apples and pumpkins fashioned into warm desserts?

Winter brings piles of snow, at least in the place that we call home. Out come the winter coats, boots and mittens … and the food that "sticks to your ribs" and warms your tummy. There's savory meats roasting in the oven, mashed potatoes and gravy, warm home-baked bread from the oven and slathered with butter to set beside mugs of steamy soup.

What's on our table reflects the season as surely as the natural world unfolding around us.

As a restaurant family we always loved the changing of the seasons, and the new flavors that each imparts. Our seasonal menus at The Pie Place Café were meant to say, "We are here together. Let us celebrate all that is good, true and beautiful."

This philosophy has been true for us since the beginning. We took over our first restaurant, the Pie Place on the hill at the edge of town in 1996 and moved in 2011 to our downtown location, The Pie Place Café and Harbor Inn, and will continue with our newest incarnation as a bakery this year, in 2016.

In our first cookbook, you came to know our neighbors and friends in the stories we shared. Relationships are key in our small lakeshore community. What better way to build relations than to sit down with friends and share a home-cooked meal? Because of the restaurant, I've been blessed to have more than my share of good friends and so many stories in this book reflect that bounty.

On these pages of our second cookbook, you will find the story of the seasons we've spent together for 20 years. You'll also find more of the recipes that you loved best in our café and that we hope become favorites in your home. We've even revealed a few held in secret until now.

For those who have visited, as you prepare these time-tested recipes, perhaps you'll remember our stories of the moments shared and will feel them in your heart, too. As you serve them at your table, we know that you'll be creating your own special memories with the ones you love.

Spring Samplings

Visitors at the end of Artists' Point. (photo by Phil Bencomo)

The Guy with the Red Suspenders

Having served the friendly folks of Grand Marais for nearly 20 years in our restaurants, we've grown to know their varied appetites and favored foods. It got so that with some folks, we didn't even need to ask. We'd walk to the table, writing down what they always had, and read it to them with confidence before they even ordered.

Case in point: Howard Sivertson and his lively family.

You know when Howard, wife, Elaine, and their happy brood arrive; laughter fills the room. They genuinely enjoy each other's company. Animated conversation flows like a waterfall spilling over sun-warmed rocks.

The Sivertsons love eating breakfast together, a hungry crowd that might require two or three tables. But hey, the more the merrier. It was fun to be their server, too, drawn into discussions of art, nature, politics, environmental issues, happenings in Grand Marais, Lake Superior and the world at large. Their energy and imagination spill over into every aspect of their life.

Howard, born to an Isle Royale fishing family, spent every summer in his youth on the island, experiencing a commercial fishing life first hand. His grandparents immigrated from Norway in 1892, living on Isle Royale until they passed away.

Liz, Elaine, Howard and Jan pose for a family portrait in 2001. (photo by Paul L. Hayden)

Howard's father and uncle started the Sivertson Brothers Fishery and Grand Portage/Isle Royale Transportation Line, continuing the traditional ways of the Isle Royale fishing culture.

Though the life of a fishing family was rigorous, the beauty of the island created a love and respect for nature. Its inhabitants inspire Howard to this day. Being part of a hard-working, yet fun-loving, family shaped his personality and attitude toward life.

And life wasn't all hard work. As Howard said in his book, *Once Upon an Isle*, "The island was a Huck Finn paradise where we were never bored."

Raised among fisherfolk on Lake Superior, Howard had a different dream. He wanted to be an artist.

After graduating with an art degree, he worked as a graphic artist in Duluth for 25 years before moving to a cabin in the woods, determined to follow his dream of being a fine-arts painter.

Hundreds of paintings and five books later, Howard is indeed a renowned artist, historian and storyteller, chronicling the history of commercial fishing and early life on Isle Royale and Lake Superior. Howard's vibrant work brings his stories to life and piques the imagination.

You can't walk through a Sivertson family gathering without bumping into an artist. Elaine paints exquisite watercolor landscapes. His children – Jan, Liz and Jeff – inherited creative genes, though the daughters became artists and the son followed his grandfather into commercial fishing.

Jan, a batik artist, owns and operates Sivertson Gallery in Grand Marais and Siivis Gallery in Duluth. The galleries feature an eclectic mix of art forms and specialize in local and regional art, as well as Inuit carvings and stone prints.

Found in the galleries are works by daughter Liz, a spirited artist who creates whimsical paintings with

North Shore themes. She's also a musician who plays the saxophone with wild abandon as part of "The Sivertones."

But … back to breakfast.

The whole family loved our Voyageur Breakfast – our famous maple sausage patties, two fluffy pancakes, two eggs any style and breakfast potatoes.

Every Sivertson ordered this breakfast; the only distinguishing difference was egg preference. So a server could write "Voyageur Breakfast" once, followed by a culinary sidebar of "over-easy," "scrambled," "over-medium," and "basted."

For this family, the "Voyageur" seemed so right. After all, Howard has written all those stories and brushed all of those paintings depicting those voyageurs of the past.

Yes, you could count on three things when the Sivertsons arrived for breakfast – laughter, multiple orders of "Voyageurs" and a talented, humble head of the clan clad in a flannel shirt and trademark bright red suspenders. His ready smile and zest for life spread far beyond just family.

The secret, of course, is that we "knew" Howard long before we ever met him. Howard's stories and paintings are one reason that we moved to Grand Marais two decades ago. Mary Lear, a pastel artist, loved his work, and a Howard original now hangs in a place of honor above our fireplace.

The way we figured it after reading his books, if there were folks like Howard living in this little lakeside village, it was the perfect place for us.

We were right.

Howard portrays Isle Royale life in "T'Dora's Rock Garden."

our secret recipe

Pie Place Breakfast Potatoes

This beloved recipe was part of our Voyageur Breakfast, and now we'd love to share it with you. Creamy and flavorful, our Breakfast Potatoes are featured every year at the Steam Bent Brunch hosted by the North House Folk School, where North House Executive Director Greg Wright always says with gusto: "There's nothing like the Pie Place Breakfast Potatoes!"

Serves 10 to 12

Amount	Ingredients
1 (30-ounce) package	frozen shredded hash brown potatoes, thawed
1 (16-ounce) carton	sour cream
1 (10.75-ounce) can	cream of celery soup, undiluted
1 cup	shredded cheddar cheese
1/2 cup	pimientos, chopped
1/2 cup	butter, melted
1 teaspoon	salt
1/2 teaspoon	coarsely ground pepper
1/2 cup	panko or bread crumbs

Instructions

Preheat oven to 350° F.

Combine the hash browns, sour cream, soup, cheese, pimientos, butter, salt and pepper into a large bowl: stir well. Spoon the mixture into a lightly greased 9x13x2-inch baking dish. Sprinkle with panko crumbs. Bake for 55 minutes or until bubbly and lightly golden brown.

Chef's note: On request, we'd put a serving on the griddle for extra crispness.

(photo by Jeremy Chase)

Blue Moose & Friends

Are neighbors a thing of the past?

Perhaps we are too busy trying to keep up with this fast-paced, technological world to take a breath and connect with those we love. Perhaps we have forgotten what it's like to have a friendly chat over the fence, to sit on a porch swing sharing a glass of iced tea, or to have a neighborhood barbecue.

Perhaps where you live, but fortunately, not in Grand Marais.

Here our neighbors are still our friends. We depend on them when the going gets rough, and we trust them to depend on us, too. We bring them chicken soup when they are under the weather. They loan us their chainsaw when that huge tree falls down in the yard. They help us

The Blue Moose garden center and gift shop. (photo by Kathy Rice)

thaw our frozen pipes, and we take time to listen and offer words of comfort when their problems seem insurmountable.

Our neighbors, Bill and Maribeth Doucette, have been such friends to The Pie Place Café family. For years, they came to the Pie Place on the hill for dinner after a long day of work.

In waiting on these gregarious folks, it didn't take long for a friendship to develop. We talked of everyday things, laughing and sharing the tales of life on the North Shore.

Bill, affectionately known as Billy D, worked at Lutsen Mountains and hired Josh, then chef at the Pie Place, to teach skiing. They became fast friends, and Bill was a father figure to Josh. Bill, Josh and Jeremy, another member of our family, began to play music gigs together – Josh on drums, Jeremy on guitar and Billy D on keyboard and doing vocals. They played classic rock – Eagles, Van Morrison, Credence Clearwater Revival and a "Proud Mary" rendition that rocked the stage.

Bill and Maribeth, a local girl, owned and operated the Snuggle Inn, a bed and breakfast in Grand Marais. Eventually the couple bought some property just down from the Pie Place on the hill. The parcel of land contained several cabins, which they proceeded to renovate.

They turned a building on the site into a gallery and gift shop of American craft and art. The hardworking duo then added a greenhouse and garden shop. The Blue Moose was born.

Maribeth, an innovative person and master gardener, began to cast her magic, planting tiered gardens of perennial flowers and herbs. Bill rolled up his sleeves, as only he does, building stone terraces and borders.

Back at the Pie Place, our family was engaged in our own renovations. Like anyone who buys an older building on the North Shore can attest, they come with myriad problems – inadequate plumbing, electrical jerry-rigging that would make an electrician shudder and foundations that shift with the coming and going of winter frost.

More often than I'd like to admit in those early days, our restaurant pipes would freeze, bursting at the most inopportune moments, as we'd discover when water seeped through ceiling tiles into the dining room.

One frosty winter night as Bill and Maribeth were enjoying dinner, water began to drip mysteriously onto their table. I stared in horror as the drip became a steady stream.

Bill, knowing exactly what was going on, stood, rolled up his sleeves and left his half-eaten meal behind, asking, "Do you have a tool box?"

Before you knew it, Bill and Josh had fixed the pipe. Our friend and plumbing savior would not hear of getting a new plate of food. He returned to his cold plate and declared, "It still tastes great!"

Maribeth and Bill by Lake Superior. (photo courtesy Bill Doucette) Our first customers, in photo below, Pastor Dale & Billy D. (photo by Mary Beams)

Many years, and many burst pipes and drywall repairs later, Bill and Maribeth faced their own challenges.

Our dear Maribeth was diagnosed with breast cancer. Just months later, Bill was discovered to have a rare leukemia requiring a bone-marrow transplant. They battled their illnesses, but couldn't care for each other, let alone open the Blue Moose or tend their cabins. It was time for some neighborliness to support a couple who helped so many others. Meals were cooked and delivered; friends took turns sitting by bedsides providing care and a listening ear.

Pastor Dale McIntire, minister of the Cornerstone Baptist Church, his wife, Linda, other clergy and friends contacted area churches to ask for help. Scores came to the Blue Moose, unpacking crates of garden pots, trees, flowers and gift items to open the gallery and garden center on time. They organized shifts, volunteering to keep the shop attended. Pastor Dale took the helm, selling flowers and greeting customers with a smile. He gave updates to all queries about our friends and passed on well wishes in return.

Pastor Dale's demonstration of love in action, week after week, was clear for all who had eyes to see. Here was a man who truly walked the talk.

As neighbors helped with the shop, Bill and Maribeth struggled with their illnesses. Sadly, our dear friend Maribeth passed away; it was hard to let her go. Bill recovered, and, though his path to healing has been slow, he lives today as he always has. Still present to those in need of assistance, he rolls up his sleeves, as is his way.

Are neighbors a thing of the past? They still live in the heart of our remote northern village.

All you have to do is look around. There is always someone you can help, and chances are, when you need it most someone will help you, too.

That's why on the first day we opened the doors at our new Pie Place Café/Harbor Inn location, we probably should have known who would be the first customers through our doors, helping us to launch our new venture.

It was our true neighbors, Billy D and Pastor Dale.

"Inasmuch as ye have done it unto one of the least of these my brethren, ye have done it unto me."
– Gospel of Matthew, 25:40

Pie Place Pecan Chicken

Our famous Pecan Chicken is dipped in a creamy honey Dijon sauce, dredged in finely chopped pecans and baked to perfection. Drizzle the moist and delicious chicken with more of the sauce, serve with rice, and you have a meal worth remembering.

Serves 4 to 6

Amount	Ingredients
2 cups	honey Dijon mustard
1/2 cup	parsley, chopped
1/2 teaspoon	garlic salt
1/4 teaspoon	salt
1-1/2 cups	pecans, chopped medium fine
4 to 6 breasts	chicken, boneless and skinless

Sauce to serve with chicken:

1 cup	honey Dijon mustard
1/16 teaspoon	garlic powder
1/4 cup	sherry
For garnish	parsley sprig

Instructions

Preheat oven to 375° F.

Put 2 cups honey Dijon mustard in a shallow bowl, blend in chopped parsley, garlic salt and salt and set aside. Chop pecans in a food processor, pulsing until medium fine, place in another shallow bowl and set aside.

Place chicken breasts between wax paper or plastic wrap and pound with a kitchen mallet (or bottom of a small saucepan) until flat, but not too thin.

Dip the flattened chicken breasts into mustard mixture, coating both sides. Dip in chopped pecans coating both sides. Place on baking sheet lined with parchment paper (to prevent chicken from sticking and for easy cleanup).

Bake chicken breasts in the preheated oven for 20 to 25 minutes, watching carefully so pecans don't get too brown.

While chicken is baking make the sauce for serving. In a small saucepan, combine sauce ingredients, whisking until smooth. Heat gently, until sauce is reduced and slightly thickened, about 15 minutes.

When ready to plate the chicken, place 3 Tablespoons of warmed sauce on each plate, swirling to create a thin layer. Lay the chicken breast on the sauce and drizzle the top with a bit more sauce. Garnish with a sprig of fresh parsley.

Bronze Age, Iron Man

The creative spark, once ignited, will have its way.

A story lives inside of you, so you write the first words on a page.

Your passion is pies, so you pull a cookbook off the shelf and try your hand at making dough.

For anything that you can imagine, just walk through the fear and take the first step.

People create because they must, because the urge is so strong that they have no other choice.

Just ask Tom Christiansen, a local sculptor who works in bronze at his foundry and studio gallery, Last Chance Fabricating.

As a young college art student, Tom fell hard for bronze casting after visiting a foundry and seeing the molten metal take shape.

He studied with noted sculptor Wayne Potratz at the University of Minnesota. Tom later became a bronze sculptor in his own right, taking on large commissions and selling his work in galleries in Arizona, Minnesota and Pennsylvania.

When we first arrived in the area, Tom's studio was housed in a small, dilapidated old building in Lutsen. Still, he pounded away, happily creating the whimsical sculptures for which he is now known. He continues to work with bronze, but also has adopted iron works, which reflects the rich red geological history of this region.

Along with the humor, there is a deep spirituality in Tom's work. Eager to mentor young people, he also enjoys passing on the wealth of information that he has gleaned in more than 50 years as an artist.

Tom and his wife, Marcia Hyatt, frequently visited at The Pie Place Café over the years and were avid customers at our Northern Impulses gallery. As often happens, it wasn't long before they evolved from guests into friends as we grew to know them well.

One Christmas after visiting Tom's gallery and buying gifts there, we had an impulse to see if he would help us create a Tibetan bowl as a gift for Cheryl.

Tom, ever the enthusiastic teacher, patiently helped us through the steps required to prepare for the actual casting.

When the day for the pour arrived, we packed a picnic lunch and a freshly baked blueberry pie, Tom's favorite, and headed for Lutsen.

The awesome experience of the pour was exciting. Our chef Josh became mesmerized as he helped Tom pour the molten bronze into our resin-bonded sand mold.

Afterward, we went to Tom and Marcia's home on Lake Superior for lunch, to talk and to wait for the bronze to cool.

A few hours later, we removed a bronze bowl from the sand mold – our internal impulse made into reality.

Cheryl was blown away by what we had accomplished, looking at

Tom, left, and Josh pour a bronze casting. (photo by Kathy Rice)

photographs that I had taken of the process from beginning to end. Though our Tibetan bowl was less than perfect, she didn't care. It was the process – and our love for her – that mattered most.

Now, years later, Tom still works at the foundry and still displays his spirit-filled pieces.

But we've created a new twist to the story.

Josh is doing an apprenticeship with Tom and has developed into an eager student. I think the two of them are good for each other.

It's said that when the student is ready, the teacher appears, and this match does seem made in heaven.

Who knows what will happen when you follow an impulse. Sometimes it takes years for the real reason to be revealed.

Friend and basketmaker, Judy Johnson, put it quite eloquently: "Josh went from one fire to another. From the fire of a chef preparing food, into the fire as an apprentice working with Tom."

Could we say from the frying pan into the fire?

Yes … I think we could.

Tom's sculptural take on "the God of Metal." (photo by Kathy Rice)

Curry Egg Salad

After having The Pie Place Café curry egg salad, Tom was hooked. An egg salad sandwich with a pungent twist and a bit of crunch, you, too, will want to serve it again and again.

Serves 4

Amount	Ingredients
1/3 cup	mayonnaise (We recommend Hellmann's)
1/2 teaspoon	Dijon mustard
1-1/2 teaspoons	curry powder
1/4 teaspoon	salt
1/8 teaspoon	pepper
6 large	eggs, hard-boiled and chopped
1/4 cup	walnuts, chopped

Instructions

Whisk mayonnaise, Dijon mustard, curry powder, salt and pepper together and set aside.

Hard-boil the eggs by placing in a medium pot of water, bringing it to a boil and then lowering the heat to simmer to cook for 12 minutes. Drain eggs and peel immediately while still warm. Dice in uniform 1/2-inch pieces.

Place chopped eggs and walnuts in a small bowl and mix in dressing incrementally. Add more mayonnaise if it's too dry. Chill it for one hour before serving.

Pounding Out a Life

The old building sits empty, a broken window pane letting shafts of light create dusty beams to the dirt floor.

As I peek through the window, my mind hears the clang of metal on metal and sees decades-gone sparks fly. Hammer on anvil forms a horseshoe, expertly fitted on an unsuspecting horse, or bends a wagon wheel back into working shape.

In the Bally Blacksmith Shop, three generations of Bally men served Grand Marais for 98 years, from 1911 to 2009.

Bill Bally, a third-generation blacksmith, learned the craft from his father. We came to know him as a Pie Place Café customer, quiet, but with twinkling eyes, who would fix a coffee machine or weld a dish rack, asking only a piece of pie or an early evening supper as pay. This craftsman also had an artistic side and made the "fish" deck chairs at the Angry Trout Café.

We came, too, to know his wife, Karen, who also grew up in Grand Marais, descended from the Holtes, an Isle Royale fishing family. Her grandfather began fishing in the 1880s. Her parents made a life as a commercial fishing family, living on Wright Island in summer and wintering in Grand Marais so Karen could go to school.

Resourceful fishing families made everything they needed – sailboats, buoys and wooden floats (called "corks"), net reels, nets and even the family cabin and fish and net houses. Any materials at hand might be fashioned into crude, but serviceable, furniture.

Karen's mother wrote a memoir, *Ingeborg's Isle Royale*, documenting the harsh life of the hearty Swedish fishermen and their families and also revealing the joys of growing up among the island creatures and delighting in the beauty of that remote, wild place.

The isolation and solitude of Karen's summers on Isle Royale created the person she would become. She had to find ways to entertain herself, learning to paint and garden. As a young girl who loved words, she started a lifelong habit of talking to herself aloud.

With a degree in counseling, Karen also loved art and beautiful objects. She stopped by our art gallery, Northern Impulses, nearly every day for a chat, often leaving with something that caught her eye. On one

visit Karen gave me a copy of her mother's book. I read it cover to cover that very night, drawn into the magic of Isle Royale and its inhabitants, human and otherwise.

After growing up in Grand Marais, Bill and Karen were married, living in the house that had belonged to Bill's parents, and renovating it for use as a bed-and-breakfast inn. Every day as regular as clockwork, the industrious couple would come to the Pie Place on the hill for an early supper. Often their clothes were paint-spattered and bits of old wallpaper clung to the bottom of their shoes. (Renovation of the home went on for years as the couple painstakingly restored the "Bally House.")

Bill and Karen enjoyed this simple daily routine, a time to unwind after a hard day's work. We reserved "their table" and looked forward to hearing Karen's detailed account of the day's progress. Bill would simply smile, sip his coffee and add an occasional nod or "Yup!"

Karen selected lamps, paintings, pillows and furniture from our gallery for the B&B. Bill came to shop, too – whenever he needed a gift for Karen.

Bill's and Karen's lives are a part of the legacy of our small town – creative folks whose parents and grandparents worked long and hard to help build our community.

In 1986, Bill worked with the Cook County Historical Society to put the Bally Blacksmith Shop on the National Register of Historic Places. He intended to preserve the history of the family business and honor those whose hard work and ingenuity shaped the community that he loved.

Bill and Karen, thumbs up to the good life. (Bally family photo)
Facing page: The blacksmith shop awaits a renewed life. (left photo by Paul L. Hayden; right by Kathy Rice)

Bill passed away in 2010 and was followed two years later by his partner in life, Karen.

I miss the conversations we used to have in those early days of our restaurant and gallery. I learned a lot about those early folks who came to Grand Marais to build a life for themselves and their families. I am grateful for the stories told and received.

Our community has joined together with the Cook County Historical Society to renovate and restore the Bally Blacksmith Shop, one of only two historic blacksmith shops remaining in Minnesota. It is a legacy to share with generations to come. Bill would be amused and happy at our enthusiasm, I think.

One day as I was going into the Cook County Co-op I heard the clanging of metal and the sound of a hammer on wood.

Inquisitive, I walked across the street to the blacksmith shop peering into the dark, dusty space through the open door.

Renovation had begun as pieces of old scrap metal were being tossed out the back door and onto an ever-growing pile.

I asked if I could go in for a few minutes and look around.

As I stood in the dusty haze of the place, old tools hanging on rusty nails and an anvil still sitting where it may have been nearly a hundred years ago, the clang of a hammer on red hot iron formed in my imagination, the energy of the place still alive.

I felt a knowing deep inside of me of how this place had been an integral part of the community in which I now live.

Bill's father, and grandfather before him, had pounded out a life among these blackened walls, meeting a vital need in this remote community.

Preserving all of this seems worth the time, effort and hard work required. It is something that both Bill and Karen's families understood.

I want to be a part of the restoration. It seems a perfect way to honor two people whose lives have touched ours. That is the real legacy, after all.

Japanese Peanut Noodle Salad

This piquant, flavorful Asian pasta salad is a favorite with our guests, and we promised we'd feature it in our second cookbook. Once you serve it, this salad also will become a favorite with your family and friends.

Serves 4 to 6

Amount	Ingredients
Dressing:	
3 Tablespoons	peanut oil
1/4 teaspoon	chili powder
1/2 cup	soy sauce (we prefer Kikkoman as it's less salty)
1/2 to 3/4 cup	peanut butter (smooth blends best)
3 Tablespoons	sugar (may need to add more to balance ginger root)
3 Tablespoons	sesame oil
3 Tablespoons	rice wine vinegar
1 to 2 Tablespoons	fresh ginger root, finely grated (season to taste, needs to be peppy)
1 large clove	garlic, put through a garlic press or finely chopped
Salad:	
1 pound	Somen noodles or thin spaghetti
2 large	carrots, slivered
4 to 6	scallions, sliced
1 cup	unsalted peanuts

Instructions

For the dressing, mix the chili powder into the peanut oil to create a "chili oil." Place the chili oil and all other ingredients into a food processor. Pulse gently until well blended. The peanut butter tends to make the dressing thick. You can thin with water, but don't overdo it. You don't want to alter the balance of flavors and it should cling to the pasta.

For the salad, cook the pasta per package directions, being careful not to overcook. While pasta is cooking, sliver carrots and slice green onions, using the white and green parts for color. Set them aside.

(photo by Mary Beams)

Once the pasta is done, drain immediately and rinse in cold water to stop the cooking process. You don't want mushy pasta. Place the pasta in a large mixing bowl, gently folding in the peanut dressing, adding it incrementally to your desired amount and stirring gently to coat. You can serve immediately. Use remaining dressing as a nice dollop on top of the salad. Then sprinkle with the slivered carrots, sliced onions and peanuts.

Chef's note: If you don't have a garlic press, splurge. You'll use it all the time, especially for dressings.

The Doll Lady

The lure of Lake Superior is strong, its energy drawing people from far and wide.

Many seek solace sitting on its rocky shores, gazing toward the endless horizon. One Pie Place guest, a poet from Wisconsin, shared that she had come to spend time near Lake Superior to write about her 20-year-old son, who had died in a sailing accident.

"I haven't been able to write about the experience, and the deep loss I feel, until now. Coming here and spending time by the lake has helped me to heal. It has allowed me to begin to let him go."

Other people come to Grand Marais to get recharged, to escape the hectic pace of city life. They go home more centered and creative, better able to face what awaits them. Jan Williamson, a Pie Place customer for many years, brings such a story.

Jan's father came to the United States from

Jan with some of her dolls (mine is on the left).
(photo by Kathy Rice)

Denmark in 1913 at age 19. He had lived in a small village close to the sea, and it was a part of him. It was no surprise, then, that he felt the tug of Lake Superior, and he made yearly trips to Grand Marais and the surrounding area. The water soothed his longing for the sea and gave inspiration to this man.

He began to bring his young daughter, Jan, up north, instilling in her his love of this vast inland sea. Jan grew up surrounded by art and creativity, nurtured by her artistic father, a poet who loved to work with wood. He made clocks and carved intricate, beautiful chess sets.

Jan became an artist, too, delighting in all the world as inspiration. She merges "found" objects into her art, passionately blending color and texture.

Her soulmate (or "my big bear" as she says), her husband, Ron, created a studio in which she gathers her materials and fashions fascinating artwork. She has envisioned, and brought to life, dolls of vintage fabric, hand-dyed lace, curly mohair sheep fleece, antique buttons, carved pewter and bone faces and even slices of antlers discovered in the local woods.

Each doll tells its own story to Jan about who it is and from where it comes. The spirit of these creations enchants me, and I'm always excited to see what new things Jan is creating.

Jan brought her newest work whenever she came for lunch. Once, after she suggested materials that she wanted, I came across some intriguing antler pieces. Perfect for arms, I thought.

Thrilled with my find, she incorporated them into her designs and brought new dolls to show me. A generous, loving person, Jan gifted me with my very own doll, Nyree, who lives in a cabin in the forest, where the trees have crept close to the Big Lake's shore. As Jan reveals: "She may sometimes be spotted amidst the trees, or on the rocky shore, gathering pine cones here, a gull's feather there and bits of colorful moss and lichen to bedeck her window sills, where the spiders are welcome to spin their homes as well."

"My dolls have a life of their own," Jan once explained. "They tell me their story, and how they emerge is really up to them."

Jan's story will forever include Lake Superior. She says it's in her soul, one that she inherited from her Danish father and like him, she finds the North Shore is her "heart place."

If you listen carefully, you, too, may hear the heartbeat of the waves and find yourself inspired by them, as Jan's father, Jens Jacob Christiansen, was for the poem he wrote that's so dear to his daughter:

I like to be near Lake Superior's shore
When bolts of lightning are cleaving the sky
When winds are howling and breakers roar
And its foam and vapors are tossed up high
The rhythm of the waves, the rise and the fall
The fierce assault on the high rocky wall
Is one of the grandest of Nature's sights
And one that has given me untold delights.
Against tempest and waves unholy alliance
The igneous rocks stand in silent defiance
As if to say "You are wasting your ire
For we, we are born of volcanic fire!
Immersed in white heat and baptized in flame
Besides, we were here long before you came
Think not we will yield, the answer is Never"
So the old feud goes on, forever and ever.

Chicken Cashew Pasta Salad

This chicken pasta salad, creamy and delicious, has long been a favorite with our guests. Cayenne pepper adds punch, and the salted cashews an unexpected crunch.

Serves 4 to 6

Amount	Ingredients
3 to 4 breasts	chicken, boneless and skinless
1 to 2 Tablespoons	butter
1 pound	bowtie pasta
1/2 small	red onion, diced
3 cups	shredded cheddar cheese
1 (10-ounce) can	salted cashews

Dressing:
1 cup mayonnaise
  (we prefer Hellmann's)
1 cup sour cream
1/4 teaspoon garlic salt
1/4 teaspoon Cayenne pepper
1 (8-ounce) carton half-and-half

Combine above and whisk until smooth. Dressing should not be too thick. Thin slightly with more half-and-half if needed.

Instructions

Sauté chicken breasts in butter on medium heat until golden brown and completely cooked through, about 3-5 minutes per side, depending upon thickness. Cool and dice into 1/2-inch pieces. Cook pasta according to package directions, drain and rinse in cold water. Do not overcook pasta.

Combine chicken, pasta, diced red onion and shredded cheddar, adding dressing to moisten mixture. Chill for one hour and then stir in cashews just before serving.

Mushrooming with Auntie Fred

Hundreds of people come from all over the United States and across the world to teach or to take classes at the North House Folk School in humble Grand Marais.

Thanks to our partnership and friendship with the wonderful folks at the North House, and because we happened to own a local eatery, we've been privileged to serve and make friends with so many of these visitors passionate about passing on and learning traditional northern craft.

Among our favorites is Fred Livesay, a longtime craftsman, North House instructor and friend, who teaches Scandinavian wooden spoon carving. When Fred comes up to the North Shore, he often brings our mutual friends, the Denglers: Tom, Kathryn and young Anja. In his North House classes, Tom demonstrates the Scandinavian craft of making "shrink boxes," a process using green wood.

Both Fred and Tom bring an earthy sensibility and intensity to their crafts. It's always a delight to connect with these creative friends.

Besides their other skills, Fred and Tom are enthusiastic mushroom hunters. On many occasions, they've invited me to accompany them on a foray into the woods to gather whatever varieties are peeking their fungal heads into the sunshine. As a child, I frequently watched my grandfather, father and uncles hunt the elusive morel mushroom and later inhaled their fecund aroma as they browned in an old cast iron skillet. With memories that savory, Fred and Tom never had to twist my arm to join them.

One early morning, I joined Tom, Kathryn and Anja as they sat in the restaurant, warming their hands around mugs of steaming hot chocolate. Our talk turned to mushrooms, and we shared our favorite recipes. Then they told me a wonderful story about Anja and Fred – "Auntie Fred!" corrected Anja, then about 8 years old.

Fred has been part of Anja's life since she was a baby. In many cultures, such a close friend to the family may be considered something of a relative, and that was exactly how Anja felt about her dear companion in all things fun. When she was just learning about familial relations, though, the subtleties of "aunt" and "uncle" eluded her. And so when Anja declared him "Auntie Fred," he didn't have the heart to correct her. He has been her favorite "auntie" from that day forward.

One spring, Tom, Kathryn, Anja and Fred came together to stay in a little cabin tucked away in the boreal forest.

Awaking early, Tom and Kathryn noticed that Anja and Fred were not in their beds. They heard hushed voices outside and peeked through the window to spy two figures clad in red-and-white flannel nightshirts stepping with bare feet gently on fallen pine

All grown up, Anja still likes to go mushrooming with Auntie Fred. (photo by Crystal Liepa)

needles. They bent intently to the dew-covered ground, eagerly searching for mushrooms.

As Tom and Kathryn listened with amusement, the two exclaimed over their finds and discussed strategies for locating more. The couple rose to make coffee and breakfast, waiting for the happy hunters to return inside.

At breakfast, Anja informed them that she and Auntie Fred gathered "fairy ring" mushrooms, which grow in a circle in the forest – a most magical find for a budding young naturalist.

That night they dined on the bounty from the forest, and Anja declared her favorite part of vacation was, of course, mushrooming with Auntie Fred.

Wild Mushroom Lasagna

For those passionate about mushrooms, this is a dish from heaven. If you're lucky enough to have an "Auntie Fred" who will go mushrooming with you, fresh forest mushrooms can be used. We use a dried forest blend, which imparts a wonderfully earthy flavor.

Serves 6

Amount	Ingredients
Mushroom filling:	
3 cups	water
2 ounces	dried porcini mushrooms (or a forest blend of morel, porcini and elephant-ear mushrooms)
2 pounds	fresh white mushrooms
l pound	zucchini (2 large), unpeeled, diced into 1/4-inch cubes
1 large	onion, chopped
3 cloves	garlic, minced
5 Tablespoons	butter
6 Tablespoons	sherry
2 teaspoons	fresh thyme, chopped
1-1/2 teaspoons	salt
1/4 teaspoon	pepper
Sauce:	
8 Tablespoons	butter
1/2 cup	all-purpose flour
5 cups	whole milk
4-1/2 ounces	Parmesan cheese, freshly grated
2 teaspoons	Dijon mustard
1-1/2 teaspoons	salt
To finish:	
18 (7x3-1/2-inch) sheets	dry, no-boil lasagna noodles (about 1 pound)
8 ounces	mozzarella cheese, freshly grated
1-1/2 ounce	Parmesan cheese, freshly grated

Instructions

In a small saucepan bring 3 cups of water to a boil and then remove the pan from heat. Stir in the dried mushrooms and soak 20 minutes. Lift out mushrooms, squeezing out excess liquid. Reserve the soaking liquid. In a sieve rinse mushrooms to remove any grit and pat dry. Chop mushrooms and transfer to a large bowl. Simmer reserved soaking liquid until reduced to about 1/4 cup. Pour liquid through a sieve lined with a dampened paper towel (to remove grit) into the bowl with the mushrooms.

Wash and quarter white mushrooms. In a food processor, pulse in 3 batches until finely chopped. In a 12-inch, heavy skillet, heat 1 Tablespoon butter over moderate heat until foam subsides. Cook one-third of the white mushrooms with 2 Tablespoons sherry, stirring until the liquid from the mushrooms is evaporated and they begin to brown.

Add white mushroom mixture to the reconstituted dried mushrooms. Cook remaining white mushrooms in 2 batches in butter with remaining sherry, in same manner and add to the final mixture.

In a skillet, cook diced zucchini in 1 Tablespoon butter until tender and then stir into mushroom mixture. In skillet, cook chopped onion in the remaining Tablespoon of butter, stirring until softened. Stir in garlic, thyme, salt and pepper and cook, stirring, until fragrant, about 30 seconds. Stir onion mixture into mushroom mixture until combined.

To make the sauce, melt the butter in a 3-quart heavy saucepan over moderately low heat and then whisk in flour. Cook this roux, whisking constantly, 3 minutes and then whisk in milk. Bring sauce to a boil, whisking constantly. Reduce heat and simmer, whisking occasionally, for 3 minutes until thickened. Stir in Parmesan, mustard and salt. Remove pan from heat and cover surface of sauce with wax paper (this keeps sauce from developing a hard skin).

Preheat oven to 375° F.

To assemble the lasagna, butter a 9x13-inch (3-quart) baking dish. Spread 1-1/4 cups of sauce in the baking dish and cover with 3 pasta sheets, making sure the sheets don't touch each other. Spread 1/3 of the mushroom filling over pasta sheets and then top with 3 more pasta sheets, gently pressing down layers to remove air pockets. Top this second set of pasta sheets with 1/3 of the mozzarella. Continue layering in same manner, ending with mozzarella (dish will be filled to the rim). Spread remaining sauce over top and sprinkle with Parmesan.

Place the casserole dish on a foil-lined baking sheet. Bake lasagna in middle of oven until bubbly and golden, about 45 minutes. Let lasagna stand 20 minutes before serving. Serve with a crisp green salad and warm, crusty homemade bread.

Chef's note: The filling and sauce may be made one day ahead, covered individually and refrigerated. If you do this, bring the sauce to room temperature before assembling the dish and baking it.

For the Love of Art

Todd and Karin Holen have a love affair with the North Shore and Grand Marais. As young lovers, they came here to restore, traversing the Superior Hiking Trail in summer, fall and winter.

After an extended courtship, Todd and Karin were married off Sweethearts Bluff Trail. A small, intimate affair, it suited them well.

Todd and Karin return to the North Shore as often as they can and used to always stop at The Pie Place Café for breakfast, lunch or dinner. We have spirited reunions with them on their anniversary, for Karin's birthday or sometimes during one of their quick getaways. We share a love of movies, reading, spiritual pursuits and art. Our conversations can last hours.

Avid collectors of art, they always go home with a painting, pottery (a personal passion of theirs) or with some other locally produced treasure. Todd and Karin frequented our Northern Impulses in its early days and when we continued to sell art and crafts in

Karin and Todd, on the trails, of course. (top photo by Patti Judalena; bottom a Mt. Josephine selfie)

a space above the Pie Place on the hill, they met Mary Lear (Pie Place Café caterer, family member and pastel artist). Mary's fall landscape pastel, just completed, became their anniversary gift to each other – a reminder of the northern forest ablaze with color.

On a trip to the Twin Cities, I got together with Todd and Karin. They took me to one of their favorite Indian restaurants. The distinctive food was fantastic; the conversation even tastier. We just never seem to run out of things to say.

On their visit north in the fall, Todd and Karin invited me to dinner at the cabin they were renting. We spent a companionable evening eating lasagna, drinking good red wine … and, naturally, talking.

Much of our conversation turned to the Crossing Borders Studio Tour, the annual self-guided tour of local artists that they come up for each September. Artists stretching from before the Grand Marais area up to Thunder Bay greet visitors to their studios and galleries, and we've spent wonderful fall afternoons together on the tour.

One of our favorites is Dan and Lee Ross, who own an awesome home and studio on the cliffs of Lake Superior. Potters and sculptors, Dan and Lee fashion clay into animal forms that embody a sense of whimsy, or primal vessels and small sculptures that seem from an earlier time. Their paintings combine paint, clay and fabric.

Karin has immersed herself in pottery for years, taking classes to perfect her skills. Attending the Northern Clay Center in Minneapolis as a student, she now teaches at the center's "ClayToGo" program. She has also worked for Silverwood Park in its "Nature Inspired Art" program and loves working with children. A graphic designer, Karin brings an earthy yet sophisticated touch to her work. Todd, a surveyor and a great cook, has also worked on "the wheel." He and Karin make bowls each year at the Grand Marais Art Colony for Empty Bowls, the community event that raises money to support local food banks.

A talented couple themselves, Todd and Karin find happiness in being surrounded by beautiful art that speaks to them. They have quite a wonderful art collection.

Art is a part of the fabric of their life together.

Karin's birthday is fast approaching. She and Todd will be arriving at the Harbor Inn on Friday. I've invited them to our house for a birthday dinner, and it's clear that they have become a part of the fabric of our life as well.

We can't wait to see them and if I hurry, I'll have this story done by the time they arrive. It will be my present for a perfect birthday.

I think Karin will like that.

(*our secret recipe*)

Pie Place Crab Cakes with Red Pepper Sauce

The first time we served crab cakes at a family dinner it was a warm, summery day. I remember that first bite, sweet with a briny hint of the ocean on my tongue. We loved them then, and our guests at the Pie Place have come back over and over again to savor this seaside delicacy.

Serves 8 to 10

Amount	Ingredients
2 pounds	cooked crab (or use imitation krab, the 90% crab-10% whitefish kind)
1 cup	mayonnaise
2 large	eggs, lightly beaten
1	jalapeño pepper, seeded and finely diced
1/2 cup	scallions or chives, chopped
3/4 cup	fresh red bell pepper, diced finely (get a large pepper and use 3/4 for the crab cakes and 1/4 for the sauce)
1/2 cup	parsley, chopped
1 cup	bread crumbs
To taste	salt and pepper
To sauté	safflower oil, just enough to fill your sauté pan to about 1/4 inch

Instructions

In a large bowl, mix together all the ingredients, tasting it and adjusting the salt and pepper accordingly. Form into patties using a 1/4 cup to measure them out.

Heat oil in a sauté pan on medium-high until slightly bubbly around the sides of the pan. Gently place cake in the oil and cook until crab cake is golden brown and crispy on one side. Then gently turn the cake and cook until it also is brown and crispy. Place on a paper towel to absorb excess oil.

Chef's note: Pie Place Crab Cakes can be prepared and frozen for later. Simply thaw them in the refrigerator before cooking them.

Imitation krab is really very good, just be sure it's 90% crab meat. It saves the time and energy required to cook crab legs, crack and de-vein them and remove the meat. After you've done that several times, which our fingers will attest that we have done, you'll try the imitation and will note very little difference in flavor.

Red Pepper Sauce:
1/4 cup fresh red bell pepper, diced finely
4 Tablespoons butter
1/4 cup all-purpose flour
1 pint half-and-half
To taste salt and pepper

Melt the butter in a pan and sauté the pepper. Add flour, stirring constantly, until you get a creamy paste, then add about a pint of half-and-half, whisking until you get a velvety texture. Season to taste with salt and pepper.

Serve sauce on the side in small ramekins or drizzled over the warm crab cakes.

(photo by Mary Beams)

Sap's Running, Spring Has Sprung

We live in a wild country where large stands of maple trees dot the landscape. Most people think about autumn and those glorious reds, oranges and golds that are gifts of the maple trees before losing their leaves to winter.

But for the Ojibwe people, maples really represent spring. As days grow warm and nights stay cold, the sap of the maples begins to flow. In the past, the Ojibwe people tapped the trees, boiling sap in birch vessels over an open fire, creating maple sugar and maple syrup, important parts of their food supply.

Today sugar bushes, named for the stands of maple, continue. Many folks, Ojibwe and non-Native, tap and boil sap to make syrup for family use, and one family we know off the Caribou Trail has created a livelihood from the maples, making award-winning maple syrup.

We have known the Cordes family – Jim, Marianne, Chris and Kirstin – since 1997, not only as neighbors and friends, but as purveyors who provide The Pie Place Café with the best maple syrup that we have ever tasted.

Those of you who have breakfasted at The Pie Place have poured Wild Country Maple Syrup over your warm, fluffy pancakes. And I can assure you that once you have tasted this maple syrup, you will definitely want to take some home as a tasty reminder of your trip to the North Shore. We even like the bottles, especially the whimsical glass log cabins filled with this northwoods ambrosia.

If you want the full authentic experience, we encourage you to visit the site of where it all happens. Not for the faint of heart, a trip to the maple stand is well worth the drive, even along the little two-track dirt road. It doesn't really matter if it's sugar bush time; the trip is particularly awe-inspiring when the leaves are in full fall color.

When you reach the small, rustic handmade sign pointing the way, you're almost there. The narrow road meanders through the maple forest, a brilliant canopy of leaves around and above you.

At the end of the road is Sawtooth Mountain Maple Syrup Company, where the maple syrup is produced. There's the sugar house where the sap is boiled, the bottling house where the syrup is put into glass bottles (glass being best for the flavor) and a tiny cabin where you can purchase the syrup.

Each part of the process is housed in old Scandinavian log buildings. The Cordes family discovered these original log buildings, moved them to the site and did some reconstruction on them. The buildings, echoes of an earlier time, add to the charm and authenticity of this family business. They are some of the things people love about making a yearly pilgrimage at sugar bush time. The real treasure at the end of the road, though, is maple syrup.

Visit the shop right at the sugar bush site. (photo by Kathy Rice)

If no one is around, don't panic. Keeping a 300+ acre farm of certified organic maples tapped and in proper running order is a full-time job. With more than 24,000 taps, Sawtooth Mountain Maple Syrup Company is the largest certified organic sugar bush in the Midwest.

Feel free to open the door of the cabin store, make your purchase and put your money in the old sap bucket hanging from a peg on the wall. It's how transactions used to be done. Feels really good, doesn't it?

Chris, Kirstin and her husband, Greg Nichols, have big plans for the property. Someday they envision another log building replicating the traditional sugar shack. Folks will be able to come with their children and trek on snowshoes to tapped trees, gathering sap from traditional wooden buckets, to boil into maple syrup. After a day in the forest, doing things in the old way, a family will leave with a bottle of maple syrup that they had a hand in making.

Until then, when the sap's running, and you have a hankering for good old-fashioned maple syrup, take a trip to Sawtooth Mountain Maple Syrup Company or look for Wild Country on a local store shelf.

(*our secret recipe*)

Maple Pecan Pie

The sap's running and our mouths are watering for Maple Pecan Pie. The Cordes family loves this pie. One delicious mouthful and you will, too.

Serves 6

Amount	Ingredients
1/2 recipe	pie dough, next page
1-1/2 cups	chopped pecans
1 cup	light brown sugar
1/4 cup	butter, melted
3 large	eggs
1 cup	maple syrup
	(Wild Country, of course)
1 teaspoon	vanilla
1/4 teaspoon	salt

(photo by Mary Beams)

Instructions

Preheat oven to 375° F.

Roll out the dough into an 11-inch round on a lightly floured surface, using a floured rolling pin, and line a 9-inch pie pan with bottom crust. Crimp edges of pie crust.

Into the unbaked pie crust, spread the 1-1/1 cups of coarsely chopped pecans.

Measure brown sugar into a medium bowl, working out any lumps. Add melted butter and stir to blend well. Add eggs, blending well and dissolving remaining sugar lumps. Add maple syrup, vanilla and salt. Pour into the crimped pie crust.

Bake about 45 minutes. Crust will be golden, filling will be brown and set until just jiggly. Let sit until room temperature before cutting.

Pie Place Pie Crust

Since we were home pie bakers before we became professionals, we have experience with a variety of basic pie dough recipes. We inherited The Pie Place recipe, which seemed pretty well based on Crisco shortening's recipe, but was adapted for larger production. Over the years we've tweaked the recipe to get the best performance from our restaurant pies. Our café recipe would be of little use to the home pie baker because you have much more freedom to experiment. The following is an easy home recipe.

(photo by Kathy Rice)

Assuming you may be new to pies, with the anxiety most first-time pie bakers hold, let me assure you that pie dough is easy and delicious, and it's enjoyable to practice refining dough to your own tastes.

Pie dough consists of flour, shortening, salt and water. It's true that certain conditions make the most tender and flaky crusts, but there is a lot of leeway within those conditions. Chilled shortening, cold water, fluffy flour all contribute to the basic chemistry of coating pellets of shortening with flour, binding them together with a little bit of moisture, rolling the dough flat and even, and counting on the baking to turn the moisture into steam. The flattened pellets, separated by the steam, create flakes of toasty, golden crust.

Though that is the chemistry of pie dough, and interesting to know, release yourself to the artistry of pie baking and allow the experience to be a joyful one. You'll do fine.

Makes enough for a 9-inch, double-crust pie

Amount	Ingredients
1 cup	shortening (or 1/2 cup butter plus 1/2 cup vegetable shortening makes the best combination). Slightly chilled can help in working the crust.
2-1/2 cups	flour
1 teaspoon	salt
1/3 cup	water
	Half-and-half, sugar and nutmeg, for brushing and sprinkling for pies with a top crust

Instructions

Cut the butter into small cubes; whisk the flour and salt together. Add the butter and shortening with a quick, light touch with a pinching motion, using your fingers, until the flour and shortening combine to form pea-size chunks. Add the water, holding back a little, and gently gather the flour mixture around the water until it holds together. Adjust in small increments with flour or more water as you go because the climate and temperature will affect how it all behaves. You want it to get just past

crumbly for the best flavor. The more you handle the dough, the more it will be very solid and not flaky and tender.

When it is the right consistency, divide into two balls, one slightly larger than the other, if you are making one double-crust pie.

Hand form the dough balls into disks about 2 inches thick. Any cracks on the edges will cause irregular shapes when you roll out dough, so make sure the edges of the disk are smooth. Wrap the dough disks in plastic wrap and refrigerate it for at least 1 hour. The dough needs to rest to organize itself into your tasty crust, and needs to be chilled when you roll it.

Have a pie pan ready. The best pans are glass or ceramic. If you are using a disposable tin, lightly grease it. Take out the largest disk, leaving the other in the refrigerator.

Lightly flour your smooth counter surface and your rolling pin, and begin with even strokes to roll the dough. Use one hand as a pivot and the other to swing the pin in an arc. As the disk flattens, turn it frequently so it doesn't stick to the counter. If you roll in only one direction you will get a rectangle; by turning the dough often you will get a circle. As the dough enlarges, keep the end of the pin inside the edge of the dough to avoid making the outside crust edge too thin.

Center the rolled pie dough on the pie plate. Cut off the outer edge of the dough to about 1 inch of overhang, then roll the overhang under so it sits on top of the pie plate edge. If you are making a single-crust pie, you will crimp this by pressing a fork in a pattern around the edge or by pinching around the edge, keeping the crust edge an even thickness.

Preheat oven to 400° F.

To fully bake this single crust, prick the bottom and the sides a bit with a fork to let steam escape. Line the crust with parchment paper weighted with uncooked beans or rice or simply put another empty pie tin (disposable aluminum) atop this crust. Bake in the 400° oven for 15 minutes. Remove the weights, turn the pie crust around and bake for another 10 to 20 minutes, depending on how evenly your oven bakes, and how golden brown you want the crust. It should be golden enough for it to taste toasty, be crispy, flaky and tender. At The Pie Place Café, we put a pie tin on top, weighted with a small beach stone from the beach across the street – one of the many wonderful things about living on the North Shore. As a rule, we don't have a problem with it sticking.

Work the scraps back into the next disk or use the scraps to make "pie cookies" by sprinkling them with cinnamon sugar and baking them for about 15 minutes.

To make a double-crust pie, arrange the bottom crust in the pie pan with a 1-inch crust overhang. Fill with the pie mixture and roll the second disk as you did the first. Make sure it's not too thick; 1/8 inch should be fine. Place it centered over the top of the pie and cut off any excess dough, leaving a 1-inch edge to match the bottom crust. Roll both crusts under along the pan edge and crimp. Brush the top with half-and-half, sprinkle with sugar and nutmeg to taste. Then cut small slits or a fancy pattern in the top of the crust to vent the steam.

Bake the pie according to its recipe directions.

24

Dr. L and Bow-Tie Friday

Grand Marais is a small town that is fortunate to have top-notch healers, from the dedicated doctors, nurses and clinicians at the Sawtooth Mountain Clinic to chiropractors, massage therapists, acupuncturists and those trained in Chinese and holistic healing modalities and psychotherapy.

This community of professionals understands that working together makes healing possible.

While in nursing, I worked at a clinic for children with severe birth defects and inherent orthopedic issues. Dr. Stilwell, an orthopedic surgeon who had seen it all, looked at each child from every aspect of his or her life. "We have to treat the whole patient," he would say. "If we only look at the orthopedic issues, we will have failed them." His results reflected his philosophy; the children loved him to pieces ... I did, too.

The dapper doctor with bow tie.
(photo by Kathy Rice)

Luckily the people in our family are a healthy bunch. Other than the occasional cold, or the aches and pain from hard work, we fare pretty well. We believe good health and aging well are consistent with how we care for our bodies. Eating balanced meals from fresh organic foods, getting exercise and fresh air, resting and making time for play and contemplation all aid in maintaining a healthy body.

However, even the healthiest body needs help sometimes.

Those of us who live on the North Shore know about sore backs and necks after a day spent cutting, splitting and stacking that winter wood supply or shoveling snow or falling on the ice.

That's where Dr. Loren Stoner comes to the rescue.

Loren, or Dr. L as I so fondly refer to him, is a local chiropractor. A master manipulator (and I mean that in the best way), Dr. L can take that hitch in your back, that crick in your neck or that numb, tingly feeling in your arm and ... voilà! Pain gone and you're on the road again.

Now, this is not magic; patients (one would be me) must do their part to stay healthy and tuned up. When pain persists, we have to examine our behavior: Have we done our exercises? Did we apply ice after the last alignment? Are we reading in bed? (Darn it, I love doing that.) You see where I'm going with this.

Loren, his wife, Becky, and his friendly staff (that would be Laurie, his competent, compassionate and capable receptionist) frequented the Pie Place for lunch on a very regular basis. We loved serving them and often catered to Loren's penchant for pie. He claimed not to have a favorite pie, loving anything and everything Mary baked on a given day.

It was not unusual for us to see Dr. L in the morning for an appointment and then to serve him lunch at The Pie Place Café a few hours later. Such is small-town life.

Another trait of Dr. L is that he's a snappy dresser and always looks dapper, whether he wears a baseball cap, sweatshirt and jeans or his professional office attire. His white coat does not conceal his impeccable clothing choices.

Soon we began to notice a fashion trend both at his office and in the restaurant. Loren always seemed to wear a bow tie on Fridays, which I must say made him look quite handsome. It's a style choice we don't often see in this day and age, particularly here in Grand Marais.

He started wearing bow ties in honor of an early mentor, Dr. Osborne, who taught about the importance of dressing in a professional manner in one's chiropractic practice. Dr. Osborne, impressed with Loren, presented him with one of his very own bow ties (a Brooks Brothers no less) in front of 100 other chiropractors at a conference. And so the tradition began.

After moving to Grand Marais, Loren noted our much more understated attire. Although he still wanted to present himself professionally to patients, he also wanted to blend into his new home.

His compromise? He proclaimed the last day of the workweek to be "Bow-Tie Friday."

More often than not, "Bow-Tie Friday" included a trip for lunch to the Pie Place for Loren and Laurie. How we looked forward to seeing the variety of bow ties sported by a person we so enjoy. Dr. L brightened our day, made us laugh and always exclaimed enthusiastically about his lunch and pie (whichever was on the menu).

Such joy helps make us healthy, too – a medical skill that comes naturally to the man in the bow tie.

Pie Place Frozen Key Lime Pie

The Pie Place family lived in Key West for a time, eating our share of Key Lime Pie, and delighting in the tropical tastes of the island. Our take on this island delicacy is frozen and more tart. A light, fresh dessert for a hot summer evening on the North Shore, this pie will remind you of tropical breezes and warm, sandy beaches.

Serves 6

Amount	Ingredients
Graham Cracker Crust:	
1-1/4 cups	Graham cracker crumbs (we like Keebler)
3 Tablespoons	sugar
1/3 cup	butter, melted
Filling for one pie:	
5 to 7	pasteurized egg yolks (numbers depends on size of yolks)
1/4 cup	sugar
1 (14-ounce) can	sweetened condensed milk
2 Tablespoons	lime zest
3/4 cup	lime juice, fresh squeezed

Instructions

To make the crust, which is adapted from the Keebler Graham Cracker Crumb package, first combine graham cracker crumbs and sugar in medium-sized bowl. Stir in melted butter until thoroughly blended. Pack the mixture into a 9-inch pie pan, pressing firmly on bottom and sides, bringing crumbs evenly up to the rim. Make sure the edge between bottom and sides is well packed, but is not too thick. Chill 1 hour before filling. For a toastier crust, bake it in a 375° F oven for 8 minutes and then cool, chill and fill.

For the filling, beat the egg yolks and sugar on high speed with an electric mixer for 5 minutes until thick. With the mixer on medium speed, add the condensed milk and lime juice. Gently blend in the lime zest by hand, spreading it evenly throughout the mixture. Pour into the graham cracker crust and freeze at least 4 hours or overnight. Once removed from the freezer, serve immediately with a dollop of whipped cream and a twist of thinly sliced lime. (It melts fast.)

Chef's note: You can make several pies ahead, cover with plastic wrap and freeze them. One 13.5-ounce package of Keebler Graham Cracker Crumbs makes enough for four crusts. When you want a quick, easy and elegant dessert … voilà.

North Shore Folk Artist

One of the many inspirational achievements of our town is the Grand Marais Art Colony. It's a natural outgrowth; many people travel here seeking the quietude and motivation that Lake Superior and the surrounding boreal forest impart. Besides visitors, this community itself is filled with artistic people, some born here and some, like us, drawn to its energy and beauty.

I and my Pie Place family have lived in Grand Marais for more than 20 years, but it still amazes me how many people I meet here reveal artistic interests or abilities. It runs the gamut of pursuits – pottery, poetry, photography, writing, painting, glass blowing, cabinet making, weaving, beading. What a rich, creative neighborhood we live in.

One day when I came out of the Cook County Whole Foods Co-op after having picked up fresh produce for our dinner entrées, I glanced across the street to Bill Bally's Blacksmith Shop.

A man in paint-splattered coveralls sat on a stump, an array of paint cans in a variety of colors spread before him. A rather makeshift paint palette to be sure, but it seemed to work for him. In front of him was an old abandoned refrigeration container, the truck long since gone, set in the tall grass. He would stand and look at the container, swipe paint on its side, adding another hue to his landscape. Then he'd step back for another look at the big picture.

In spite of the hour, and the fact that we would shortly be serving dinner at the café, I was drawn to go over and talk with this most unusual "plein air" painter.

I introduced myself. He stood up and took my hands in his paint-speckled ones.

"My name is Lyle Saethre, and I am an artist."

"I can see that."

Lyle began to tell me a most wonderful and touching story.

"When I was a little boy I went to school in Grand Marais. Bill Bally and I were in the same grade and always good friends. I remember that school wasn't so easy for me, and that I preferred coloring and

Some of Lyle's work on the walls of the Beaver House (left) and Lyle with his little brother Dale (right). Lyle was very young when he was discouraged from following his artistic passion. (left photo by Mary Beams; Saethre family photo)

art stuff. Well, my mother could see that she had a budding young artist in her midst, and one year for Christmas she gave me some paper and a small watercolor set. Oh, I can tell you, I was thrilled to get her gift. Someone had gotten me like no one else, and I loved her for that.

"I just started painting and painting. I wanted to paint everything I saw around me. Well, that didn't last too long because the boys in the school started to tease me. I remember that Bill tried to encourage me, and even took a few swings at my tormentors. One day I came home after school and threw all my paintings, drawings, paints and brushes away. I never painted again. I decided it would be easer to try and be like the other guys. But I sure missed painting.

"When my mother died and I was going through her things, I found an old wooden box under her bed. When I opened it, there were my brushes, watercolor set and all the pictures I had painted as a youngster. My mother must have taken them out of the trash and tucked them away. All I can say is that when I opened that box of paints, something inside of my heart opened up, too. I started painting, and I haven't stopped since.

Lyle's street art is inspired by many diverse things, including this bit of Lake Superior history at the Beaver House. (photo courtesy the Saethre family)

"Have you seen the painting on the Beaver Bait House? Well, I painted that. I use old house paint or anything that people want to get rid of. I take all this old paint and use it to make something beautiful. There were a lot of buildings around town in need of painting. So I'd ask the person who owned it if they'd mind if I painted a mural on it … free of charge, of course.

"Bill is still supporting my art. He commissioned me to paint the side of this old truck bed. I like to do paintings about the area, the history. Some folks might not see this as art, but it makes me happy. Hopefully it makes other people happy when they look at it, too."

I was spellbound by this passionate, humble man. I felt moved to tears that his deep inner need to create had been shut away for so many years. How painful that must have been, as if a part of him had gone to sleep for a long, long time.

Yet his mother left him a parting gift and legacy. She knew, as a mom, that someday when the voices of the world were muted and could no longer hurt him, her boy would be ready to take up his brushes and paint once again.

I praised Lyle for his work and mentioned that folk art, the simple art of everyday people like him, was very much in demand these days. Museums like the Smithsonian had glass cases full of paintings, carvings and pottery, and auction houses sold pieces for astronomical amounts. I concluded by saying that I have always been a lover of folk art. "I think there is spirit and love in this type of art. It was a way for people to express what was inside them."

"Well you don't say." Lyle responded modestly.

When it was time to go, I took those wonderful paint-splattered hands in mine. "Lyle," I said, "you just keep on painting."

He looked at me with a huge smile. "Why, I can't do anything else!"

Apricot Almond Crunch Pie

Soft golden apricots bathed in amaretto and topped with a crunchy topping. Are your taste buds alive with anticipation? Use fresh apricots when available (it's worth the pitting), but canned works well.

Serves 6

Amount	Ingredients
1/2 recipe	pie dough, page 23

Crumb topping:

3 cups	all-purpose flour
1 cup	light brown sugar, tightly packed
1/2 teaspoon	salt
1/2 cup	butter, melted

Filling:

3/4 cup	sugar
1/3 cup	all-purpose flour
4 cups	apricots (1-3/4 pounds), sliced and pitted (or 3 of the 15-ounce cans of apricots in light syrup or juice, drained)
2 Tablespoons	amaretto (or 1/2 teaspoon almond extract plus 2 tablespoons water for non-alcohol version)
2 Tablespoons	butter
1/3 cup	sliced almonds, toasted

Instructions

Preheat oven to 375° F.

Roll out dough into an 11-inch round on a lightly floured surface, using a floured rolling pin, and line a 9-inch pie pan with bottom crust.

To make crumb topping, mix flour, brown sugar, salt and melted butter in a large bowl. Blend thoroughly, rubbing out lumps with a wooden spoon or by hand. Set aside for topping. To toast almonds, spread in a single layer on a baking sheet and bake for 8 minutes in preheated oven. Keep an eye on the almonds during the last minute or two so they don't burn. When they smell fragrant and are golden brown, they are done. Keep oven at 375°.

In a large bowl combine sugar and flour. Drain apricots thoroughly and discard juice and place fruit in the bowl. Add amaretto; toss with dry mixture until coated. Place fruit in crust, dot with butter.

In medium bowl, mix toasted almonds and crumb topping thoroughly. Sprinkle mixture generously over the apricot mixture. You will use about 2 cups of crumb topping. Store any remaining crumb topping in refrigerator for up to two weeks.

Bake in center of a preheated oven for 45 minutes, or until crust and crumb topping are golden brown. Fruit will be soft and juices will bubble thick and clear. It's best served warm.

Summer Tastings

Downtown Grand Marais. (photo by Phil Bencomo)

Cultivating Community

Jeanne Wright at Rutabaga Ridge Homestead. (photos by Joan Farnam)

I love to count the blessings in the rich and marvelous community where we live.

Beautiful sunsets reflecting off the surface of Lake Superior bless us. Friendly waves from neighbors as they drive by bless us. And the fresh farm-grown produce that arrives weekly during the growing season from our local Community Supported Agriculture (CSA) group is the most flavorful blessing of all.

No wonder it brings to mind thoughts of love.

In a local newsletter by "three farmer friends" in Grand Marais, Jeanne Wright wrote a column called "Taste of Love." She starts by quoting Erin Barnett, co-founder of LocalHarvest, supporting CSAs. "Love changes the food we eat for the better, and that is one reason people search for locally produced food."

Then Jeanne goes on to write, "Well, certainly your food is well loved. It begins when we first put the seeds in the rows, gently cover them with soil, water and then anxiously await the first sprouts, excited but nervous like expectant parents. Each day the little plants are visited. Sometimes weeded, sometimes watered, sometimes propped up, sometimes sung to, we hover, we tend, we love. So, when you bite into that veggie, savor the moment and taste the love."

Olya, chicken wrangler, on the job.

For those of you who have been Pie Place Café customers, or read our first cookbook, you know our philosophy about the food that we serve echoes that sentiment: The Pie Place, where the first ingredient is always love.

So we take it one simple step further, food grown with love and prepared in the same way.

In our small rural area, we get to see the relationship of the farmers to our food. Our CSA friends, Melinda Spinler (Maple Hill Farm), Erik Hahn (Leaping Greenly Gardens) and the Wrights, Jeanne, Greg and daughter, Olya (Rutabaga Ridge Homestead), work to produce the food we thrill to receive each week during our rather short growing season. They battle late northern springs, too much rain (or not enough rain) and a host of pests – cutworms, rabbits, deer – with the grace, patience and determination of Mr. Green Jeans.

To celebrate the bounty, we CSA friends and neighbors share favorite recipes and gather for occasional potlucks to savor the flavor of homegrown food.

So add to our blessings both good food and good friends.

One CSA potluck at Rutabaga Ridge Homestead stands out in my memory. During the tour of the greenhouse and beehives, Olya arrived on the scene with her chicken Brownie tucked under her arm. She then showed off the chicken coop and her treasured chickens. Olya presented those CSA members attending a basket of farm-fresh eggs gathered that morning and laid by her feathered friends.

Seeing a young person so deeply connected to the earth and to the creatures that provide us with food filled me with hope. It speaks well of the future of our food sources, our community and our planet. It connects again the relationship of the food we grow, cook and serve to customers, family and friends.

Whether farmer, local restaurant chef or family meal maker, the thing that most honors this sacred gift, the blessing of good food, is love.

Gazpacho

This is a perfect summer soup for those of you who have a garden or are members of a local CSA. Served cold, it is refreshing and a great way to use the summer's bounty. I suggest you try serving it the way we did in the café, too, garnished with the Roasted Corn Sorbet that follows.

Serves 8 to 10

Amount	Ingredients
10-1/2 cups	tomato juice, divided (any brand you enjoy; organic is great)
12 medium	tomatoes, diced, divided in half
3 cups	cucumber, finely chopped, divided in half
1-1/2 cups	red onion, chopped, divided in half
1-1/2 cups	celery, finely chopped, divided in half
3/4 cup	green pepper, finely chopped, divided in half
6 Tablespoons	parsley, minced (we use both curly or flat-leaf, whichever is fresh)
9 cloves	garlic, minced
2	jalapeño peppers, seeded and minced
6 Tablespoons	red wine vinegar
6 Tablespoons	fresh lime juice
6 Tablespoons	olive oil
3 teaspoons	cumin
1-1/2 teaspoons	red hot pepper sauce (or to taste)
To taste	salt and pepper

Instructions

In a food processor or blender, put 3 cups tomato juice, half of the tomatoes, half of the cucumber, half of the red onions, half of the celery, half of the green pepper and all of the parsley, jalapeños, vinegar, lime juice, olive oil, cumin and hot pepper sauce. Process or blend until almost smooth.

Pour into a large bowl and add the remaining tomato juice and vegetables; this gives the right blend of smoothness and texture for the soup. Add salt and pepper. Cover and chill for several hours or overnight so that the flavors blend and the soup is cold.

Chef's note: This recipe makes a gallon of soup. If this seems more than you'll use or your garden/CSA isn't producing fully, feel free to cut the recipe in half. Since you are using really fresh vegetables, it will last in the refrigerator for several days. Garnish with a dollop of Roasted Corn Sorbet (next page). The flavor of the sorbet melting into the soup is an unexpected delight to your palate.

Roasted Corn Sorbet

"Roasted Corn Sorbet, you said?" That was almost always the response when we served a dollop atop our garden fresh gazpacho in summer. After the first refreshing spoonful, our guests were convinced that it was a great idea.

Makes 1 quart

Amount	Ingredients
6 ears	fresh sweet corn
2 Tablespoons	butter, melted
1/4 teaspoon	salt
6 cups	water
2 Tablespoons	sugar

Instructions

Preheat oven to 450° F.

For roasting the corn, first husk the corn and remove silk. Brush each ear with melted butter and sprinkle with salt. Wrap the ears in foil, placing the packet on a cookie sheet in the oven. Roast the corn for 20 to 25 minutes until fully cooked.

To prepare the sorbet mixture, remove roasted corn from foil and drag the tines of a fork through each kernel to split it. Don't remove them from the cob, though.

Place the ears of corn in large saucepan and cover with 6 cups water. Bring to a boil, reduce heat to medium and then boil covered for 5 minutes. Remove from the heat and let the corn cool in cooking water.

Slice the kernels from corn ears, discarding cobs. Reserve cooking water.

Place the corn kernels in the bowl of a food processor with 2 cups of the reserved cooking water. Purée for 2 to 3 minutes until the kernels are finely chopped. Transfer in batches to a sieve placed over a large bowl. Strain corn liquids by pressing the kernels on the sides of the sieve with a wooden spoon to release juices. Strain the liquid a second time to remove any bits of corn. Discard any solids. Add enough of the remaining cooking liquid to make 3-1/2 cups and stir in 2 Tablespoons of sugar.

Chill in refrigerator for a couple hours until cold.

Place the mixture in the metal container of an ice-cream maker. Churn in an ice-cream maker using directions for Pie Place Vanilla Ice Cream on page 71. When done, transfer the sorbet to a 1-quart container and freeze for at least 3 hours before serving.

The Forest for the Trees

Brian, left, and Ken planting for the future on their property. (photo by Brian Fulmer)

Grand Marais clings to the edge of Lake Superior, the boreal forest stretching for thousands of lush green acres toward Lake Saganaga and the Canadian border.

The Big Lake, town and forest attract folks for various reasons. Some come to visit and slow down in their lives. Others, drawn to the quiet beauty, come to make a home.

Whatever the reasons, a magical energy seems to call them. I like to think it may be the voices of the trees, and for some that is true.

Ken Palmquist and Brian Fulmer are partners who share a love of the forest. Though city dwellers, they travel to Grand Marais and the Gunflint Trail as often as their busy lives allow.

They became regular Pie Place customers, stopping for breakfast on every visit and even settling at "their table." One visit as I served them breakfast and coffee refills, I noticed a vast array of architectural and design magazines spread out between them. As an interior designer, I am always interested in what people are doing on the home front. Were they building a new home, renovating an existing house or restoring an old cabin? I've talked many a harried couple through home construction.

Brian and Ken offered that they were building a cabin on the Gunflint Trail. They had purchased property and were putting up a building in which to live until their home could be completed. Their eye for design came through in the ideas they shared and in their choice of a painting that they'd bought from our artist friend, Tim Young, for their home.

Each spring after, Brian and Ken would get seedlings from Hedstroms Lumber Company, a family-owned lumber yard that gives away tiny pines every year to aid in replenishing the surrounding forest.

The couple endured backbreaking weekends to plant trees on their property. On these "work weekends," they'd trudge wearily into the restaurant, a weekend's growth of beard on their faces, and, more than once, ticks scrambling on their flannel shirts.

We would feed them and prepare a box of their favorite scones for the trip back to civilization. Once as they were leaving, Brian said that they had five seedlings left from the spring bundle, but they didn't have the energy to plant one more tree. Would we like them? A lover of trees, I was thrilled. They handed over the gift, and off they went south.

In the midst of one of Brian and Ken's frequent trips, the notorious Ham Lake forest fire broke out. That Saturday, as they planted trees on the crest of a hill, Ken looked up and saw smoke billowing above the tree line. They didn't know it, but the Ham Lake fire had started and was well under way.

That night, after a hard day's work, Brian and Ken went to the Trail Center for supper and learned that they had seen the beginnings of what was one of the worst fires in Minnesota for a century. Like scores of others on the Gunflint Trail, they were evacuated to Grand Marais, where they sought lodging and settled in to wait out the fire. By mid-week, they tried to get back to their beloved property and cabin, but with the fire still raging, they were turned away.

I can tell you this, when you see smoke so thick that it blocks the sun, fear rises up in you, even if it is 90 miles away. We were uneasy for ourselves, but more so for others. The forest fire was in the Boundary Waters Canoe Area Wilderness; those hiking, camping and canoeing needed to be found and evacuated. Volunteers also rushed to the area to assist in stopping the fire and protecting homes.

It seemed like hundreds of people poured into Grand Marais. Restaurants prepared food for the evacuees, and the Pie Place Café staff made more egg salad than you can imagine and baked huge trays of brownies and cookies. We bought every known bag of potato chips in town to take to the Red Cross to distribute to those evacuated from the BWCAW.

Many of our friends and neighbors – Doug Kline, Bill Doucette, Dan Fitzgerald – are volunteer firefighters. They grabbed chain saws, jumped into their trucks and headed up the Gunflint to help.

People from Grand Marais who ferried supplies back and forth to the trail were eager couriers of the pies we sent to those battle-worn firefighters. They did stop the fire after two weeks, but not before 75,000 acres had burned and 140 structures, many of them homes, were lost.

Brian and Ken were two of the lucky ones; their property was untouched.

Jan Sivertson was not as lucky. Her cabin burned, but she still had an after-the-fire party at Sivertson Gallery for all who wished to attend. "When something like this happens," she said, "we can be sad for what we have lost, or we can be grateful that we are still here. We must turn and look to the future."

A hardy community, the folks of Grand Marais and the Gunflint Trail did just that.

Fires actually are part of the normal life cycle of the centuries-old boreal forests. Blazes restore the forest, clearing underbrush, bringing new growth and adding nutrients to the soil. But we who live among the trees have only short lives, and the fires devastate our landscape.

The next spring after the fire, our community gathered for the "Gunflint Green Up." Hundreds of people donated hundreds of hours, planting tens of thousands of trees to begin reclaiming the burned out areas. Once again, area restaurants rose to the occasion, providing food for the hungry tree planters. Brian and Ken were there, too, eager and seasoned tree planters.

Trees provide us with shade, beauty and life-giving oxygen. At times of stress, just being near trees brings me solace. What I sometimes forget is that trees live through many human lifetimes and have survived many fires of the past. Next time I'm sitting quietly in the forest, I'll remember to listen most carefully. The trees have secrets to tell.

Tomato-Gouda Soup

Gouda cheese comes from a small farm village with the same name near Amsterdam. Yellow and firm, its flavor intensifies with age, often resembling a fine Parmesan cheese. The nutty quality of the cheese and the delicate flavor of summer savory make this a memorable soup and is essential to its final character.

Serves 6

Amount	Ingredients
2 Tablespoons	butter
1 large	onion, sliced
2 (28-ounce) cans	Italian plum tomatoes, with juices
1-1/2 cups	chicken broth
1/2 cup	heavy cream
1 teaspoon	dried summer savory
1/2 teaspoon	celery seed
3/4 cup	Gouda cheese, grated for adding on top
For garnish	fresh parsley, chopped

Instructions

Melt butter in a medium-size, heavy saucepan over medium heat. Add onion and sauté until tender, about 8 minutes.

Add tomatoes with their juices, summer savory, celery seed and chicken broth. Break up tomatoes with spoon. Simmer 30 minutes.

Add cream and bring to simmer. Season to taste with salt and pepper, then generously garnish the hot soup with grated Gouda and chopped parsley.

(photo by Mary Beams)

Painting at the Fish House

*"When I come up here (Grand Marais), and I see that great big horizon line,
all the crooked thoughts in me straighten out."*

– Birney Quick, founder of the Grand Marais Art Colony

In the summer of 1947, young Birney and Marion Quick traveled to our village of Grand Marais. Birney, an avid fly fisherman, loved the Minnesota Arrowhead region and had been coming to the area since he was a young lad.

This time, though, fishing was not on his mind.

Twenty eager students awaited him to teach the first session of his "Outdoor School of Painting." The class was to launch a bigger idea. A professor at the Minnesota College of Art and Design, Birney envisioned an art colony, where people could come together, inspired by the beauty of the Big Lake area.

That vision became a reality when he and fellow MCAD professor Byron Bradley founded the Grand Marais Art Colony in 1947 (and now is the longest-lived art colony in the state).

Birney, a charismatic and magnetic personality, and Byron, an artist with a calm, easy manner, became the dynamic duo teaching classes and hosting fish fries, using fresh fish from local fishermen whose fish houses lined the shore. Soon artists could be seen painting plein air (in the open air) on Artists' Point. "Clothesline art shows" quickly became a part of Fisherman's Picnic, an annual local event since the 1920s. Byron's wife, Emma, recalls strolling along the shore eating smoked cisco on a stick, looking at paintings clipped to clotheslines draped along the street.

Others migrated up and joined the lively group. In the 1980s, artist Harvey Turner moved to Grand Marais with his wife, Lois. Often the whole group – Marion, Byron, Emma, Harvey and Lois – showed up to dine at the Pie Place on the hill. Birney had passed on before we moved to Grand Marais, but we looked forward to visits by the others, their lighthearted conversation full of wit, heart and, of course, art.

Sarah and Lydia painted at the fish house by their father, Byron. (photo courtesy Minnesota Historical Society)

Jane Burley, another friend of The Pie Place Café, participated in the "Part Time Painters Group" and joined this talented group of friends. Jane owns a wonderful old fish house that I have loved since we came to Grand Marais.

I imagine the fisherman working within those rough-hewn walls.

One spring, our friend Tim Young offered to give our family a painting lesson. Jane's old fish house seemed the perfect venue, and she eagerly agreed to our plan, but warned we'd need to do a little sweeping and dusting as it hadn't been used for artwork in quite awhile.

We packed a picnic lunch, a bottle of wine plus water, paints, brushes and canvases and off we went for a day of art.

As we opened the old fish house door, shafts of

sunlight fell across the rustic wooden floor. In the corner, an easel stood covered with cobwebs and years of dust. A blank canvas sat on it, awaiting brush strokes of color. A cluster of old brushes rested in a paint-spattered mason jar next to the easel. An empty wine bottle with several crude, yet wonderful pottery wine glasses sat on a rickety table in the center of the space.

Off to one side, an old kick-wheel held a half-formed clay pot, patiently awaiting its maker for the final shaping.

Obviously, this place welcomed more than just fisherfolk. People had created here, and the energy of that was as palpable as the smell of oil paints that permeated the dusty room. Who had been here?

Turning to look at Jane in the doorway, I saw a memory flit across her face. She remembered; this fish house had been where Birney, Byron, Harvey and other artistic folks had come to relax in the companionable way that friends have.

I completely understood. Chefs will always cook, artists will always create. With the atmosphere thus already creatively charged in the fish house, what a day we had. Tim, a wonderful teacher, patiently took his fledgling students through the subtleties of mixing paints, choosing brushes best suited to our paintings and how to "look at the landscape" and then recapture it on canvas.

After hours painting the scene outside the fish house windows, we devoured our sandwiches and raised a glass in gratitude to those who had inspired us. Our family never met Birney, but we felt as if we'd spent the day with him and his creative cohorts.

Birney's work was featured in a 1965 story by the Minneapolis Tribune (above) while Byron, on left, and Birney were featured in a 1970s-era Grand Marais News-Herald doing their famed fish fry (below).

Birney Quick envisioned an art colony where people could come together and make art, inspired by the beauty of the place he loved. Nearly 70 years later, that vision remains vital and ever-growing. People flock to Grand Marais to teach and learn about the arts, appreciating the expressive energy that exists. Our Pie Place family first came to Grand Marais because as artists we, too, were drawn here. We believe beauty is an essential need.

Art, it turns out, is the beat in the heart of our lakeside community.

"As we walked through the woods, every once in a while we'd find one of Birney's pictures nailed to a tree, way up in these inaccessible places almost.
He'd leave it there and then the next day work on it again."

– Lois Turner

Peasant Loaf Picnic Sandwich

The perfect picnic sandwich, this artisan loaf tied in a colorful bandanna will add unexpected fun to your lunch and your day. After all, every day is the day to create something beautiful.

Serves 4 to 6

Amount	Ingredients
1 (10-inch) round	peasant/artisan bread
1 (6- to 8-ounce) jar	prepared pesto
1/2 pound	ham, salami or pastrami, sliced (or a mix of all)
1/3 pound	provolone or Gouda, sliced
1/2 cup	black olives or pitted Kalamata olives, sliced
1/2	red bell pepper, sliced
1/2 small	red onion, sliced
2 small	vine tomatoes, sliced
To sprinkle	coarse salt

Instructions

Take 10-inch round bread, slice off top 1/2 inch. Scoop out some bread. Cover the underside of the loaf top and inside the loaf with prepared pesto.

Fill with ham, salami or pastrami (or a mix of all, if you are adventurous), layering bottom and sides of bread with meat. Next layer with provolone or Gouda, sliced black olives, red pepper, red onion, tomatoes and a sprinkling of coarse salt. Finish with layer of meat.

Cut into 4 to 6 wedges. Tie in a colorful bandanna around sandwich loaf to hold individual slices together until serving. Place in your picnic basket with chips, homemade cookies and lemonade. It's a creative presentation, and one that will inspire your picnic guests.

(photo by Mary Beams)

What a Girl's Gotta Do

Let me introduce you to Carolyn Dry – architect, inventor, charitable mastermind, a Pie Place Café customer for years and my dear friend.

Her home and her materials research firm, Natural Process Design Inc., are in Winona, but she feels as much at home in rural Grand Marais.

Carolyn's can-do philosophy drew me to love her, and we've enjoyed many adventures together because of that attitude. We've slogged through early morning dew in the woods to find wild bee balm. We've attended events, classes and movies at the North House Folk School, tagged along on the local art colony's annual Tour D'Art and lunched together while solving the problems of the world (at least to our satisfaction).

She helped our family create the nonprofit HEART Foundation – Healing and Education through Art – to support art programs in Minnesota prisons.

When life gives you aprons, make a party dress - that's my friend Carolyn's philosophy. (photo courtesy Carolyn Dry)

Carolyn also has rowed in the annual Dragon Boat Race and participated in the art colony's Plein Air event, using lipstick to color her winter landscape.

When she wanted to know how it felt to exhibit artwork, she didn't wait for a gallery to seek her out. She rented studio space at the art colony, and then invited friends to create art for the show. She started a group to clothe and find shelter for homeless teens in the Twin Cities. She donated money so that every Minnesota prison could create a garden, giving the men and women inmates the chance to plant food, get fresh produce and experience how those tasks, well done, can bestow a sense of achievement.

Her list of accomplishments goes on and on. A brilliant mind with a huge heart, Carolyn constantly inspires me.

The world, meanwhile, inspires her professionally. She once noted how the coral reef repairs itself, and then proceeded to develop a concrete with the same properties. From that, the Navy hired her to design self-repairing wharves. In addition, her concrete absorbs carbon dioxide from the atmosphere while putting oxygen into the air. Incredible!

Carolyn travels extensively throughout the world for her work and postcards arrive regularly from Cuba, France, Iceland – taking me along vicariously with her vivid descriptions of life in other countries.

On one visit to Paris, Carolyn's luggage was lost for two weeks. With only the clothes on her back, Carolyn trekked the streets of Paris in search of the perfect outfits until her luggage caught up to her. The only things she found to her liking were colorful aprons, which she bagged and took back to her hotel. That night she was invited to go with newfound friends to a rather fancy Paris eatery. With no appropriate clothes for the occasion, Carolyn was not thwarted. She safety-pinned three Parisian aprons together and … violà! The perfect party dress. Needless to say, Carolyn was the life of the party. (One of those aprons now resides in a drawer in our kitchen.)

Carolyn's approach to life reminds me that to live life fully, one must take risks, defy the shoulds and should-nots and follow the still small voice within to "do what you gotta do."

Parmesan Basil Chicken Salad

We have done many fabulous chicken salads at the Pie Place Café over the years, and Carolyn loves them all. This one has a wonderful nutty, garlicky taste. A great way to use the basil from your herb garden, this chicken salad can stand alone served on fresh greens or can be served sandwich style.

Serves 4 to 6

Amount	Ingredients
4 breasts	chicken, boneless and skinless
2 cups	mayonnaise
2 cups	fresh basil, finely chopped
4 cloves	garlic, finely chopped
4 Tablespoons	pine nuts
6 to 8 large stalks	celery, peeled and coarsely chopped
1-1/3 cups	Parmesan cheese, freshly grated
To taste	salt and pepper

Instructions

Poach chicken breasts, covered in water, in medium sauce pan until done (about 6 to 8 minutes). Don't over poach; you want the breasts to be moist. To check for doneness, remove a breast from the water and make a small cut with a knife to see that meat is no longer pink. Cut the chicken into 1/2-inch cubes and transfer to a large bowl.

In a food processor, purée the mayonnaise, basil, garlic and pine nuts. Pour it into the large bowl over the chicken and mix in the celery and cheese, tossing it all well. Season with the salt and pepper and serve with watercress for a salad option or on bread as a sandwich.

To serve as salad, divide over 4 medium bunches of watercress or arugula, large stems removed. To serve as 4 sandwiches, use 8 slices of our French bread (see page 99).

(photo by Kathy Rice)

Going Through Fire

I have loved pottery most of my life, but it was only when I came to live in Grand Marais that I explored it "hands on." That's one advantage of living in such an artist-rich community.

Our art gallery featured the work of many local and regional potters, raku being my personal favorite style with the rich earthy glazes made by the heat of the flames.

I met Kristi Downing at the Pie Place on the hill, and, as so many others have, I fell in love with the colorful, joy-filled free-spirited woman immediately.

We shared our mutual love of raku, and she told me about her studio, kkd pottery, hugging the shore of Lake Superior on Hat Point.

Kristi, a breast cancer survivor, held women's retreats at kkd pottery for others struggling with the uncertainty and fear of this disease. She wanted her studio to bring healing and hope for those who found their way to her. Her studio and tiny cabin, bought from up the shore and ferried along Lake Superior on log skids, are symbols of Kristi's indomitable spirit and zest for life.

Kristi helped me to embrace life fully. One fall day many years ago, I threw 17 pots on her potter's wheel in one day. It was one of the most intense, enjoyable experiences of my life. I'd never done pottery before that day, but as the clay came alive beneath my hands, emerging into its own unique shape, something magical happened within me. Something primal and familiar was reborn inside me.

Kristi applauded all of my attempts, far less than perfect. "You must have been a potter in a past life!" she exclaimed. From that time on I was hooked.

That year for Christmas, each of my family members received a raku tea bowl underneath the tree.

In the early days of our restaurant, free time was in short supply. However, we soon learned that to stay balanced while maintaining the rigors of a restaurant life, we needed to take time to rest, play and restore.

Cheryl suggested a "Raku Day" at kkd with Kristi. Kristi eagerly agreed to have us out for an afternoon. We told her we'd bring a fresh baked pie (which she loved) and a picnic lunch. Unfortunately, just prior to our day at the studio, Kristi fell while gathering morels in the forest and broke her arm. I offered to reschedule, but Kristi assured me that the day would go on. Her cousin Kurt Anderson would be there to help.

We arrived at the studio, eager for our day to begin, and Kristi lovingly introduced us to "Kurtie," as she called him. As with his cousin, we hit it off immediately with Kurt and enjoyed an incredible day of glazing, hauling water and firing our pots. After a picnic on the shore and hours of laughter and fun, our friendship with Kurtie was sealed.

A beaming Kristi on her beloved shore of Lake Superior. (photo by Layne Kennedy)

Several years and many pots later, Kristi's cancer returned. Though she must have known for quite some time the seriousness of her recurrence, Kristi participated in Crossing Borders, an annual studio tour she'd been a part of year after year. On the day we stopped at kkd pottery during the tour, Kristi was resting in the cabin, garnering the strength to do a raku firing later in the afternoon.

We didn't get to see Kristi, but I felt especially drawn to a small primitive pot. I had always wanted a "Kristi pot" and today seemed the day to get it.

A week later, I received a call from Kurtie. After Crossing Borders and her last raku firing, Kristi decided it was time to go to the hospital. Not long after, our dear and creative friend passed away, leaving behind a legacy of hope, love and soulful pottery. Kristi had done what she loved, with all of her heart, until the very end.

At Kristi's request, her family and friends joined together at the Hovland town hall to party in celebration of her glorious life. Amid the music, dancing, good food and flow of wine, you could feel her joyful presence. All of us who loved her know that she crafted her grace-filled life as expertly as she formed her pottery and, fired in the kiln of hardships, she showed us how to become, like a great pot, beautiful and strong.

Split Rock Chicken Brie Sandwich

We made these grilled sandwiches and served them to Kristi and Kurt for our pottery day at Kristi's studio. We sat on the beach and savored these delightful sandwiches, then, at the end of our day, tired but happy, went home with beautiful raku pots and wonderful memories.

Serves 4

Amount	Ingredients
8 slices	artisan bread of your choice, about 1/2-inch thick (we like our French bread, recipe page 99, or a sourdough)
5 to 6 Tablespoons	unsalted butter, softened
1/4 cup	apple butter (store-bought or we used homemade from our apple trees)
1 pound	roasted deli chicken, sliced fresh
1/2 pound	Brie cheese, thickly sliced
1 bunch	arugula, stems trimmed

Instructions

Spread each of 4 slices of bread with 1/2 Tablespoon of butter (on the outside part of sandwich). Next spread the opposite side with 1 Tablespoon of apple butter (inside part).

Top each slice of bread (apple-butter side) with a couple of slices of chicken. Cover the meat with arugula leaves, then layer with sliced Brie.

Spread the remaining 4 bread slices with 1/2 Tablespoon of butter (outside part). Lay them, buttered side out, on top of the first batch and press gently.

Heat a large cast-iron or other heavy skillet over medium-low heat. Add the remaining 1 Tablespoon butter and let it melt to evenly coat the bottom of the pan. Add as many sandwiches as comfortably fit (either 2 or 4, depending on pan size). Cook 2 to 3 minutes until the bread is golden brown and the cheese begins to melt. Flip and cook 2 to 3 more minutes to brown the other side of bread. (Add another Tablespoon of butter and cook any remaining sandwiches.) Cut the sandwiches and serve hot.

Nitty Gritty Dirt Gals

We all know the desire for fresh, organic homegrown vegetables, eggs, cheese, chickens, honey and other edibles is sweeping across the country. For those of us blessed to have grown up on or near a farm with fresh food, it seems like rediscovering the wheel.

In our fast-paced, technical world, time for family gardens does seem a thing of the past. Luckily, CSA – Community Supported Agriculture – has blossomed across the country, giving people the ability to get fresh produce even without their own garden and reconnecting them to something vital and real.

Coming from a family of farmers, I know what it takes to grow crops, feed and milk cows, plant and harvest a garden. I remember the effort of "putting up" the harvest in shiny glass jars to save for a tasty winter meal. It is a labor of love and, in an earlier time, the way many families survived.

That's why I so appreciate Robin Raudabaugh and Gigi Nauer, owners of The Nitty Gritty Dirt Farm, a CSA located in Harris, just an hour from Minneapolis. Situated on the Minnesota prairie, the farm yielded 100 shares a week, including fresh eggs and honey, for those who helped to support it.

As farmers, it's hard for Robin and Gigi to get time away from the daily chores, but they do manage occasional quick trips to the North Shore. The women, partners in business and in life, love canoeing, hiking and snowshoeing on the Gunflint Trail. One trip, they stopped at the Pie Place for a bowl of soup before heading out to put in their canoe. We hit it off right away, and two hours later we were still talking. That is a conversation still going on today. And the travel has been in both directions.

We've had "farm weekends" at the Nitty Gritty Dirt Farm, doing the things that real farmers do. We've fed lambs, cleaned the fleeces of newly shorn sheep, milked goats and made cheese. We've sampled some incredible homemade wine (Robin makes the best Malbec I've ever had). One visit, I brought my spinning wheel to spin yarn, but we became so darn busy talking, I never got around to it.

Robin and Gigi are frequent welcome guests and always arrive laden with gifts – honey from their bees, maple syrup tapped and boiled on their property, homemade wine, glass jars filled with garden produce and music and songs from Gigi, an accomplished musician and music teacher. Sometimes, we actually manage to get in some spinning.

Gigi and Robin taking an Up North break from farming; Robin and Gigi on the farm with Gigi's daughter Katie, and the roadside philosophy of their Nitty Gritty Dirt Farm. (photos courtesy Gigi Nauer)

Robin and Gigi have raised and butchered 30 free-range chickens for our family several years in a row. A few years ago, we got two lambs from the farm. In a true farming spirit, they traded homegrown food for meals at the Pie Place Café and a good night's sleep at the Harbor Inn, the way things used to be done.

Best of all, Robin and Gigi bring us the gift of their presence and a deep abiding friendship.

As if running a farm and CSA were not enough, Robin is a minister of the United Church of Christ. Living so close to the land, that deeply rooted spiritual connection brings meaning to her sermons and those whom she serves.

A few years ago Robin and Gigi decided to quit the CSA and cut back a bit on farming. They felt it was time for a quieter, more contemplative life. Four hundred plantings of grape vines and hundreds of raspberry and strawberry plants later, they were negotiating to sell fruit and grapes to a local vineyard. All I can say is, "Once a farmer, always a farmer."

Things are changing, though, in this couple's life. They just closed on a 20-acre parcel of land nestled in the woods not far from our home in Grand Marais. They plan to put the farm up for sale and head north for a new beginning.

Who knows what these two dynamic, tireless women will do next. You can bet that it will be something amazing, and, with them as new neighbors, we'll get to be a part of it.

Café Bistro Salad with Goat Cheese Croquettes

This salad is great for a summertime bistro lunch. Served atop organic field greens, these simple, easy-to-make croquettes will add the crowning glory to any salad. Use either of the two simple flavorful vinaigrette options here, and your family and friends will ask you to make this salad again and again.

Serves 2

Amount	Ingredients
Croquettes:	
2 (8-ounce) tubes	goat cheese, dry (plain or herb)
3 Tablespoons	all-purpose flour
2	eggs, lightly beaten
1 cup	panko (Japanese bread crumbs) or regular bread crumbs
2 Tablespoons	butter
Salad:	
3 cups	organic field greens
1 cup	cherry or grape tomatoes, halved
1/2 cup	walnuts, toasted
Lemon-Basil Vinaigrette:	
1/2 cup	olive oil
1/4 cup	lemon juice, fresh squeezed (about two large lemons)
1 teaspoon	honey
1 Tablespoon	fresh basil, finely chopped
To taste	salt and pepper

Combine olive oil and lemon juice in a shaker bottle. Add honey and basil plus salt and pepper to taste. Shake or stir with an emulsifying whisk. (Note: I got an emulsifying whisk for my birthday one year and love it. They are pricey, but well worth it.)

Honey-Mustard Vinaigrette:

1/2 cup	olive oil
1/4 cup	white wine vinegar
1 Tablespoon	honey
1-1/2 teaspoons	stone-ground mustard
To taste	salt and pepper

Combine olive oil and white wine vinegar in a shaker bottle. Add honey and stone-ground mustard plus salt and pepper to taste. Shake or stir with an emulsifying whisk.

Instructions:

To Prepare Croquettes: Take the goat cheese (in a tubular shape package) and slice into four 1/2-inch-thick slices. Dredge in flour, dip in egg, then dredge in Japanese panko or regular breadcrumbs.

These croquettes can be made ahead of time, refrigerated and sautéed just before you are ready to plate your salads.

When ready to prepare the salad, spread the walnuts evenly on a baking sheet and place in a 350° F oven for 5 to 8 minutes (this can be done ahead of time). Remove and set aside.

Melt butter on medium heat in a non-stick skillet and place the croquettes in the skillet, sautéing until lightly golden brown, just a few minutes on each side.

Arrange greens on plates, place warm croquettes on top of greens, add halved tomatoes and toasted walnuts. Drizzle either Lemon-Basil or Honey-Mustard Vinaigrette (two Pie Place Café favorites).

Chef's note: Always keep a good olive oil, white and red wine vinegars, honey and a piquant mustard on hand. With these, you can make a simple, yet flavorful, vinaigrette whenever you need one. Be inventive, adding your favorite fresh herbs. I love making dressings. Once you get the hang of it, you will, too.

(photo by Mary Beams)

Finding the Words

Life brings us remarkable people to enjoy and cherish, and then sometimes takes them away long before we are ready for them to go. I try to remember this when making time to be together with any of my friends and family.

It is during those times of heart-shredding loss that we become acutely aware of how precious life is, how much a loved one, no longer here, meant to us.

I met Ted Haaland and Maria Faust one summer day at the Pie Place on the hill. They were visiting Maria's parents, Chuck and Helen Faust, and spending time at their cabin in Hovland.

I liked Ted and Maria immediately, an outgoing couple dedicated to each other and excited at the prospect of building a summer home on Lake Superior.

Though the couple had a full life in Winona, Minnesota, surrounded by friends who shared their passion for food, gardening, art, music and poetry, they enjoyed time spent on the shore, where they roamed with their various adopted dogs, taking in the rugged beauty of Grand Marais.

Ted and Maria were a creative couple, and they often stopped at our gallery to look for lamps, rustic furniture and art for their almost completed home on the shore.

Maria had an eye for the right things, selecting unusual pieces to add character to their vacation home. I looked forward to their visits as we never seemed to run out of things to talk about. The couple, always generous with their time, were a joy to be with, and I felt fortunate to call them friends.

Maria was a tower of strength when Ted was diagnosed with non-Hodgkin's lymphoma and underwent chemotherapy followed by a long road to recovery. Ted was her life, and she did everything she could to make sure he was comfortable and had the best care possible.

They spent as much time on the North Shore as they could during Ted's confinement and recovery, and I think being here did them both good.

Maria had a way of bringing folks together, surrounding herself with interesting and imaginative people. She knew how to live life fully, and I must say that spending time with her and Ted was truly a gift.

In the early summer of 2012, Maria's parents, Chuck and Helen, returned to their cabin for the summer and stopped at the restaurant. Dear friends for years, I was happy to see them, asking how their winter had been.

I could tell by the look on their faces that something had happened. I feared the announcement that Ted had passed away. What they told me gave me a jolt of shock and sadness I could not have expected.

Maria had gotten a rare and fast-growing ovarian cancer. Three months after the diagnosis, she was gone. Grieving the loss of this remarkable daughter and wife, Chuck and Helen had tried unsuccessfully to get Ted to travel with them to the cabin. He seemed unable, unwilling to leave the home that he and Maria had lovingly created together.

From the grief, Ted found an unexpected place of solace.

Ted and Maria, a remarkable and devoted couple whose love lives on. (photo courtesy Ted Haaland)

"I woke up one morning early after Maria's death and felt a poem," Ted explained. He sat down in the kitchen and started writing. He hasn't stopped writing since then. Ted has written more than 3,000 poems and more than 200 each of haiku and sonnets. Marie always loved poetry, and that sentiment seemed to spill over into her husband after her death, giving him a voice for his sadness and loss.

As Ted so aptly puts it: "I don't think writing poetry causes grief. I think the grief enables me to write the poetry."

Wanting to create something positive in memory of his beloved wife, Ted endows the Maria W. Faust Sonnet Contest each year in conjunction with the Great River Shakespeare Festival in Winona. The contest, originally created by Winona's first poet laureate, Professor Jim Armstrong, has drawn the works of poets not only from Minnesota, but from all over the world.

Finding the words for his grief through poetry has been a catalyst for the annual event and something that I suspect would make Maria very happy indeed.

I, too, am a lover of poetry, but finding the words are harder for me. Instead, I have found the words of a lovely poet and now gift them to Chuck, Helen and Ted in honor of Maria.

These touching verses helped me in grieving the loss of our dear friend Cheryl. They brought me solace at a time when I felt particularly raw and alone, the missing of Cheryl taking me to my knees at times.

I pray it does the same for my friends in remembering Maria.

Ascension

And if I go,
while you're still here…
Know that I live on,
vibrating to a different measure
— behind a thin veil you cannot see through.
You will not see me,
so you must have faith.
I wait for the time when we can soar together again,
— both aware of each other.
Until then, live your life to its fullest.
And when you need me,
Just whisper my name in your heart
… I will be there.

— by Colleen Hitchcock,
used with her generous permission

our secret recipe

Mary's Pie Place Potato Salad with Black Olives

Our guests love The Pie Place Café potato salad, asking for the recipe over and over. Now here it is, the perfect accompaniment for a summer picnic on the shore or lunch in your own backyard.

Yields 1 gallon, serves a picnic crowd of 16 to 20

Amount	Ingredients
7 to 8 pounds	potatoes, Yukon gold, all similar in size
1 dozen	eggs, hard-boiled
2 (6-ounce) cans	medium black olives, drained and cut in half (you may leave olives whole if you wish)
1 cup	red onion, finely diced
To taste	salt and pepper

Dressing:

4 cups	mayonnaise (Hellmann's)
2 cups	sour cream
To thin	milk (dressing should be consistency of tomato soup)
To taste	salt and pepper

Instructions

Choose potatoes that are similar in size so they cook uniformly. Wash them and leave the skins on, place them in boiling salted water, enough to cover an inch above the potatoes. When they are fork-tender but not too soft, remove them and rinse in cold water. When cooled enough to handle, remove the skins. Dice in uniform 1/2-inch cubes.

Hard-boil the eggs by placing in a medium pot of water, bringing it to a boil and then lowering the heat to simmer to cook for 12 minutes. Drain eggs and peel immediately while still warm. Dice in uniform 1/2-inch pieces.

While potatoes and eggs are cooking, prepare the dressing by whisking ingredients together in a medium bowl. Chill until you are ready to dress the potato salad.

Place all cooled ingredients, including the olives and onions, in a large bowl and mix with dressing until moistened. Save extra dressing to add later as potatoes will absorb dressing and salad will need refreshing. Season with salt and pepper to taste. Keep the salad well-chilled until ready to serve.

Chef's note: Since this recipe makes a large, picnic-sized quantity, feel free to reduce it by half for a smaller amount.

Northern Barbecue

Southern barbecue has been a family favorite since our beginnings, and I must say that my first experience with this barbecue was one of sublime awakening.

Cheryl Polson, our menu planner extraordinaire, once lived in Georgia. I believe she was a "Southern girl" at heart, and Cheryl made the best barbecued ribs in the world. Yes, this seems a rather large claim to make, given all the barbecue in all the world, but when you've had the best, you just plain know it.

A couple of decades ago, our family took a three-week trip to Georgia and Tennessee, visiting all the haunts that Cheryl loved. We immersed in southern cuisine and its broad range of culinary delights. We sampled everything from grits, biscuits and gravy in ma-and-pa diners to succulent steaks that were cut tableside to our specifications in a high-brow restaurant called the Peddler. Of course we had great downhome BBQ ribs, too, in an old-fashioned joint called

Cheryl hugs our official "barbecued rib taste tester," Manny. (photo courtesy the Alvarez family)

"The Barbecue Pit." We ended up eating there at least once nearly every day, basically salivating at the sight of those ribs piled on the huge indoor grill and glistening red with hot, spicy sauce. And if your mouth is not watering at the thought of it, you've never tasted southern barbecue.

At the end of our vacation, we offered to take the entire kitchen staff of "The Barbecue Pit" home with us, which, except for the fact that we have snow, seemed like a good idea to them, too. Even so, when we took over the Pie Place, there was no question Cheryl would have barbecued ribs on the menu.

Cheryl and Josh set about perfecting her already perfect barbecue sauce, jotting out the recipe on a piece of paper blessed in barbecue sauce and now preserved for posterity – a transcendent, sacred writing for followers of great barbecue. The two also adapted a dry rub, applied to the meat prior to an eight-hour slow-cooking process. After that, the ribs were placed on our outdoor grill and slathered with layer after layer of barbecue sauce until they were caramelized and flavored to perfection. Cheryl grilled a batch of ribs for the family so we could test this northern barbecue before deciding to offer it in the restaurant. The vote was unanimous; those ribs with that sauce were on the menu. From that moment, we quickly became known for our barbecued ribs. People came from miles around to savor them – a heavenly plate overflowing with succulent ribs, cole slaw and an ear of fresh sweet corn.

One night our dear friends Manny and Cheryl Alvarez came in for dinner. These constant, committed customers had been coming to the Pie Place for longer than even I could remember. Like so many others, they have become dear and trusted friends, whose children and grandchildren feel like our own.

That doesn't mean, though, that they are pushovers when it comes to good food. Seeing our new BBQ dinner on the menu, Manny, who loves barbecue, proclaimed that he knew good ribs and was pretty particular about them. He'd already tasted the best, but he'd give ours a try.

I placed the heaping plate in front of him, ribs straight from the grill, and watched him. Manny took his first bite, and a broad smile spread over his face. He jumped up from the table. Quickly striding to the kitchen, he flung the door open. Grabbing Josh, he enveloped him in a huge bear hug. If memory serves me, there were tears in his eyes when he exclaimed, "Those are the best ribs I have ever tasted!"

From then on, whenever Manny and Cheryl came for dinner, you can guess what he ordered. He became our official "barbecued rib taste tester." The ribs, of course, are as important as the sauce. We always got ours from Marlo Larson, the butcher at Johnson's Grocery. Once when he was out, we tried another brand. Josh knew immediately they were not acceptable, but he still asked Manny to test them. One bite and our taste tester gave a thumbs down. "No way, man. I know the best, and these aren't it."

Our lives are filled with memorable firsts – first kiss, first dance, first canoe trip, first run alone down the ski hill. We probably did a thousand pounds of ribs at the Pie Place, and quite a few of those pounds were eaten by our official rib taste tester. But to this day, Manny remembers – and speaks fondly about – his first taste of barbecued ribs at the Pie Place. We could just hug him for remembering.

our secret recipe

Cheryl's Barbecue Sauce

I'd never really had barbecued ribs until I tasted Cheryl's. I clearly remember that hot summer day as she stood patiently at the grill brushing baby back ribs with her special sauce. Now we share it with you.

Makes about 1 quart

Amount	Ingredients
1 (64-ounce) bottle	ketchup
1/2 cup	Worcestershire sauce
1 Tablespoon	Tabasco sauce
2 to 3 cups	brown sugar
2 cups	vegetable oil (Wesson)
1 cup	apple cider vinegar
1/2 cup	lemon juice (bottled)
1 Tablespoon	garlic salt
1/2 cup	sherry
2 Tablespoons	Italian seasoning
3/4 cup	honey

Dry Rub for Ribs:

1 cup brown sugar
1/4 cup Lawry's seasoned salt
1/4 cup garlic salt
1/4 cup celery salt
1/4 cup onion salt
1/2 cup paprika
3 Tablespoons chili powder
2 Tablespoons pepper
1 Tablespoon lemon pepper
1 teaspoon dry mustard
1/2 teaspoon ground thyme
1/2 teaspoon Cayenne pepper

Sift together sugar and seasonings in a bowl; store in an airtight container. This dry rub is adapted from one created by Chef Paul Kirk.

Instructions

Combine all ingredients in a large bowl and stir until brown sugar is combined completely. (Base amount of brown sugar on how sweet you like your sauce.) This recipe makes a lot, but keeps in the refrigerator for months.

The sauce works for chicken, burgers and mixed into meatloaf, but if you want to try ribs, here's what we suggest. For 2 racks of baby back ribs (we like John Morrell; look for lean): Preheat oven to 250° F.

Remove membrane from back of ribs and place on high-sided baking sheet with bone side down. Liberally coat ribs with dry rub (sprinkle, don't rub!). Put 1/2 inch of water into the baking sheet. Wrap foil tightly over the baking sheet and ribs. Bake for 3 hours or until meat is tender. Check ribs after 1-1/2 hours, and add more water if necessary. Be sure to re-seal foil tightly so meat does not dry out. Once ribs are cooked, remove from oven and let cool.

Apply more dry rub and place cooked ribs on a grill heated to 325° F or a low setting and with the hood closed. Slather with barbecue sauce. Turn frequently and continue to brush with sauce, allowing it to caramelize for about 20 minutes.

Brushstrokes of Life

Some people, given the life they have lived, inspire us to greater heights, help us to see the world in a fresh way and change us forever. These people leave a mark, like brushstrokes on a canvas, that remain vivid even after they depart this earthly plane.

And you just never know when or where you will meet these fellow travelers.

I met Kenny Dumdie, Marilyn Taus and their daughter, Rochelle, in the Pie Place when they came in for lunch on their way to visit Marilyn's mother, Harriet, who lived on the Gunflint Trail.

Marilyn, Kenny and Rochelle carry on a tradition of lodge keeping. (photo courtesy the family)

Harriet Taus was the daughter of Charlie and Petra Boostrom, who owned Clearwater Lodge off the Gunflint. Founded in 1915, Clearwater is the oldest log lodge in Minnesota. Charlie, a master builder, constructed the main building and cabins on Clearwater Lake. Petra, an excellent cook, fed 13 children and hundreds of guests. She baked bread in the wood-burning stove every day but Sunday; I imagine smelling the fresh bread wafting through the lodge. Harriet remembers a fresh pot of coffee ever waiting on the stove. Her mother cooked for all the fishermen who came to Clearwater Lake.

While all 13 children were needed to help run the lodge, Harriet assured me there was plenty of "fun time." The Boostroms owned and ran the lodge for nearly 30 years, and it remained home for Harriet and later, for her daughter, Marilyn, who loved to spend summers at the lodge her grandfather had built.

The deep connection to the Gunflint Trail meant Kenny and Marilyn spent much time there as a young married couple and soon brought their children to experience the Boundary Waters Canoe Area Wilderness, always coming back to the place that nourished their souls.

As a young girl, Marilyn painted pictures of everything, and the Gunflint Trail especially inspired her. At college, she completed a degree in art and embarked upon a career as a prolific artist. Though her first love was ceramics, she expanded into drawing, painting and sculpture. Her fascination with all art forms culminated in a teaching career at Cambridge Community College. Her fascination with the Gunflint Trail motivated her to bring students there in the hope that they would be as inspired by the natural beauty as she had been.

Kenny, also an artist, works in many mediums, including glass blowing and leatherwork, and has participated in the North Shore's Crossing Borders Studio Tour of local artists for many years. It was only natural, since, as Kenny says, "We felt at home here."

Kenny, Marilyn and Rochelle's visits to "grandma's place" meant we got a chance to spend time with them, too. As fellow artists, we always found much to talk about, an endless stream of conversation that seemed to pick up wherever we had left it on the previous visit. Josh, my son, our chef and also an artist, loved Kenny and Marilyn. He gravitated out of the kitchen and onto the sun porch of our restaurant on the hill whenever they came for lunch. When they visited the sun porch, Kenny and Marilyn's favorite place to dine, it transformed into a classroom for inspiring conversation about art.

They regaled us with stories. Once they talked about a trip to Italy, where they painted, took stone-carving classes and foraged for Carrara marble, quite possibly in the same quarry that Michelangelo had frequented. Josh was engrossed with their tales and encouraged by their interest in his drawings. That's the kind of people they were – always excited about life and ever willing to share their time, knowledge, exuberance and love.

It was only later that we were to discover that for years Marilyn, who had breast cancer, had been undergoing rounds of chemo and radiation therapy. She fought a courageous battle against this disease, determined to enjoy her family, friends and the life that inspired her art until the end.

Very few people I've known have lived life so fully as she did in the midst of dying.

Marilyn continued to come to the North Shore and Gunflint Trail. She helped her mother build a new cabin on the trail. Marilyn designed and helped to fabricate an etched-glass door, painted landscapes for the walls and little murals on the wooden risers of the loft staircase. Her ceramics and sculptures, placed here and there, became loving reminders of her presence.

"She's driven," Harriet confided in me. "It's as if she is leaving parts of herself behind."

At the end of autumn in 2006, Marilyn, Kenny and Rochelle made what I knew would be their last trip to the Pie Place and to the Gunflint. Very weak, Marilyn insisted on a stop at the restaurant for their traditional lunch before going to her mom's newly completed cabin.

They dined on the porch, the sun streaming in on Marilyn's face. "How beautiful she is, and how full of light," I remember thinking. We talked nonstop, as always, until this time Marilyn said she was tired and that they needed to go.

I walked them to the front door, my arms around them all. Before she turned to leave, I said to my creative, courageous friend, "I just want you to know that you, and the life you have led, have inspired me."

"Thank you," she said with a smile. Then she was gone.

Marilyn passed away in February 2007, surrounded by family and friends, and ready, I believe, to see what new, exciting things awaited her.

In the spring of 2011, Marilyn's paintings, along with those of her friend Margaret Carroll, were exhibited at the Johnson Heritage Post Art Gallery in Grand Marais. Kenny worked hard to gather Marilyn's paintings from family, friends and the couple's own collection; he had always wanted to show her work in Cook County.

Clearwater Lodge, the oldest log lodge in Minnesota. (old postcard)

"She was an artist," he explained. "That was her life."

So this became his tribute to Marilyn – wife, mother, artist and friend.

Kenny called me weeks before the exhibit. He wanted to have a party at the Pie Place after the opening. "That would make Marilyn so happy."

We eagerly agreed, helping Kenny plan the menu of foods indigenous to the area, recipes that were their favorites. Marilyn would have loved the party with lots of good food, plenty of flowing wine and a room full of friends and family sharing memories and laughter.

One of Marilyn's dear friends, a glass blower, presented us with beautiful vases as a "thank you" for the party. Kenny gifted us with one of Marilyn's still life paintings, delicate little wildflowers from her beloved Gunflint Trail.

We will cherish them always, brushstrokes of a life painted on our hearts.

Grand Marais Summer Fruit Salad

What a wonderful way to savor the season. This fruit salad is perfect for picnics or outdoor barbecues. We include two dressings; both are family favorites. You'll be hard-pressed to decide which you like best.

Serve 4 to 6

Amount	Ingredients
1 (16-ounce) package	fresh strawberries, hulled and quartered
3	bananas, peeled and sliced
1/2	cantaloupe, seeded and cut into 1-inch cubes
1/2	honeydew melon, seeded and cut into 1-inch cubes
4 cups	seedless watermelon, cut into 1-inch cubes
1-1/2 cups	shredded, sweetened coconut, toasted for garnish

Instructions

Preheat oven to 375° F.

Prepare all the fruit, except the bananas. Mix fruit in a large bowl, evenly distributed. Put the fruit into a storage container and refrigerate to chill.

Spread the coconut on a baking sheet and toast in the oven for 5 to 7 minutes, stirring frequently (to a nice golden brown.) Keep an eye on the coconut; it burns easily.

Take out the fruit. Add in sliced bananas and divide equally onto a bed of mixed greens for each serving. Drizzle on the dressing (Caribbean Banana or Kathy's Creamy Yogurt) and garnish with toasted coconut.

> **Caribbean Banana Dressing:**
> 3 bananas, very ripe
> 1/2 cup cream of coconut
>   (we like Coco Casa best)
> 4 Tablespoons rum extract
> 2 Tablespoons lime juice
> 4 Tablespoons honey
> 1/8 teaspoon nutmeg, freshly grated
>
> In a blender or food processor with a steel blade, combine ingredients. Process until smooth. Chill for 1 hour. The extra will keep 2 or 3 days; it turns brown but still tastes great.

Kathy's Creamy Yogurt Dressing

Amount	Ingredients
1 (32-ounce) container	plain or vanilla yogurt
3 to 4 Tablespoons	honey
1 Tablespoon	vanilla (amount depends on using plain or vanilla yogurt)
1 to 2 teaspoons	cinnamon

Instructions

Combine all ingredients in a medium bowl and stir until completely blended and yogurt is smooth. If you like a sweeter or spicier flavor, add more honey or cinnamon. If you use vanilla yogurt, mix all ingredients (but the vanilla) first and taste. Some brands will have enough vanilla and you don't need to add more. This recipe provides a large amount of dressing. It will keep two or three days. This incredibly simple, flavorful dressing, served over fresh fruit, is perfect for summer.

Lure of the Lake

This is how it all begins.

In 1928, Millie Okeson first came to the North Shore as an eager teenager on a family trip from Rush City. Each following summer, they came to Lutsen Resort, where Millie's older sister, Emma, worked as a seasonal waitress. In those days, Highway 61 was a dirt road, cars were slower and the trip took all day. But once the family arrived the weary, dusty and often bumpy trip was forgotten. Awaiting them was Lake Superior, its rocky shore, the fragrant pines … and two weeks of fun.

After she grew up and left home, Millie continued to come north in summer. Soon a husband, Ray Huppert, was joining her, and Lutsen Resort remained a favorite getaway. Next came their baby daughter, Carolyn, carried along to Grand

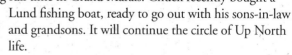

Carolyn and Chuck will move to Grand Marais thanks to a legacy started with Millie (below). (photo by Kathy Rice)

Marais or to Port Arthur (now Thunder Bay), with perhaps a stop at Gooseberry Falls along the way. Like her mom, Carolyn grew up with Lake Superior summers. Quickly the lure of the lake got into her blood.

Now 87 years from Millie's first visit (and many vacations later), daughter Carolyn and her husband, Chuck, own a vacation home on the shore a few miles from Grand Marais. Chuck spent his own memorable summers fishing in the Boundary Waters Canoe Area Wilderness, dipping for smelt, canoeing and exploring the lakes and forest with his teenage friends.

Chuck and Carolyn Berg found us when we first took over the white bungalow Pie Place on the hill.

They loved to eat and talk in equal measure, adding spice to our restaurant life. Chuck, quite the teaser, brought his dry, often quite outrageous, humor.

"Stop it, Charlie. Stop it!" would come Carolyn's exasperated scold. Chuck just smiled and kept teasing.

Next to the shores came Chuck and Carolyn's children, Vicki, Patti and Andi, and their spouses. One grandchild was named Orla Ray for her great-grandpa. She and Lucas, Adam and Nicholas make up the fifth generation, and we hope they carry on the family North Shore tradition.

With few obligations in the city, Chuck and Carolyn happily spend as much time as they can in their northern home. Chuck, an avid collector, loves all things old, collecting stamps, books, cameras, dishes and furniture. For years, he bought and sold antiques, acquiring items on foraging trips. As any lover of antiquing will tell you, the hunt is as much fun as gaining the treasure.

Chuck and Carolyn plan soon to move, living full time in Grand Marais. Chuck recently bought a

Lund fishing boat, ready to go out with his sons-in-law and grandsons. It will continue the circle of Up North life.

As a guest told me one summer morning, shifting her gaze from the harbor, "I just can't stay away from Lake Superior for too long. There is something about it that draws you back again and again."

So true, I thought.

Just ask Chuck and Carolyn Berg.

Swedish Salmon and Potato Casserole

A dish prepared in the Swedish tradition, this creamy salmon casserole is flavored with fresh dill. For those who love Lake Superior fish, it's a crowd pleaser.

Serves 10 to 12

Amount	Ingredients
3 Tablespoons + 1/2 cup	butter, melted
1/2 cup	dried bread crumbs
3 pounds	Yukon gold potatoes, peeled and cut into thin slices
1 teaspoon	salt
1/2 cup	dry white wine (or water)
3/4 teaspoon	white pepper, freshly ground
1 pound	salmon, cut into about 20 pieces
4 teaspoons	fresh dill, finely chopped, divided
6 large	eggs
3 cups	heavy cream
For serving	lemon wedges

Instructions

Preheat oven to 350° F.

Place salmon in a lightly oiled ceramic baking dish, season with a sprinkling of salt and pour 1/2 cup dry white wine (or water) over all. Tightly cover the dish with nonstick aluminum foil. Bake for 10-15 minutes. Remove salmon from oven and poaching liquid, placing filets on a plate, and cool to room temperature. Once salmon is cool enough to handle, gently cut into 20 or so pieces for layering in the casserole.

Increase oven temperature to 425° F.

Lightly grease a 9x13-inch casserole dish with 1 Tablespoon of melted butter. Coat the greased casserole with 3 Tablespoons of bread crumbs. Lay about a third of the potatoes in the casserole dish, overlapping in a shingle pattern. Season with 1/4 teaspoon salt and white pepper. Lay half the salmon slices over the potatoes and sprinkle with 1 teaspoon chopped dill. Lay half the remaining potatoes on the salmon, again in a shingle pattern. Season with another 1/4 teaspoon salt and white pepper. Lay the remaining salmon over the potatoes and sprinkle with 1 teaspoon chopped dill. Arrange the rest of the potatoes on the salmon and season with 1/2 teaspoon salt and 1/4 teaspoon white pepper.

Whisk the eggs with the heavy cream and 2 Tablespoons melted butter in a medium bowl. Pour the mixture over the potatoes and salmon, and then wrap with aluminum foil. Place the casserole dish in the oven and bake on the middle rack for 30 minutes. Remove from the oven, peel away the foil and sprinkle the remaining bread crumbs over the top. Place back in the oven and bake, uncovered until the top is golden brown and the potatoes are tender, about 30 minutes more. Remove from the oven and allow to cool for 15 to 20 minutes before serving. Sprinkle on the remaining 2 teaspoons of chopped dill. Serve, drizzled with the remaining 1/2 cup melted butter and garnished with lemon wedges.

How's That for Love

I am passionate about love stories.

One such story stirred me at an early age. In *Mrs. Mike*, a true story, a Royal Canadian Mountie and his young bride, Kathy, travel by dogsled into the Canadian Northwest to Hudson's Hope to live among the Cree Indians, French Canadian trappers and employees of the Hudson's Bay Company. Their love endures and grows amid the hardships.

Mrs. Mike stirred my imagination and opened my young heart to the power of love. I've read this treasured book almost every year (in winter, of course) since I was 12.

I have given copies of the book to my niece, Rachel, my daughter-in-law, Anna, and other dear friends. To me, it is a love story for all time, and one of which I will never tire. Whenever I hear a tale of love found, I'm held in rapt attention.

Curt Hort and Louise Davis caught my attention the first day they came into the restaurant several years ago. This couple obviously was in love. Holding hands and engaging in an actual conversation, they clearly liked each other immensely.

A woman from New Orleans and a German Jewish man? Yes . . . when it's all about the love. (photo courtesy the Davis family)

Their love radiated outward. Charming and full of life, Curt and Louise raved with gustatory ecstasy about each and every bite, making them a pleasure to serve.

Some love stories, of course, grow gradually. Curt and Louise were friends for many years, both married to other people. Then Curt's dear wife died, and Louise had an unfortunate parting with her husband. They found support in each other through these difficult times, and what started as a strong friendship blossomed into romance.

But there is another twist.

Louise, a spunky petite woman, minces no words in her description of the situation: "A 94-year-old German Jew marries a 74-year-old Southern Episcopalian from New Orleans … how's that for love!"

The most unlikely matches really can be made in heaven.

They married in 2000, still keeping each other young and vital. Both exude an inspiring, hope-filled zest for life. Louise loved to cook for her family and friends while her nonagenarian husband would often encourage a brisk walk along the shore after their meals.

"Curt is the love of my life," says Louise. "There is absolutely no one like him. He is every woman's dream."

Whenever Curt and Louise arrived, I could expect a lively kiss on the cheek from Curt. Louise did not mind; she knew his heart.

"I love women," Curt once explained to me. "My mother got me and my father out of Germany after Hitler started rounding up the Jews. She saved my life, what more can I say? I have loved women ever since."

Curt's family, then Horwitz, spent the years of 1939 through 1947 in Shanghai, China, in a Jewish ghetto. When the Japanese occupied Shanghai, Curt was placed in a concentration camp and spent nearly five years there from 1941 to 1945.

After Curt finally made it to America after years of adversity – "but at least alive" – he was forced to change his surname from Horwitz to Hort to avoid the sad predominance of anti-Semitism in Minneapolis in the late 1940s and early '50s. "This was the only way that I could get a job, and I had a family of four to feed." But, true to Curt's sweet and loving nature, he let go of the past as best he could, determined to live a happy life. In short, Curt chose love and forgiveness over fear and hatred.

In the end, he got his reward in the form of his late-in-life bride. "I was having a lot of health problems when Louise and I came together. She got me exercising, started fixing me good, healthy foods and just loved the dickens out of me. Just think of that? Two women saved my life, Mother and Louise."

Curt felt he was given a second chance after he and his family left Germany and then escaped China. "When you are faced with the possibility of death, I can tell you that you don't take life lightly. I made a decision that no matter what, I intended to live my life to the fullest."

With Louise, he led that full, active and happy life. They did everything together. Louise's children and grandchildren adored Curt and gave him a family once again. He lavishly doted on them; they were his treasure.

"You can have all the money and possessions in the world," Curt told me once with tears in his eyes, "but if you don't have love, you have nothing!"

How refreshing it was to see these lovebirds embrace life and each other.

My moral for this story is that we truly are never too old for love. It can sneak up on us when we least expect it. It may look far different than you imagined possible. But if it finds you, at whatever age, embrace it. There's nothing better than a love story.

When All That's Left is Love

When I die
If you need to weep
Cry for someone
Walking the street beside you.
You can love me most by letting
Hands touch hands, and
Souls touch souls.
You can love me most by
Sharing your Simchas (goodness) and
Multiplying your Mitzvot (acts of kindness).
You can love me most by
Letting me live in your eyes
And not on your mind.
And when you say Kaddish for me
Remember what our
Torah teaches,
Love doesn't die
People do.
So when all that's left of me is love
Give me away.

– Rabbi Allen S. Maller,
reprinted with the poet's kind permission

This story is in fond memory of Curt, whose love continues in our hearts.

Poached Salmon with Caper-Chive Mayonnaise

Poached salmon alone is a perfect complement to a fresh summer salad, but with this preparation the capers add a wonderfully salty counterpoint to the sweetness of the fresh fish.

Serves 4 to 6

Amount	Ingredients
4 to 6 filets	fresh salmon (about 4 ounces each)
To coat dish	vegetable oil
To taste	salt
12 small sprigs	fresh dill
1 stalk	celery, thinly sliced
1 large	leek, white part only, thinly sliced
1	bay leaf
3 whole	white peppercorns
1/2 cup	white wine
1 head	bib lettuce or butter lettuce
1	lemon, thinly sliced or cut in wedges
Additional sprigs	fresh dill

(photo by Mary Beams)

Instructions

Preheat oven to 325° F.

To poach the salmon, lightly oil a shallow ceramic baking dish large enough to hold all of the filets with space between each. (Or salmon may be poached in two batches.) Season the filets with a little salt and place them in the bottom of the dish. Place one sprig of dill on top of each filet and scatter sliced celery, sliced leek, bay leaf and peppercorns between them. Pour in the white wine. Tightly cover the dish with nonstick aluminum foil. Bake the salmon for 20 minutes. The top of the foil will puff up as the salmon filets cook.

Caper-Chive Mayonnaise:

1-1/2 Tablespoons	fresh lemon juice
1 teaspoon	Dijon mustard
1 teaspoon	tarragon vinegar or white wine vinegar
1 cup	mayonnaise
1/8 cup	capers
1/8 cup	fresh chives, snipped
Pinch	sugar
Pinch	salt

Combine the lemon juice, mustard and vinegar in a small bowl. Add the mayonnaise and whisk thoroughly. Fold in the capers and chives. Season to taste with sugar and salt.

Remove the salmon from the oven and insert a thermometer into the thickest part of one of the filets. The temperature should register between 130° and 135° for fully cooked salmon. At this point, peel the foil back halfway and cool the salmon to room temperature before serving, about 20 minutes.

To plate the salmon, wash the lettuce leaves and pat them dry. Place them on a chilled platter and arrange the filets on top. Garnish with lemon slices and sprigs of dill; serve mayonnaise on the side.

Sydney's & Summer

Everybody on the North Shore loves summer. Out-of-town visitors and local residents all seem to have places to go and things to do to help shrug off the long, cold winter while soaking in the fleeting warmth of the sun.

We mark summer, in part, with the annual openings of some favorite food shops. We can't wait for that first warm crispy doughnut from the World's Best Donut Shop or creamy frozen custard from Sydney's.

Bruce and Pam Block and their girls, Tara, Yvonne, Anna, Sydney and Ellie, together operate Sydney's Frozen Custard, a family-owned business right on the shore of Lake Superior. Even before it opened, their son, Rush, stood shoulder to shoulder with Bruce helping to construct the building and then to make additions and improvements as Sydney's grew.

This fun-loving, hard-working family has created a unique place to relax, eat and visit with friends, where a friendly face and good conversation always awaits. I like taking my custard for a leisurely stroll along the shore outside the restaurant.

Like many of the businesses in Grand Marais, The Pie Place Café and Sydney's long supported each other, not only as business owners, but as friends. The eldest daughter, Tara, worked at the Pie Place on the hill while she was still in high school. She brought an eager and willing spirit to everything she did from waiting tables to decorating sugar cookies to washing dishes. It was a joy to have her as part of our restaurant. For me, who had never had the fun of decorating Christmas cookies with a daughter, she brought a cheery experience to life.

The family opened Sydney's Frozen Custard, named for the baby of the family at the time, daughter Sydney, in 2003. Featuring rooftop and patio seating on the shore, Sydney's fast became a favorite place for our family to "wind down" after a long week in our own restaurant. Bruce, Pam and the kids did the reverse, coming to our restaurant, too.

Chef Bruce takes a break during the busy summer season. (photo by Mary Beams)

Over the years, both businesses have seen changes. Bruce built a beehive bread oven to bake rustic hand-thrown pizzas and expanded his seating capacity by creating a glass-enclosed space with a fireplace and lake view.

The Pie Place Café moved to the location on the harbor, expanding to include more seating, and took over the Harbor Inn, which we still operate.

One sunny summer day, while savoring our frozen custard and visiting with Bruce and Pam, we had an epiphany. We made homemade bread; they made frozen custard. Could we use our culinary expertise to help each other out?

And so it began. The Pie Place Café made pizza dough for the pizzas at Sydney's. The Blocks, in turn, delivered homemade frozen custard for us to serve with slices of pie.

In the true spirit of community, it was a match made in heaven.

Such cooperation is one of the many things we love about living in Grand Marais. We approach life with knowledge that we are all in this together. When one business prospers, we all do. What we do for one another

comes back a thousand fold. There is no keeping score. We help because it is the right thing to do. We help because we see how hard everyone works to fulfill their dreams and to create a good life for their families. The world would be a better place if we all began to nurture each other.

At the end of each summer, we're sad when Sydney's closes its takeout window and we must go through a bit of custard and pizza withdrawal as a result.

But the time we're without them is what makes the places and the food we love so special. We never take those flavors – and the experience of strolling the shore, custard in hand – for granted.

All through the winter, we can count on the arrival of summer. We can count on the friendship between our two restaurant families.

And when the weather warms, we can count on Sydney's to serve up our favorite frozen custard.

Cajun Meatloaf

Meatloaf seems to be everyone's family favorite. Remember the "Blue Plate Special," a blast from the past? Meatloaf is comfort food that brings back childhood memories for many of us. Here's a recipe we've served often at the Pie Place on the hill, one that will add a little pep to your memories. Our guests love meatloaf at dinner with mashed potatoes and gravy or at lunch as a warm or cold sandwich. This photo shows it with Cheryl's BBQ sauce (page 52).

(photo by Mary Beams)

Serves 6 to 8

Amount	Ingredients
4 pounds	hamburger
2 cups	bread crumbs
1 (28-ounce) can	crushed tomatoes
1	green pepper, chopped
1 teaspoon	pepper
1 teaspoon	ground red pepper
1 teaspoon	salt
1/2 cup	chopped onions
1-1/2 Tablespoons	jalapeño pepper, seeded and finely chopped
2 large	eggs

Instructions
Preheat oven to 375° F.

Place all ingredients in a large bowl and mix until thoroughly combined. (It's OK to use your hands.) If the mixture looks a bit dry, add another egg. Shape meat mixture into loaves; two smaller loaves bake best in the oven, or make individual loaves for each person, which is a nice serving touch.

Place large loaves in bread pans or small ones on a baking sheet, leaving space between each loaf. Bake on a rack positioned in the middle of the oven for 45 minutes to 1 hour. Baking time depends on the size of loaf and your oven temperature. Check by placing knife in the loaf to make sure the hamburger is done (no longer pink). Do not overbake or meatloaf will be dry.

If you are preparing the meatloaf for later, after it's baked, you can wrap each loaf in plastic wrap and freeze. They'll be available for a quick and easy meal later. Just thaw the loaf, cut into slices and warm in a skillet.

Craft & Community

*"I want to live in a society where people are intoxicated
with the joy of making things."*

– William Coperthwaite
A Hand Made Life, In Search of Simplicity

It's called North House Folk School, and it's a living, breathing entity beside Lake Superior in our small town of Grand Marais.

Its campus bustles with vibrant life as students come from around the world to learn traditional northern craft, immersing in the community that is North House.

Instructors from Minnesota, Wisconsin, Iowa, North Carolina and Alaska, as well as Canada, Sweden, Norway and Finland, travel here to teach time-honored skills. There's Vladimir Yarish from Novgorod Province in Russia who teaches weaving of birch bark and the art of tuesi, birchbark storage containers. Or Robin Wood from the United Kingdom, inspiring students "to make the very best wooden bowls and plates that bring a little quiet beauty into everyday life."

A happy crew on the schooner Hjørdis from North House Folk School. (photo by Caleb Mattison)

While students learn new (old!) skills, they also develop new friendships. A weekly community pizza bake takes place at the handmade masonry and brick oven. From just outside the blue building, one of several brightly painted timbered structures on campus, laughter and cheery voices echo across the commons as the North House community breaks crust together.

Since its founding, North House Folk School has become as much a part of our community heartbeat as the Great Lake and boreal forests that surround us.

Local boatbuilder Mark Hansen, with the support of his wife, Wendy, founded the folk school in 1997 along with a group of innovative volunteers. Together they conceived of 23 courses that captured the story of traditional northern crafts.

The first North House catalog was created, with one slight problem. The fledgling group had no classrooms. "If this is supposed to happen, we will find a way" became the hope-filled mantra of these visionary folks.

Find a way they did, teaching a kayak class in a building adjacent to the Grand Marais Coast Guard Station by the Grand Marais Harbor.

I remember those early days well. Mark and his students frequently came to the Pie Place on the hill after a day of kayak making, warming themselves with a hearty bowl of soup.

Mark's booming laughter and enthusiasm cheered the hearts of all around him. He and many others made the vision a reality. He still teaches there, but now also operates Hansen Boat Works.

Today, nearly 20 years later, North House Folk School is alive and well, offering more than 400 courses, taught by 100 or so experienced, passionate instructors. They don't worry about classrooms anymore; their school campus in the heart of Grand Marais is nestled along Lake Superior. Classes take place in brightly colored buildings warmed by wood fires; laughter and camaraderie and gathering occurs in the inviting student commons.

The *Hjørdis*, a two-masted sailing schooner, bobs expectantly beside the dock while handmade wooden skiffs lay overturned on the rocky shore, awaiting a voyage in the harbor.

Greg Wright, executive director of North House, appears to be the perfect person for the helm. Positive and outgoing, Greg's enthusiasm is infectious. His friendly manner quickly makes you feel a part of the North House family, which in fact you are.

Boatbuilder Mark Hansen, happy by the water, naturally. (photo by Kate Watson)

But Greg is the first to acknowledge that success depends on the committed full-time staff – Jessa Frost, Kay Costello, Russ Viton, Kate Watson, Kaitlyn Bohlin, Andrew Beavers and Matt Nesheim. The help, though, goes beyond even them. Hundreds of volunteers work tirelessly to make classes and events possible.

And there is plenty to volunteer to do. From fish boils and potlucks to concerts, folk dances and seasonal events, many hands and hearts create the warmth and welcome felt as soon as you walk onto campus. There's the Winterer's Gathering & Arctic Film Festival, Wooden Boat Show, Northern Fibers Retreat, Family Weekend, Unplugged and Wood weeks. Plus there are those 400 classes.

The Pie Place Café has had a relationship with the North House since the beginning, feeling deeply connected and committed to those who have brought so much to our remote community. We've happily fed students and staff, catering large events, feeding musicians before the Unplugged concert and providing lunches for classes.

Every year, we prepare the Steam Bent Brunch, an annual gathering held during the Wooden Boat Show. We have served more than 200 eager brunchers in a sitting with ticket sales raising money for North House. It's also a great way to say "thank you" to our friends who work so hard to make the folk school a success.

We've even been students ourselves. Our family has taken many classes at North House throughout the years, enriched by the hands-on experience and welcoming energy of the place.

At the end of a class, you leave having learned something and having accomplished something you didn't necessarily think you could. You also leave knowing you've forged new friendships, making you part of something bigger that will change the world.

Mary Beams, our Pie Place "Pie Lady," conceived of "the Fearless Pie Baker" classes at North House, trading places as a student to become the teacher (along with our other Pie Lady, Katherine Goertz).

That's the way it is at North House – today's teacher may be tomorrow's student. Learning from each other makes a community exciting, full of life and full circle.

And building community is actually what the North House Folk School is all about.

"This is about doing, making things happen, and finishing something.
There's a healing thing that happens when you work with your hands. It's not about efficiency;
it's not about proficiency. It's about learning to be a human being with all your senses."
– Mark Hansen, boatbuilder, woodworker, instructor

Lattice Raspberry Pie

Raspberries taste of summer like nothing else can, whether in a bowl with cream and sugar, plucked from a bush while hiking in the woods or baked in a pie and topped with homemade ice cream. Made with a lattice top, this recipe is a showy pie to bring out for guests. But I just bet your family will love it, too.

Serves 6

Amount	Ingredients
1 recipe	pie dough, page 23
5 cups	fresh or frozen raspberries
1 cup	sugar
3 Tablespoons	cornstarch
2 Tablespoons	butter
2 Tablespoons	half-and-half
2 Tablespoons	sugar
For sprinkling	nutmeg for top of pie

Instructions

Preheat oven to 375° F.

Roll out half the dough into an 11-inch round on a lightly floured surface, using a floured rolling pin, and line a 9-inch pie pan with bottom crust.

In a large bowl, toss fruit, sugar and cornstarch, mixing thoroughly. Place fruit mixture into the pie pan and dot generously with the butter. Top it with a rolled pastry crust, brush with half-and-half, sprinkle with sugar and nutmeg. With a sharp knife, cut small vent holes for steam to escape. Or use a lattice top (instructions next page).

Bake for 1-1/2 hours, checking at intervals after 1 hour, until crust is golden brown and juices are thick and bubbly. If you've used a lattice top and it's getting a bit too brown before the pie is quite done, "tent" the top loosely with foil and continue baking.

Chef's note: If your oven bakes unevenly, you might want to turn the pie 180 degrees after about 45 minutes.

(photo by Mary Beams)

How to Do a Lattice Top

A lattice on a pie is made by layering alternating strips of dough over and under to make a patterned top. The patterns you may create are many, depending on the width of the strips you cut and the space you leave between each strip.

Juicier pies with fresh, canned or frozen fruits will need strips that are closer together. Drier pies will tolerate wide spaces between strips. It's fun to experiment with patterns as you get familiar with lattices.

To form a lattice, roll an 11-ounce crust dough patty into a rectangle about 11 inches wide and 18 inches long. Using the back of a knife (or a pastry cutter), cut strips: you will need 14 to 18 strips, depending on the width of the lattice pieces.

Lay an X of two strips at right angle to one another in the center of the pie (one vertical and one horizontal strip). Lay two more strips, one on each side of the X.

Now, fold the center bottom strip back and place a strip across the two strips still laying on the fruit.

Next fold those two strips back, place a strip across the pie and lower the folded parts back onto the pie.

Keep working your way across the pie one strip at a time, always folding back the strips underneath, laying a new strip on the top of those still on the fruit and then setting the folded part back over the newly placed strip. What's underneath is always folded up, a strip is laid across the remaining strips, the folded up strips are then laid back down and the new "underneath" strips are folded back.

When all the pie is covered, trim the overhanging strips and crimp the edge all the way around the pie.

Pat or brush half-and-half onto the surface, sprinkle with sugar and nutmeg. Bake per pie instructions.

Chef's note: If the pie isn't quite done, but the lattice top is getting a bit too brown, "tent" the top loosely with foil and continue baking.

(photos by Mary Beams)

Paints, Bees & Blueberry Pie

I still remember one of the first nights in our new home in Grand Marais.

That morning while having coffee at the Waltzing Bear, we met Tim Young, a local artist who had a studio and gallery called "The Caboose," literally an old railroad car situated on Highway 61.

Welcoming us to the community, Tim invited our family to an art opening for his friend and fellow artist Tom McCann. Eager to meet the folks in our new town and get acquainted with the local art scene, we gratefully accepted.

I immediately liked Tom, a humble, articulate person with an open-hearted spirit. The collection of his paintings featured at the opening showed Grand Marais at night. They inspired me to realize that there is light even in darkness; Tom's nighttime images exuded an ethereal light.

Tom loves to paint in the open air, being close to his subjects, whether a beautiful sunset on the open water or an intriguing weathered old building.

One of his favorite locations to paint on Lake Superior is Rossport, a tiny Ontario village where he has become friends with many of the locals, hearing their stories and painting life there.

Tom also became a friend of our Pie Place family. Working as a cartographer for the Superior National Forest, Tom ordered "lunch to go" nearly every day. Since the Pie Place on the hill was situated across the street from the forest headquarters, all Tom had to do was amble on over.

No matter what his luncheon choice, he always ordered a slice of blueberry pie.

One summer day, we became the proud owners of a pie refrigeration unit. Sadly, once it arrived, it was much larger and heavier than we had anticipated. Josh,

Tom in his element at Quetico Provincial Park at the boundary waters. (photo by Nancy Haarmeyer)

being the only "man on deck," scratched his head as he looked at the heavy beast sitting in the middle of our driveway.

How in the world were we going to get this monster into the restaurant?

I had an idea! I called Tom, explained our dilemma and promised him a whole blueberry pie if he could pull together a work crew to muscle the fridge into its new home.

An eager crew of six men appeared at our back door within five minutes. After much huffing and puffing, along with out-of-the-box thinking and muscle, the deed was done. And never a happier group have I seen as those six men walked back across the street, each with a slice of blueberry pie in hand.

We often see Tom and his wife, Nancy Haarmeyer, around town, participating with enthusiasm in all the wonderful things that our small community offers.

Nancy, a fiber artist, is active in the Grand Marais Fiber Arts Guild. Her work appears at the yearly Christmas Fiber Guild Bazaar and in area galleries and shops. The couple also is active in the Grand Marais Art Colony, with their work frequently on display in the Great Hall exhibitions.

Art shows aren't the only places we spot them. The lively couple loves to dance and we often see them at the North House Contra Dances, kicking up their heels for a reel or two.

One summer day, I happened upon Tom at the Java Moose, the local coffee shop down the street from

The Pie Place Café. Knowing I am a beekeeper, he asked, "Do you have any dead bees I could have?" A little confused, I assured him that I did indeed. Tom went on to explain that he was immersing himself in Japanese sumi-e black-ink painting and wanted the deceased honeybees as models.

I went home and filled a tiny box with the most beautiful bees I could find. After a life of pollination, they would be Tom's models. A life of service never ends.

Several months later, I saw Tom again as he was taking paintings into the Betsy Bowen Studio. He thanked me for the bees and gifted me with a painting of them. I was thrilled, as you might imagine.

Tom has a life of service, too. He'll continue to paint, and we will continue to seek out his paintings.

This artist and friend is a vital part of our community, of the place we now call home.

Blueberry Sour Cherry Pie

There's nothing like the marriage of summer blueberries and sour cherries. Each mouthful of flavor yields the subtle essence of a summer forest. Those of you who like blueberry pie will love this unexpected combination of sweet and sour.

Serves 6

Amount	Ingredients
1 recipe	pie dough, page 23
3-1/2 cups	fresh or frozen blueberries
1-1/2 cups	fresh or frozen sour cherries (pitted)
2 teaspoons	lemon juice
1/2 teaspoon	almond extract
1 cup	sugar
3 Tablespoons	cornstarch
2 Tablespoons	butter
2 to 3 Tablespoons	half-and-half
For sprinkling	nutmeg for top of pie
1 teaspoon	sugar

Instructions

Preheat oven to 375° F.

Roll out half the dough into an 11-inch round on a lightly floured surface, using a floured rolling pin, and line a 9-inch pie pan with bottom crust.

In a large bowl toss fruit, lemon juice, almond extract, sugar and cornstarch, mixing thoroughly. Place fruit in pie crust. Dot with butter.

Top with a rolled pastry crust. Crimp and then brush with half-and-half. Sprinkle with nutmeg and sugar. Cut a vent hole in the center of pie with a thimble, or make slits with a sharp knife.

Bake for 1-1/2 hours, checking at intervals after 1 hour, until crust is golden brown and the juices run thick and bubbly.

We Were Waiting for Them

Summer on the North Shore is a happy time. Children of all ages (yes, adults, too) congregate along the Lake Superior shore to fill brightly colored plastic buckets with beach stones, skip rocks across the water and occasionally chase a few squawking Canada geese into the waves.

For so many of us, summer means the open water and a beach, whether an inland lake or our great inland sea.

At The Pie Place Café, summer was a time to renew acquaintances with old friends from afar, picking up where we left off the summer before.

Summer meant catching up on all that happened when these friends were not by the Big Lake. We talked about the end of a school year, a new job, an engagement or wedding, a book published, a health concern, children growing like weeds or perhaps the sad loss of a loved one. What a difference a year can make in the course of life.

One year, the return of our longtime friends Chris and Julie Gilbert brought news of a most wonderful, life-changing surprise.

The couple had been trying to adopt a baby for quite some time, investigating adoption from China. Like many hopeful adoptive parents, they'd spent hours filling out papers, attending meetings and interviewing with agency staff and then waiting … always waiting.

Many times, their hopes were raised, only to be dashed by one legality or another. A whirlwind trip to China had been met with disappointment. Discouragement set in. When would they hold "their child" in their arms?

The portrait of a family: Julie, Sam, Jesse and Chris beside Lake Superior. (photo by Julie Gilbert)

Their desire to be parents, though, was stronger than the wait and the bureaucracies. They continued the long, arduous process of finding their child, and each summer we'd get an update.

Then one glorious summer day, I looked up to see Chris and Julie coming through our front door with a smile, a wave … and a baby stroller.

As I rushed over, the beaming parents picked up their beautiful baby boy.

"Kathy, meet Sam." Sam had found his way home!

Clearly thrilled by parenthood, Chris and Julie took to the task like seasoned veterans. They adored Sam, as parents tend to do, and I knew that this little boy had chosen his parents well. They waited for him through the pregnancy of his birth mother, who decided to give him up for adoption.

Julie was in the delivery room for Sam's birth. As she watched Sam arrive into the world, Julie told me, "I felt something in my heart, and heard myself saying, 'Oh, there you are.'"

A couple of years later, in the summer of 2010, as Chris and Julie were considering a second adoption, they received a call. Sam's biological brother would be entering the world in about a month. Would Chris and Julie be willing to adopt him? They started packing as soon as they hung up the phone.

Eagerly they retraced their earlier journey to pick up their newest son. This time Chris got to be in the delivery room, too, when Jesse was born. They arrived home to present Sam with his baby brother on Labor Day.

Julie later mused to me, "We tried so hard to adopt a baby from China, but it just never worked out. Only now do I realize that we were waiting for Sam and Jesse."

Not all families come into being the same way, but this family was certainly meant to be.

After I left regular work at The Pie Place Café to focus on other pursuits (writing cookbooks, for one), I didn't always see those people I have come to know and love. But a couple of summers ago while having pizza at Sydney's, the local eatery owned by our friends Bruce and Pam Block, I watched a sunny summer montage unfold on the beach outside the window.

A couple sitting on a bench kept an eye on their two vigorous boys running along the shore, throwing stones into the pounding surf.

"Be careful, Sam!" the man shouted to be heard above the waves. "Watch out for your brother."

Even though I couldn't see their faces, I knew immediately who this family was.

Jumping up from the table, I ran out to them, hugging Chris and Julie and exclaiming about how much the boys had grown.

They called Sam and Jesse over to me.

"You don't remember Kathy, but she was one of the first people in Grand Marais to meet you when you were a baby," they told Sam.

Both boys politely said, "Hello," and then raced back to their joyful play.

Yup, summer in Grand Marais is definitely fun for children. And how blessed we are to get to meet them when they first arrive.

Pie Place Homemade Vanilla Ice Cream

I remember summer Sundays when my mom, dad, sister, brothers, aunts, uncles, cousins and I went to my grandparents' farm to make homemade ice cream. It took a whole family as the men took turns cranking the old-fashioned ice cream freezer. Store-bought just isn't the same. Today's electric ice cream makers are easier, but the creamy end result remains the same. Give it a try … you're in for a treat.

Makes 1 gallon, enough for 16 to 20 1-cup servings

Amount	Ingredients
2 pints	half-and-half
2 cups	sugar
2 Tablespoons	vanilla extract
1 bean	vanilla, cut in half and scrape out the soft inner part to use
1/2 gallon	heavy cream (8 cups)
per instructions	rock salt and ice for ice cream maker
1/2 cup	water

Instructions

Combine 1 pint of half-and-half with sugar and microwave for 2 minutes, or warm in a saucepan on medium-low heat for 2 minutes until sugar is dissolved. Stir well.

Combine sugar mixture, the rest of the half-and-half, vanilla extract, soft inner part of vanilla bean and heavy cream, stirring until well blended. Pour mixture into the inner metal container of your ice cream maker to the "fill" line.

Place ice cream paddle into metal container, put on lid and place container with ice cream mixture into ice cream maker. Before you add ice and rock salt, start machine to make sure everything is aligned and working properly. Place ice on bottom of the ice cream maker around the inner metal container, about 2-1/2 inches thick, then add three large handfuls of rock salt scattered over ice. Make sure the salt is evenly distributed in the freezer compartment. Repeat until bucket is full. Ice and salt will be between the ice cream freezer and the inner container housing the ice cream liquid.

Plug in the maker, and while the freezer is rotating, add 1/2 cup water, pouring it evenly over the ice. Wait for ice cream to be completed. This requires some patience for those who usually just buy ice cream from the freezer compartment at the grocery store. Expect an hour, but check after 45 minutes.

You will know when the ice cream is done, as the machine will begin to slow down (if it stops rotating, it's done; don't burn out the motor). This is because the liquid inside the metal container has turned firm and the paddle is working hard to turn in the ice cream. However, if you're not quite sure, unplug the freezer, lift off the top unit, then lift the inner lid to see if the ice cream is the consistency you want. DO NOT take the container out of the ice until you are sure the ice cream is done. If the ice cream is not quite set up, add a bit more ice and salt, layering as before, and continue the process.

Keep in mind that homemade ice cream is a much softer consistency than the ice cream you buy in the store. Though you can store it in the freezer to get a harder ice cream, the real treat is ice cream straight from your ice cream maker.

The Quest for Walter

When the Pie Place family first came to the North Shore, we yearned for connection to this wonderful wilderness. We made trips up the Gunflint Trail to hike, cross-country ski and fish.

One of our favorite spots was Golden Eagle Lodge, built in 1945. Often we'd pack a picnic, trek up the Gunflint and rent a pontoon for the day. We'd motor around Flour Lake looking for fish. Sometimes when the fishing was slow, we'd peel off our T-shirts and jump into the cool clear water. One day, while we were in the water, a mother moose and her calf apparently had the same idea. They swam toward us until, as startled as we were, the mom turned and herded her gangly youngster back to shore.

No doubt such adventures encouraged the Baumanns to buy Golden Eagle Lodge in 1976 after camping at Flour Lake with their four boys for years. We met John and Irene Baumann and their son and daughter-in-law, Dan and Teresa, on one of our first trips there. After their years of backbreaking work, the lodge, cabins, campsites and naturalist center had become a destination for many.

We liked these friendly, hard-working folks immediately and spent many memorable hours boating, swimming and fishing on Flour Lake and staying in a cabin nestled among the trees. In the evening, we'd fry the day's catch in a cast iron skillet. If the catch consisted of one meager fish for our family of 13, we each still exclaimed over our single succulent bite. The stars never seemed brighter than at Golden Eagle Lodge, and the tremolo of loons woke us to the morning sun.

The hard-working, fun-loving Baumanns: Jonathan, Brianna (in back), Teresa, Dan, Zach and Neeko. Below, Irene and John. (photos by Dan Baumann)

We learned more about the lodge family, too. John had a passion for pie, and so a tradition was born. We brought a fresh baked pie whenever we visited. John never turned down whatever we brought.

On one fishing trip, Dan told us about a large walleye living in a cove on the east side of Flour Lake. Many had hooked the wily fish, only to have it break their line and swim away. That was it for Cheryl, our family fisherman. The elusive walleye became "Walter," and the hunt for him was on.

From that day forward, we would float silently in the cove, trying every lure, worm, cricket or other bait to entice Walter to our hooks. To the consternation of all on board, I imagined Walter treading water mere inches from the pontoon, a huge smile on his fishy face.

For years, our annual custom was to take one last excursion on the pontoon at summer's end. Poles and fishing gear put away, we savored the vibrant fall colors and listened to the last loon calls. We always motored over to Walter's cove, wishing him a hearty farewell until next summer.

Every autumn, Irene would say, "Don't take the pontoon out of the water just yet. The Pie Place kids haven't been up." That's the kind of folks they are.

Six years ago, our beloved Cheryl passed away. One of her parting wishes was that we spend a weekend in "our cabin" at Golden Eagle Lodge. She urged us to eat great food, play games and take the pontoon to Walter's cove. Cheryl asked for some of her ashes to rest in the cove, one of her favorite places in this world. I like to think that Walter welcomed her there, and at last she met the fish she could never catch.

On our last morning there fulfilling Cheryl's wish, I went to the dock to watch the sunrise. A mournful loon called to me. She rose from the water, wings outstretched and her head raised to the sun. Like me, her time had come to leave Flour Lake, but she seemed full of life, eager for what awaited.

For a brief moment, the ache in my grieving heart melted away. All that remained was the sun, the lake and the promise of a new life. Cheryl would love that. I must tell her.

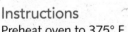 *our secret recipe*

Bumbleberry Pie

Bumbleberry merges all the summer fruits we love and you can taste the subtle flavors of each in every delectable bite. A Pie Place favorite.

Serves 6

Amount	Ingredients
1 recipe	pie dough, page 23
1-1/2 cups	blueberries
1-1/2 cups	sliced strawberries
1 cup	raspberries
1 cup	rhubarb, sliced
2 Tablespoons	lemon juice
1 cup	sugar
1/3 cup	all-purpose flour
2 Tablespoons	butter
1/4 cup	coarse sugar for sprinkling (Mary likes turbinado)

(photo by Mary Beams)

Instructions
Preheat oven to 375° F.

Roll out half of the dough into an 11-inch round on a lightly floured surface, using a floured rolling pin, and line a 9-inch pie pan with bottom crust.

In a large bowl, gently mix the fruits with lemon juice and toss with sugar and all-purpose flour. Place fruit in the unbaked pie shell, dot with 2 Tablespoons butter cut into small pieces.

Using a medium grater, shave remaining patty of pie dough over the pie, taking care not to compact the shavings, but to cover all the fruit. If the patty is too moist to shave well, dip it liberally into flour and work it through. If you prefer a traditional top crust, roll the dough on a floured surface, place on top of fruit and crimp. Sprinkle generously with coarse sugar over the top. (Regular sugar will be fine if that's what you have.) If you decide on a traditional top crust, cut slits into the crust to vent steam. Place pie pan on a baking sheet. This is a juicy pie. Bake for 1 hour, and up to 1 hour and 20 minutes. The juices will thicken and run clear and bubbly, the top will be golden brown when done.

Autumn Bounty

Autumn adds color to Artists' Point. (photo by Bob Berg)

How Would You Like Your Eggs?

As a restaurant described in *Minnesota Monthly* as serving the best breakfast on the North Shore and touted by Andrew Zimmern of Food Network fame as serving jam that is "orgasmic," The Pie Place Café had a reputation to uphold.

We did consider The Pie Place Café a "happening place" when it came to breakfast, featuring our famed Maple Sausage Patties conceived of by Cheryl during the infancy of the Pie Place on the hill.

But the essence of a good old-fashioned American breakfast, as we know, is the egg, and in taking any breakfast order, the mantra was "How would you like your eggs?"

People are very, and I mean *very*, particular about their eggs. Everybody knows just how they want their eggs and they express that in ways that sometimes defy one's grasp of the human language. We had to become familiar with all the nuances of egg communication.

Poached, over easy, over medium, over hard, fried, basted, hard boiled, no jiggly whites, egg in a hole, dippy – you get the picture.

And believe me when I tell you, the perfectly prepared egg can make a person's day, and we treated it as that important. Many people trusted us as their breakfast place of choice.

Steve Nielsen, Nancy Starr and their lively family came to The Pie Place Café for over a decade of breakfasts. Their gang brought a playful energy and we looked forward to seeing and serving the family.

Steve, quite the tease, is not beyond shock value as he needles and cajoles. I learned to give as good as I got, sometimes mock threatening, "If I didn't like you so much, you'd be finding these eggs on your head." Which Steve loves, of course.

I recall quite clearly the first time that Steve and Nancy came in for breakfast. I recited my breakfast mantra, asking Steve how he'd like his eggs.

"Hard as heck!" came the reply.

OK, a new descriptor to add to our egg preparation list.

From that time on, when Steve, Nancy and their robust family came for breakfast, it was clear how he wanted his eggs. Case (or egg carton) closed.

Nancy and Steve have been coming to the North Shore since the 1950s. Both are avid outdoors folks who love the serenity of the forests, lakes and rivers nestled in the Boundary Waters Canoe Area Wilderness.

To the good life with Steve and Nancy.
(photo courtesy the couple)

Nancy worked at Hungry Jack Lodge in the early 1990s, bartering good old-fashioned hard work for room and board. Longing to be on the Gunflint Trail and Hungry Jack Lake, she cleaned cabins and anything she could to secure her stay. Nancy scrubbed more logs than she'd like to remember, but she was happy and that was all that mattered.

After years of spending as much time as they could on the North Shore, Steve and Nancy bought property on the outskirts of Grand Marais, planning to live here full time as soon as they retired.

They made frequent trips from the Twin Cities to clear land, had a driveway put in and began work on their future home.

They always seem to have an eager crew of children and friends. For this close-knit family, work weekends became fun weekends. For our part, all we had to do was keep their bellies full.

One Saturday morning the gang came in for breakfast before heading off to another hard day of labor.

The morning was frantic with guests and feeling more than a little stressed, I went into "efficient mode." Already knowing how he wanted his eggs and jumping right in to the business at hand, I looked at Steve and, before I could stop the words, I said, "You're the guy who's …!" You know what came next.

Once it was spoken, I was mortified. My face burned with embarrassment. Getting ready to flee (the only thing I wanted to do just then), Steve burst out laughing, gales of it spilling all over the place.

I started laughing, too, along with everyone else at the table. Awkward moments do pass quickly, if we can laugh at ourselves. I will forever be in Steve's debt for helping me to save face that fateful morning.

Last summer I happened upon Nancy beside a local antique shop. She and Steve were making the final move and would be living here soon.

Shortly after, Steve and some fishing buddies, including his granddaughter Piper, stopped in for breakfast before heading into the BWCAW.

Even though it's taken years for Steve and Nancy to make the move here, it seems as if they've been part of the fabric of Grand Marais all along.

We come to know so much about the lives of the people we serve, their hopes and dreams, their ups and downs, and, perhaps most importantly, how they like their eggs.

Potato, Leek and Mushroom Frittata

A frittata is an open-faced omelet often baked in a cast iron skillet that can go from stove to oven to table. A change from more traditional egg dishes, a frittata can be served at breakfast for a more hearty meal. Or it's perfect with a salad for a light supper.

Serves 4

Amount	Ingredients
2 small	potatoes, unpeeled, scrubbed, cooked in salted water for 10 minutes and sliced moderately thin
1 Tablespoon	olive oil
1	leek, slice the white end only
1 cup	mushrooms, sliced
9 large	eggs
1/2 cup	half-and-half
3 Tablespoons	white wine
1/2 teaspoon	salt
1/4 teaspoon	pepper
1/2 cup	Parmesan cheese, grated

Instructions

Slice the cooked potatoes. Heat olive oil in a large oven-safe pan and sauté leeks for 5 to 7 minutes until tender. Add mushrooms, sauté for 3 minutes. Add potatoes and sauté for 5 to 10 minutes until done. Mix eggs, half-and-half, wine, salt and pepper with whisk; pour over potatoes, leeks and mushrooms. Cover and cook about 5 minutes over low heat until the bottom of the mixture has set, but it's slightly uncooked on the top. Sprinkle with Parmesan. If skillet has a wooden handle, wrap it in foil. Complete by broiling a few minutes in oven until cheese is melted and top is golden. Slice into wedges and serve with fruit for breakfast or a salad of organic field greens for a light supper.

"Snappy Bacon"

Gunnar, a happy, snappy kid. (photo by Lisa Kollander)

Children have been such a wonderful part of our years as a restaurant family. One of the joys of operating this kind of business has been to see babies and small children grow into incredibly bright, self-reliant young adults who leave the nest of family and strike out to build the life they are called to live.

Each child seems to have unique words to describe what he or she wants to eat and how it should be prepared. In the kitchen, Josh learned, based upon "guest check speak," which young diner was out in the restaurant ordering.

"Dippy eggs" meant Grace and Keegan, who insisted, "How else are you going to dip your toast into the yolk?"

Some youngsters, encouraged to make the "healthy choice" perhaps of celery sticks over chips, would lament, "OK, I'll make the healthy choice."

Josh tried to help make the meals fun. He folded chocolate chips into pancake batter artfully making happy faces. I think he enjoyed making playful creations as much as those eager young guests liked to receive them. Many a crayon drawing was sent back to the kitchen as a "thank you" for a job well done. Sometimes "our kids," those we knew well, asked to see the chef cooking. When not busy, Josh would agree, a big smile on his face.

After the two-penny tour, the children often returned to their table with exclamations: "Wow, Mom! I got to go into the kitchen!"

Gunnar Olson has been traveling to the North Shore with his dad and mom, Larry Olson and Lisa Kollander, since he was a tadpole. Gunnar loves the water and spends hours throwing stones in the Lake Superior swells. On each trip, he ambles over rocks, collecting treasures on the beach and in the forest. Many such acquisitions ended up proudly displayed on the breakfast table with detailed explanations of what they were and where he had found them. An inquisitive boy, Gunnar seems fascinated by life and brings that enthusiasm to his family's trips to Grand Marais.

Since Gunnar and his parents started having breakfast at the Pie Place from our early days, we watched him grow from a rather shy little guy into a handsome, outgoing young man.

As passionate as Gunnar was for his gathered treasures, he was equally clear about his breakfast preferences – crisp bacon and a toasted English muffin with cream cheese oozing into the crevices. It was his standard fare. Asked how he liked his bacon, Gunnar replied with childlike simplicity. "I want snappy bacon." Seemed clear to me, but I glanced at Lisa for culinary confirmation. "He means crisp," she whispered. So "snappy bacon" became a standing order whenever this family arrived in the morning.

Things have changed since those early days … our restaurant moved from the hill to the harbor across from the lighthouse and now into a new phase. Josh left the kitchen for other artistic pursuits, and I am writing cookbooks. Some things remain the same, though. Larry, Lisa, and Gunnar still love coming to Grand Marais and I suspect that for breakfast, Gunnar still prefers his bacon "snappy."

Spicy Bacon

Like Gunnar, our family loves bacon. The Cayenne in this recipe creates a "snappy" flavor that will delight your taste buds. What a great way to wake up your morning.

Serves 6

Amount	Ingredients
1-1/2 Tablespoons	light brown sugar, packed
1/4 rounded teaspoon	Cayenne pepper
1/4 rounded teaspoon	black pepper
1 pound	bacon, thick sliced

Instructions

Preheat oven to 350° F and put oven rack in middle position.

Stir brown sugar, Cayenne and black pepper in small bowl until well blended.

Arrange bacon slices in 1 layer (do not overlap) on a large broiler rack. Bake 20 minutes. Turn slices over and sprinkle evenly with spice mixture. Continue baking until bacon is crisp and a deep golden color, 20 to 30 minutes more. (Check bacon every 5 minutes so you don't overbake).

Transfer bacon to paper towels to absorb grease.

Chef's note: You can use regular-sliced bacon, too, but use shorter baking times.

(photo courtesy cyclonebill)

Robbie Burns & a Cabin in the Woods

The McDonald clan (photo courtesy of the McDonalds)

The McDonalds from the Isle of Skye.

The name evokes so many images. A mountain glen, verdant green against a gray sky. The McDonald plaid, clan colors wrapped around the waist of a hearty Scotsman. A bagpipe whose voice wails over the sea. Or perhaps an old man before a fire in an ancient stone cottage, waving his smoking pipe as he spouts a Robert Burns poem at the top of his lungs.

I love these visions, but as I shake out of my reverie, a different image comes to mind: Duncan and Evelyn McDonald, faithful Pie Place Café customers and friends for nearly two decades.

Having lived, gone to school and worked in Michigan for much of their life, they are kindred spirits to me, a Michigan girl born and raised. After retirement, they moved to Grand Marais. They bought a cabin on Gunflint Lake, a home in town on Lake Superior and then split their time between the two.

They've spent many happy summers at the cabin with their daughter, Deborah McDonald, son-in-law, Ed Hyman, and grandchildren, Cameron and Devon. Worlds away from their California home, the boys spend hours hiking, boating, fishing, exploring and gathering memories – like the time Devon proudly reeled his catch to his grandpa's waiting net only to find a glaring loon, beak clamped ferociously around the fish, confronting them as if to say, "Hey! That's my fish!"

Since the family often visited the Pie Place, we watched the inquisitive boys grow into capable young men, eventually going off to college to pursue careers in medicine and filmmaking.

Their grandparents remain young at heart. Evelyn goes to Zumba, is auxiliary president for Cook County North Shore Hospital & Care Center, works in the Garden Club and tries to keep Duncan out of trouble. Duncan, always busy at the cabin, still finds time to get together with a group of local guys for coffee most mornings. They've spent months each year in California going to their grandsons' sports events.

Back in Grand Marais, keeping the cabin ready for family visits can prove challenging.

Once a fisher (a relative of the weasel) chased a squirrel in winter, likely skittering down the cabin chimney. The sharp-toothed fellow apparently spent much of the season trying to leave. When the McDonalds opened the cabin in spring, they found the tragedy of a dead fisher and his unfortunate prey nested in the sofa cushions and their gnawed cabin much in need of renovation.

On one July Fourth weekend, straight-line winds laid waste to thousands of acres of old-growth trees, cutting a jagged swath on the Gunflint Trail. Their cabin was spared, but Duncan and Evelyn lost hundreds of trees, including 40 towering virgin white pines.

Then there were bears on porches and docks washed away by turbulent waves. With the spirit of all who choose to live here, they pushed up their flannel sleeves each time and put their piece of the wilderness back together again. The year of the blowdown, they planted hundreds of seedlings, and each fall they mulch and wrap the young trees over days of backbreaking work. The trees, by the way, are growing nicely.

Duncan and Evelyn came to The Pie Place Café most Sundays for breakfast. True to his Scottish heritage, jovial Duncan delights in teasing. He's been trying to get a job as The Pie Place "pie taste tester" for years. I tease him back, which is only fair, telling him I need a picture of him in his family tartan. He sheepishly offers Evelyn as the girl for the job. "She bought a kilt in the McDonald plaid when we were there."

Duncan and Evelyn have made numerous trips to Scotland, once visiting the Isle of Skye, Duncan's ancestral home. They visited an elderly cousin, who regaled them with old photographs and family stories. That gentle old Scotsman quoted verses from Robert Burns in a loud and melodic brogue, and I can almost hear, "My heart's in the Highlands, my heart is not here. My heart's in the Highlands a-chasing the deer …"

So you see, my imaginings are not too far off. We have the clan of McDonald right in our own backyard. Maybe with a little coaxing and a piece of pie, I can get Duncan to quote a verse or two.

Black Bean Soup

This hearty soup will warm your cockles as you snuggle in front of the fire on a frosty fall evening. Fit for the likes of Robbie Burns and those who love poetry or prose, this spicy soup is for the strong of heart.

Serves 4 to 6

Amount	Ingredients
3 Tablespoons	extra-virgin olive oil
1 large	dried bay leaf
1	jalapeño pepper, seeded and minced
4 cloves	garlic, minced
3 stalks	celery with greens, chopped
1 large	onion, chopped
1	red bell pepper, seeded and 1/4-inch dice
3 (15-ounce) cans	black beans (keep 1 can undrained)
2 Tablespoons	cumin
1-1/2 teaspoons	coriander
To taste	salt and pepper
1 to 3 Tablespoons	hot sauce, divided (we use Cholula sauce)
2 cups	chicken or vegetable stock
1 (15-ounce) can	diced tomatoes
To garnish (optional)	sour cream, sliced green onions, diced red bell pepper

Instructions

Pour olive oil into a medium soup pot and heat over medium-high heat. Add bay leaf, jalapeño, garlic, celery and onion. Cook 3 to 4 minutes, stirring occasionally. Add red peppers; cook 2 minutes.

Drain and rinse 2 cans of beans, add to the pot. Take remaining beans and juice and mash with immersion blender or a fork. Add mashed beans to pot and season with cumin, coriander, salt and pepper and 1 Tablespoon of hot sauce along with stock and tomatoes. Bring to a low bubble. Let simmer for 15 minutes. Add more hot sauce to desired spiciness.

Ladle into soup bowls and garnish with sour cream, green onions and red pepper.

(photo by Mary Beams)

Storyteller of the Gunflint Trail

Snuggling under my warm winter blanket, I began to re-read *A Wild Neighborhood*. After all, tomorrow I planned to write about the author, an illustrious teller of tales (one of my favorites), John Henricksson. As I read his words, John's strong, commanding professorial voice comes into my head.

Then thoughts of John and his wife, Julie, warm my heart. They have been devoted Pie Place Café friends for many years. I first met the couple when they came in for lunch on a rare hot summer day.

John, in his authoritative way, requested shade.

"Excuse me?" I countered, rather confused.

"My dear," said John, equally perplexed. "I need a shaded spot for our dog!"

John and Julie in their wild neighborhood.
(photo by Nace Hagemann)

Now I understood. I told him to pull his car to the back of the restaurant and park under the large tree outside the kitchen window. I offered a bowl of water, which seemed to please him immensely.

When they were properly seated, I approached the table to take their order. "Since we have never eaten in your establishment," John said, looking at me gravely from under bushy brows, "you will have to tell me what is good and what to order."

I did just that, and by the look on his face I knew that I'd guided him well. Feeling as if I had passed a crucial test, I relaxed. This distinguished man was to become a friend.

After that day, John and Julie came to the Pie Place weekly on their trips into town from their cabin on the Gunflint Trail. John's stern demeanor soon gave way to light-hearted banter and storied conversation peppered with the couple's lively life on the trail.

Editor, author, historian and naturalist, John is an acute observer of the natural world that surrounds his summer home in the boreal forest near the Boundary Waters Canoe Area Wilderness. His stories bring the forest creatures alive. From his writing, one feels a kinship, reverence and compassion for those often displaced wild neighbors and a rather fierce desire to protect them. I think perhaps that is part of John's plan as he artfully introduces you to a culture far more akin to us than we realize.

In *A Wild Neighborhood,* John talks of Makwa, Ojibwe for Bear, and an animal he portrays as "most like a man." John writes with great affection about the antics of bears, something we who also live in this neighborhood appreciate.

As new local restaurant owners, we quickly found out what we call a dumpster translates loosely to a popular "food truck" for the bears. We had a steady influx of guests at the dumpster for breakfast, lunch and dinner. Apparently we got a good reputation among bruins – "Have you eaten here? If not you must give it a try!" – because we had bears in the crab apple trees, inside the dumpster, in the bee yard and even meandering into the parking lot during broad daylight peering into customers' cars.

One summer a mama bear, a yearling and two small cubs showed up. We named them (sorry, John) Thich, Nhat and Han and stuck to Mama for the matriarch. Our place provided balanced meals for her growing family, and, my goodness, a mother can't be cooking all the time, can she?

It was a summer to remember.

Many of Mary "the Pie Lady" Beams' paintings are of bears, our adopted symbol of The Pie Place Café. So, John is right. We are neighbors to these wonderful inhabitants of the great North Woods. Sometimes it's hard to live with them, but as they were here first, we should give it our best. If humans and these usually gentle, inquisitive creatures are much alike, we'll be doing ourselves a favor in the end.

For those who haven't met John and Julie Henricksson, I invite you to pick up *A Wild Neighborhood* and introduce yourself. You'll come to know and love them along with their woodland friends … just as I did.

(*our secret recipe*)

Radish Dill Soup

Without a doubt, this soup is among the most requested – and until now well-kept secret – recipes at The Pie Place Café. Even if you can't imagine a soup from radishes, one taste and you're hooked. Creamy and delicious, this beautiful soup is adapted from an old Shaker recipe. You asked … and here it is.

Serves 6 to 8

Amount	Ingredients
1/2 cup	butter (1 stick)
1 medium	onion, peeled and diced
4 heaping cups	red radishes, trimmed, cleaned and thinly sliced
2 Tablespoons	fresh dill, minced (or 1 teaspoon dried dill weed), plus extra for garnish
1/2 cup	all-purpose flour
4 cups	chicken stock
1 cup	heavy cream
1 cup	half-and-half
To taste	salt and pepper

Instructions

In a large soup pot, melt the butter over low heat. Add onions, radishes and dill; cook until the vegetables are translucent, about 5 to 7 minutes, stirring often. Stir in the flour and cook 2 to 3 minutes; do not allow it to brown. Stir often. Stir in the chicken stock until smooth and simmer the soup over medium heat, 15 to 20 minutes or until the vegetables are tender. Again, stir often.

Carefully purée the soup in batches in a blender or food processor, then return to the soup pot. Stir in the cream and half-and-half, and season with salt and pepper. Heat to just below a simmer; do not let it come to a boil.

Ladle into bowls, and garnish with a sprig of fresh dill. Ta-da!

(photo by Mary Beams)

What Would Genghis Do?

Traditional cultures have lived in round houses for centuries, from yurts on the Mongolian steppe to the wiigiwaam (or wigwam), a structure built of bent-over saplings covered with birchbark and woven mats by the Ojibwe people, to the tipi of the Plains people like the Dakota.

Yurts, or "gers" as they are traditionally called, have been in use since the time of Genghis Khan. As many as 50,000 house families in Ulaanbaatar, the capital of Mongolia, to this very day.

The North House Folk School offers a class in making your own yurt, first taught by Mark Hansen and Kurt Buetow.

You can visit a yurt on the North House campus, or spend time in a yurt village, glowing from within, during the annual Winterer's Gathering. Hardy folks bring their moveable homes to spend a weekend for arctic films, winter survival classes, chili and companionable fun, snug and warm in their yurts despite the outside frigid temperatures.

All Kurt needs for happiness is a yurt and a pony. (photo by Jody Slocum)

I first met Kurt Buetow and his wife, Jody Slocum, when he began teaching the yurt class. They would come to the Pie Place on the hill for breakfast before class each morning.

Kurt and Jody care deeply about the environment, the world and the people with whom they share our global community and planet.

Kurt, an inventor by nature, always looks for ways to solve problems big and small. He adores the outdoors, cultivating a deep connection as he strives to live ever closer to harmony with the earth.

Jody is a talented fiber artist. She's traveled many times to Guatemala and other Latin countries to help women in local villages set up fair-trade weaving cooperatives. These enterprises give women opportunities for more prosperous lives by empowering them with skills to produce indigenous crafts for a greater world market.

Jody and her friend Mary Anne Wise founded "Cultural Cloth," a store in Maiden Rock, Wisconsin, and an online marketplace that establishes direct relationships with fiber artists in many countries. This opportunity gives resilient people in many places around the world a way for cultural expression in the form of the beautiful items they create, as well as a way to help make a living.

Our family shares many interests in common with this couple, including a love of yurts.

Cheryl and I had a mutual dream of owning a yurt. After spending a night in one of the yurts at Poplar Creek, owned by Ted and Barbra Young. we were hooked. We began an active and energetic search for the perfect yurt.

Kurt, a yurt enthusiast who has made six or seven of his own, encouraged us to take his class.

However, we felt drawn to purchase a traditional ger from Mongolia, and after extensive research, we found FIRE, the Flagstaff International Relief Effort Project.

A nonprofit in Flagstaff, Arizona, FIRE Project acts as the middleman to get handmade Mongolian yurts shipped to folks in the United States. Proceeds from the sale of the yurts then go directly to needy families in Mongolia. By buying our yurt through FIRE, a young mother and recent widow was able to get her own yurt so that she and her children would not be homeless.

One day our 22-foot yurt finally arrived, having come across the country wrapped in felted wool. It was a relatively small bundle, about 5 feet in diameter, from which would emerge the yurt of our dreams.

Bundle to "bungalow" perplexed us, though. That's where Kurt came in.

Kurt enthusiastically became a part of our yurt raising, along with three friends, Rick Anderson, Jane Reyer and Gavin Stevens, who arrived ready to work one fall morning.

Eight of us stood in a circle, undoing the hand-felted wrapping that would itself become the walls. The earthy smell of the steppe (or what we imagined anyway) wafted into our nostrils. Piles of yak-hair rope and brightly painted poles lay helter-skelter on the ground. We found writing on the canvas, obviously in Mongolian. If these were the directions, they didn't help. We looked at Kurt, who was scratching his head.

We were all more than a bit overwhelmed at the task before us until Jane, a pragmatic Buddhist, quipped, "What would Genghis do?"

That broke the ice as we all laughed. We rolled up our sleeves and got about the business at hand.

All day, whenever we came to a cog in the wheel – and I mean this quite literally as the roof poles we were trying to connect to the circular Tono kept falling out and clobbering us in the head – someone would speak the plaintive: "What would Genghis do?" Often, less-than-holy frustrated expletives might be the echoed cry.

Nearly eight hours later, our industrious group had erected the yurt, something a Mongolian family could do in a little over an hour (but then, they could probably read the directions).

But we had done it together and added a unifying refrain that kept us going until the end.

Rick brought sweetgrass, and we smudged the interior and exterior of the yurt, each saying a few words to consecrate this space that would be used for prayer, meditation and gathering.

We set up an old wooden table in the tall meadow grasses outside the yurt. We sat together, tired yet happy, to share supper.

The yurt stood serenely in the last rays of the late afternoon sun, as we raised a glass of wine to those gentle nomads on the other side of the world. Because of them, our dream had been fulfilled.

Our yurt had come home.

A yurt in the boreal woods? An unusual sight, but a natural fit and a great gathering place for friends and family.
(photo courtesy Kurt Buetow)

Saffron Butternut Squash Soup

There's nothing like a spicy squash soup to celebrate autumn's harvest. This flavorful soup will warm your tummy on a frosty fall night. Set a festive table among the trees and enjoy those last warm fall days al fresco. Other squash can be substituted, like the heritage squash shown in the photo below.

Serves 6 to 8

Amount	Ingredients
1 (about 3 pounds)	butternut squash, halved and seeded
1 large	leek
1/4 cup	butter
Pinch	saffron threads
1 cup	dry white wine (we like a chardonnay)
2 medium	carrots, diced
4 cups	chicken broth
1/8 teaspoon	ground cinnamon
1/8 teaspoon	nutmeg
1/8 teaspoon	ground red pepper
1/4 cup	heavy cream
1/2 teaspoon	salt
1/4 teaspoon	ground pepper
Garnish	Crème Fraîche, recipe page 115

Instructions

Preheat oven to 375° F.

Cut squash in half lengthwise and bake for 1/2 hour.

Cut and discard green top from the leek. Cut white portion into slices.

Melt butter in a soup pot over medium heat; add leek slices and saffron, and sauté 5 minutes or until leek slices are tender. Add wine, and cook 1 to 2 minutes. Add squash, carrots, broth, cinnamon, nutmeg and red pepper. Bring to a boil. Reduce heat, and simmer, uncovered, 20 minutes or until squash and carrots are tender. Remove from heat, and cool slightly.

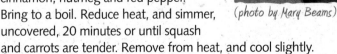

(photo by Mary Beams)

Process squash mixture, in batches, in a blender or food processor until smooth, stopping to scrape down sides. (A handheld immersion blender can also be used.) Return squash mixture to soup pot. Add cream, salt and pepper; simmer 10 to 15 minutes or until thickened. If the soup is too thick, thin with chicken broth. Garnish with Crème Fraîche, if desired.

Hungry Jack & Pulled Moose

As someone who believes in the interconnectedness of all beings on this wonderful planet, I frequently see my philosophy come to life in our northern community. Anywhere you look, you find the lines between families.

Take, as an example, the business founded in 1954 by Harry and Margaret Nolan. The Nolans opened Sunset Point resort on the Gunflint Trail, from which they guided canoe and fishing trips in the Boundary Waters Canoe Area for nearly 30 years.

In the early 1980s, the Nolans sold their resort to Jack and Sue McDonnell. Moving into the original cabin beside Hungry Jack Lake, the McDonnells changed the name of the business to Hungry Jack Outfitters, which they operated for nearly a decade.

David and Nancy with their northwoods boys, Ben and Will. (photo by David Seaton)

Then in 1991, David and Nancy Seaton bought Hungry Jack Outfitters. The McDonnells, meanwhile, built a bed-and-breakfast inn a few miles from Grand Marais. And here is where our connection comes in. The Pie Place Café delivered meals to guests at the Dream Catcher B&B for several years … until we bought it as our home.

At the restaurant, the McDonnell and Seaton families made another connection, in a way. Jack McDonnell's mother, Betty, and David Seaton's mother, Carrie, each frequently ate at The Pie Place Café. We enjoyed their youthful exuberance and recognized in them an adventurous spirit that lives on in their children and grandchildren. When Carrie passed away, David asked us to cater her memorial service. We were honored to do it, and the threads of our shared lives wove together even more.

Food, of course, is our link to so many local families and it's one we shared with the Seaton family, too. Which is why their family's "legendary feast" is a story I so enjoy.

Through Hungry Jack Outfitters, David and Nancy have carved out a life in the North Woods that they love. David makes guitars, and Nancy creates art inspired by the natural world. As one might expect, their sons, Ben and Will, are growing up inquisitive, thoughtful and closely connected to the land and lake.

One afternoon, David and Ben stopped at the Pie Place for lunch. David ordered our Pulled Pork Sandwich with Bleu Cheese Dressing, a Pie Place best seller. As he ate, David shared a humorous story that anyone who lives in Grand Marais would appreciate and understand.

Planning Ben's high school graduation party, David and Nancy pondered what food to serve. A barbecue seemed festive and appropriate. Ribs, pulled pork, a pig roast – so many choices.

Ben had something else in mind.

That winter, their friend's vehicle had collided with an unsuspecting moose that had wandered onto the road. David and Nancy ended up with the moose, butchering it and filling their freezer to the brim.

When they asked Ben what he wanted for his graduation feast, he had a practical idea. "We've got plenty of moose. Let's serve 'pulled moose!'"

Pulled moose it would be, and word spread far and wide as to the barbecue's origin. Guests arrived,

eager to partake in this woodland bounty, slow-cooked and slathered with sauce.

And so, an unexpected harvest became the foundation of a shared community experience and a way to celebrate one young man's accomplishment and our ties to him and his family.

Pie Place Pulled Pork Sandwich

Summer barbecues bring us together. Be it hot dogs on a stick over an open fire, ribs sizzling over coals or a savory pulled pork slathered in barbecue sauce, you can create a party atmosphere anytime.

Serves 8 to 10

Amount	Ingredients
1 (4-pound)	pork butt (we prefer bone-in, bones allow for more flavor)
1/4 cup	Lawry's seasoned salt
12 ounces	Coca-Cola (do not use the diet soda)
8 to 10	hoagie or hamburger buns

Instructions

Place pork butt and other ingredients in slow cooker (crock pot) on low heat until it falls apart, 6 to 8 hours. Remove the meat from the slow cooker and remove the bones and some excess fat. Pull (shred) pork until desired texture and add some of the juices from the slow-cooker.

Put a portion of pork on a bun and add desired amount of Cheryl's Barbecue Sauce (recipe page 52). Serve with our Creamy Bleu Cheese Dressing and …. yum

Creamy Bleu Cheese Dressing

The earthy flavor of bleu cheese makes the perfect culinary partner for our sweet barbecue sauce.

Serves 6 to 8

Amount	Ingredients
1/2 cup	Danish bleu cheese or gorgonzola, crumbled
1 Tablespoon	apple cider vinegar
1/2 cup	mayonnaise
1/2 cup	sour cream
1 Tablespoon	fresh chives, chopped (or 1 teaspoon dried)
1/4 teaspoon	dry mustard
1/8 teaspoon	ground marjoram
2-3 drops	Worcestershire sauce
To taste	salt and freshly ground white pepper

Instructions

In a small bowl, mash 6 tablespoons of the bleu cheese into the vinegar. Once the mixture is fairly smooth, whisk in mayonnaise, sour cream, chives, mustard, marjoram and Worcestershire sauce. Season with salt and pepper to taste. Add remaining cheese and chill until ready to serve. If dressing thickens in the refrigerator, thin with a bit of milk, but go easy. You don't want to diminish that great bleu cheese flavor. If the ingredients separate, you can whisk them gently. The dressing will keep up to two weeks in the fridge.

All Ground Up

One might not think of it, given our northern climate, but our tiny shoreside community produces a wonderful abundance of local foods.

Fresh catch from the local fish market, maple syrup from an organic sugar bush, fresh produce from our local CSA (community supported agriculture), wild rice parched over an open fire and homemade sausages – just thoughts of it all can make my mouth water.

Planting, gathering, harvesting and making these culinary riches depends, of course, on the skills and talents of those who live here. We are fortunate that many fine folks born or drawn here come with a sensibility to the ways of an earlier time, with a creative spirit and a desire to be contributing members of a close-knit community.

Craig, center, mixes it up with Dennis Chilcote and Lou Pignolet mix it up.
(photo by Kate Watson)

So many who choose to reside here aspire to live an ordinary life in an extraordinary way.

Take, for example, Craig and Dianne Peterson, who moved north and became important threads in the fabric of Grand Marais. Dr. Craig, a retired dentist, and Dianne, the wife and mother who Craig says playfully "took care of three kids – me and our two children," purchased a small cabin on an inland lake in 2006. The energetic couple adapted to northern life in true Norwegian spirit and, over the years, added on to their cabin three times, creating a beautiful home to enjoy with family and friends.

They brought much more than their energy and hospitality north. Craig, a self-proclaimed foodie, brought his skills in preparation of charcuterie, wild game and sausage making.

It was while living in Waseca, Minnesota, that they learned to make their own sausage, eventually demonstrating sausage making at Farmamerica, a Minnesota agricultural interpretive center. Emphasizing organic ingredients and healthy foods, they continued to teach sausage making and smoking techniques in Grand Marais at the North House Folk School. For more than 17 years, they've offered the classes, which were featured in the *Minneapolis Star-Tribune*. They've also been active volunteers at North House, proving to be roll-up-their-sleeves folk who add enthusiasm and friendliness to events.

Besides North House, Dianne volunteers with the Cook County Historical Society, at the First & Second Thrift Store, the Cook County School District Education Foundation and several groups at Bethlehem Lutheran Church.

Quite an amazing resume for a couple in retirement, but then, retirement takes on a whole new meaning in this town we call home.

Craig and Dianne dined at The Pie Place Café from the beginning of their new life on the North Shore

Craig and Dianne enjoying the simpler life outdoors.
(photo by daughter Kara Miller)

and soon their lives intertwined with ours. Eventually, many of our menu items were chosen to highlight the sausages crafted by Craig and Dianne. This energetic couple fills a culinary niche savored by local sausage lovers.

The Petersons became part of another creative aspect of our lives, frequenting Northern Impulses, the art gallery we once operated in an old log building beside Lake Superior. That building inspired one of the works that I sold there. I combed the shore, gathering driftwood, pieces of old metal, small stones and moss washed up by the waves. Then, glue gun in hand, I constructed miniature dwellings reminiscent of early fishermen's cabins. They were an instant hit, and as long as there were waves, I had plenty of materials.

Craig and Dianne bought several of my cabins. They reminded Dianne of the old dwellings she had been drawn to on their trips to Norway. She even brought one of my "Superior Shanties" across the ocean to Norway. On a recent visit, Dianne told me she saw it still sitting in a place of honor on the fireplace mantel, bringing me a pleasant feeling of being part of the family there, too.

A few folks come to Grand Marais thinking they want to enjoy the quiet only to find it too remote, too far from the trappings of the city. They soon leave, returning to what they know.

But many do come to seek a simpler life, where what matters most is community, a connection to those around us, to nature and to its silent, sometimes turbulent beauty.

I believe that is what drew Craig and Dianne to the area, and much to the betterment of our community, I'm sure that these friends are here to stay.

Cider Baked Beans with Chicken and Sausage

Handcrafted sausages have become a thing of the past in most places, but not on the North Shore. The North House Folk School offers a sausage-making class, and Marlo, our local butcher at Johnson's Grocery, offers a vast array of homemade sausage. This dish is in homage to the old-world craft of sausage making. Rich and savory, it is the perfect meal for a cold autumn night.

Serves 4

Amount	Ingredients
1/2 pound	dried white beans, such as navy
2 cups	water
1/3 pound	slab bacon, cut into 1/2-inch cubes
3/4 cups	leeks, chopped, just the white part
1 cup	yellow onion, diced to 1/2 inch
1 cup	celery, diced to 1/2 inch
1 Tablespoon	garlic, minced
2-1/2 cups	fresh apple cider
2 Tablespoons	apple cider vinegar
6 thighs	chicken, boneless, skinless
2 Tablespoons	olive oil
4	bratwurst (or artisan sausage of your choice)

Instructions

Place the beans in a small saucepan with 2 cups water. Bring to a gentle boil and cook for 10 minutes. Remove from the heat, cover and let stand for 1 hour. Drain and rinse the beans.

Preheat oven to 350° F.

Place the bacon in a medium skillet over medium-high heat, and cook until the bacon begins to brown, about 3 minutes. Drain. Add the leeks, onions, celery and garlic, and cook until they soften, about 5 minutes longer. Reduce the heat to medium, add the apple cider, apple cider vinegar and the beans. Continue to cook until the mixture begins to thicken, about 20 minutes.

Meanwhile, quarter the chicken thighs. Heat the olive oil in a medium skillet and brown the chicken on all sides, about 5 minutes. Cut the bratwurst into 2-inch chunks.

Add the chicken and sausage to the beans, and transfer the mixture to a greased, 3-quart casserole dish. Bake for about 2 hours, until the beans bubble and the top browns.

Chef's note: If the beans are still firm after 2 hours, add 1 cup more of cider and continue to bake until the beans are soft.

(photo by Mary Beams)

Healing Stones

As a family of artists, we often find ourselves drawn to the creativity in others. We get inspired by the variety of ways in which people express themselves, and our restaurant seemed, in turn, to pull those imaginative and talented people through our doors.

Often our guests who were taking classes at the Grand Marais Art Colony or the North House Folk School brought their artwork into the Pie Place. They showed us their progress, knowing they'd be supported enthusiastically by fellow artists. We understand perfectly that expression is the "breath of life" to those who must make art.

I find that art has a way of making sense within a frightening and confusing world. I've seen art heal wounds hidden deep inside us, communicating deeply when mere words seem inadequate.

Perhaps the best example of this came to us through Ben and Xenia LaBaw, Pie Place Café customers who for years came up regularly from Rochester.

Ben grew up as a farmer's son, surrounded by fresh fruits from his father's farm in California. He loves peach pie, as you might expect. He can discern where a particular peach was grown and when it was picked based upon its flavor. Xenia has a sweet tooth, favoring our Pie Place Café chocolate chip cookies, decadent by any standards.

These two, Ben, a photographer, and Xenia, an accomplished artist and writer, have spent a lifetime merging their creative passions and helping others.

A courageous woman, Xenia personally knows the transformative power of making art. She survived childhood abuse and finds healing through creating, using painting to restore and guide others who also experienced childhood traumas.

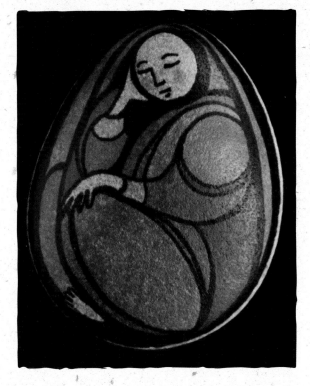

These examples of Xenia's work show how naturally her paintings complement the stones. Facing page: Their cards use images and words to help healing. (photos by Ben LaBaw)

She has found the soul of her work, though, not on a canvas, but on something more raw and substantial, something provided by Lake Superior. She paints on stones that she and Ben gather from along the rugged North Shore coast. The energy of these stones fueled a way for Xenia to release inner torment and convey the possibility of internal peace.

One day Ben and Xenia asked Mary and me to join them for lunch at The Pie Place Café. Xenia wanted to show something to us, to get our artistic opinion. What she had were photographs, taken by Ben, of paintings that she had done on those Lake Superior stones gathered over the years.

God understands lonely

Mary and I were overcome by the beauty of Xenia's work, how each stone matched perfectly the image she'd chosen for it. Xenia felt that the stones themselves had directed her painting, and that after working on hundreds of stones, she felt free for the first time in her life, free of the shame that often comes from childhood abuse and free to cope with the pain that it carries.

Ben, a pillar of strength on his wife's healing journey, had turned the images into cards or "touching stones" with the intention that Xenia's art could be used to inspire and heal others. A faith-filled couple, Ben and Xenia keep God, their refuge in any storm, at the center of their lives. Their work reflected their faith.

We urged Xenia to get her work published as focus cards, images to help people in meditation, prayer or centering in their daily lives. Xenia was encouraged by our enthusiasm.

The couple are now speaking to groups about childhood abuse and healing, and they do use these powerful images to reach those whose lives have been filled with fear and shame from the past.

Their cards have a wonderful life of their own, delivering powerful messages of faith, forgiveness, healing and love.

Last Christmas, each of the women in our household was gifted with a beautiful box of touching stone focus cards.

When I contemplate these beautiful images and sentiments, I understand more fully that healing is a process that requires courage, patience and self-acceptance.

Those who suffer tragedy or abuse cannot be made whole overnight, but their life and their trust can be rebuilt, one stone at a time.

our secret recipe

Isle Royale Harvest Chicken Casserole

We've been preparing this dish since the early days of the Pie Place Café, and it never ceases to delight our guests. Tender sautéed chicken breasts, nutty wild rice and water chestnuts meld with a delicate creamy sauce. This meal always makes folks exclaim, "What's in that recipe?" Now you know.

Serves 4 to 6

Amount	Ingredients
2 (6.5-ounce) boxes	long grain and wild rice mix
1/4 cup	butter, divided
3/4 teaspoon	salt, divided
2 to 3 breasts	chicken, boneless and skinless, cooked
1 small	onion, chopped
4 stalks	celery, chopped
2 (8-ounce) cans	water chestnuts, sliced
4 cups	shredded cheddar cheese
2 (10-ounce) cans	cream of mushroom soup
1 (16-ounce) carton	sour cream
1 cup	milk
1/2 teaspoon	black or white pepper
1/2 cup	soft bread crumbs (a great way to use leftover bread; just pulse in your food processor)

Instructions

Preheat oven to 350° F.

Prepare the rice per package instructions. While the rice cooks, put butter and 1/4 teaspoon of salt into a skillet and sauté the chicken breasts until they are golden brown and tender. Remove cooked breasts from skillet. Once the chicken is cooled, dice into 1/2-inch pieces and place in a large bowl, adding rice when it's done. Add more butter to the skillet and lightly sauté onion and celery 6 to 8 minutes. Slice water chestnuts in 1/8-inch slivers and add to skillet along with the chicken pieces.

In large mixing bowl combine cheddar cheese, soup, sour cream, milk, salt and pepper, whisking until smooth and creamy. Pour the sauce over the cooked chicken, rice, onion, celery and water chestnuts stirring until the mixture is completely covered and creamy. There may be sauce left. You don't want the casserole to be dry, but you don't want it soupy either.

Melt butter in a skillet over medium heat, add bread crumbs, stirring constantly until golden brown.

Pour chicken mixture into a lightly buttered 2-quart baking dish and bake at 350° for 35 to 40 minutes. Sprinkle the top of the casserole with bread crumbs during the last 5 to 7 minutes of baking.

Chef's note: You can prepare this casserole ahead, cover with plastic wrap and refrigerate 8 to 24 hours before baking. Use any extra sauce to refresh any leftovers you might have because the rice will absorb the sauce.

Dinner Guest of Your Choice

Some people never seem to age. They stay forever young, forging on ahead to live every moment on life's timetable to the fullest.

That pretty much sums up my friend Nancy Newman, a happening woman who can talk politics, books and current events with the best of them. Nancy surrounds herself with friends of the same ilk, those destined to heed the beat of a different drummer.

Nancy lives in the Twin Cities, where she keeps busy, ushering at Minneapolis and St. Paul theater events, attending book readings, going to museums, dining out

Nancy makes a big splash wherever she goes — even at Gooseberry Falls State Park. (photo courtesy Nancy Newman)

with her vast array of friends and being a companion for an elderly lady in the area. City life excites her, yet she will call a friend (or friends) at the drop of a hat for a "quick trip" to refuel in Grand Marais and the North Shore and to hike, cross-country ski or do whatever activity sparks her fancy.

I first met Nancy, as I've met so many great people, when she stopped at the Pie Place for breakfast. As a voracious reader, I'm always on the hunt for a new read. Waiting on Nancy, I asked about the book she was reading. She launched into a detailed description of the plot, the writing style, other books the author had written and others like it. Well, this girl was destined to be my friend, which is exactly what happened.

We started exchanging book suggestions regularly and I looked forward to Nancy's returns.

Each visit, Nancy brought a lively group of women who fast became my friends, too. We had enlightening conversations about politics, books, men, environmental issues and life. We covered it all.

One afternoon when Nancy and the girls arrived for lunch after a morning of hiking, we were engaged in an animated discourse. A customer got up to use the restroom, and her dining companion leaned over and said, "Do you mind if I join your table? Your conversation is a lot more interesting than mine."

Nancy tells a great story about one of her favorite authors, Carl Hiaasen, who writes fabulously funny, thought-provoking books about zany Florida characters, some you love and some not so much. Having lived in Key West for 10 years, we've enjoyed Carl's many books, laughing our socks off as we read excerpts aloud.

Anyway, one night at a New Year's Eve dinner party, the question was asked, "If you could invite eight people you wanted to be dinner guests in your home, who would they be?"

Nancy didn't hesitate; she named Carl. Then, as is her style, she wrote Carl a long letter about two of his books and included this postscript: "Have you ever played the game of naming the eight people (living or dead) whom you'd like to invite to a dinner party? I did on New Year's Eve, and you were on my list."

To her surprise, Carl wrote a postcard thanking her for the "lovely letter" and saying that he was honored to be on the guest list for her imaginary dinner party. When Carl came to a book reading and signing at a St. Paul bookstore, Nancy was there to meet him.

Nancy's lesson was quite clear. "If you like a book and want to write to the author, you should do it.

Some authors write back and some don't, but I have a collection of letters and emails that warm my heart with their gratitude and graciousness. Writers are no different from anyone else – they, and we, love to be praised, right?"

Nancy and our friends Lynne Bergman, Cathy Hegg, Ann Smith and Denise Woods came for their annual fall hike again recently and what a splendid visit we had. I always learn something new, such as Ann getting a pilot's license back when that was "not the thing for a woman to do … thank you very much!" Each of these women have balanced the roles of wife, mother, career woman and friend. We laughed till we cried and raised our mimosa glasses to strong and powerful women everywhere. How proud I feel to be a part of this wonderful sisterhood. As I've often told Nancy, "I want to be like you when I grow up."

Nancy's taught me this special thing (and so much more): If there's someone you'd like to invite for dinner, take courage in hand and call or write. You never know what might happen.

Chorizo Stuffed Peppers

Who says you can't get what you want living in a small town? Our local butcher, Marlo, makes the most awesome chorizo we've ever had, and we've spent time in Key West. These flavorful, spicy stuffed peppers are redolent of Cuban cuisine. Served with Grilled Peach Salsa, all I can say is "mmmmm!"

Serves 4 to 6

Amount	Ingredients
Stuffed Peppers:	
4 to 6 large	red bell peppers (or a mix with green peppers is nice)
1 pound	ground chorizo
1 (8-ounce) package	yellow rice (use Vigo)
1 Tablespoon	olive oil
1 large	onion, diced
1 (8-ounce) package	frozen corn
1/2 small	jalapeño pepper, seeded and finely diced
2 medium	fresh tomatoes, diced
2 cups	shredded cheddar cheese (16 ounces)
Grilled Peach Salsa:	
5	fresh peaches, halved with pits removed (or 2 pounds frozen peaches)
1 Tablespoon	olive oil
2 small	jalapeño peppers, seeded and sliced to grill
1/4 cup	fresh parsley, chopped
2 Tablespoons	balsamic vinegar
To taste	sea salt and fresh-ground pepper

Instructions
Preheat oven to 375° F.

To stuff the red peppers, cut tops from the peppers, remove the seeds and membranes and set aside. Save top with stem for presentation.

Bring large pot of water to boil, submerge peppers and tops in boiling water for 8 to 10 minutes, until peppers are soft but still have firmness. While peppers are cooking, brown chorizo in large skillet, drain and return to pan. Cook yellow rice per package instructions.

Place onions, corn and jalapeño in a different skillet with olive oil, sauté on medium-low heat until onion is transparent, about 6 to 8 minutes.

Once rice is cooked and onions, corn and jalapeño are sautéed, add them to browned chorizo with diced tomatoes and 1 cup of the shredded cheese. Season with salt and pepper to taste. Remove peppers from boiling water. Rinse with cold water to stop cooking process, drain and stuff with chorizo/rice mixture (there will be some left to use as a bed under the pepper).

Place in a baking dish and bake for 25 to 30 minutes. Sprinkle the remaining 1 cup shredded cheese on peppers during the last 5 to 7 minutes of bake time to melt. When ready to serve, warm remaining rice, place on plate and set pepper on chorizo/rice with pepper top and stem as a garnish. Serve with Grilled Peach Salsa on the side.

To make the salsa, grill the peaches and jalapeños on medium-high. Brush with olive oil. Turn peaches and jalapeños after 10 minutes and continue grilling about 20 minutes more until juices bubble. Remove from grill and cool. You don't want to burn the jalapeños, so watch them carefully.

Combine peaches, jalapeños and other ingredients in a food processor; pulse until mixture is blended, but coarsely chopped. Place salsa in a glass jar and refrigerate until used; remains good for up to four days in fridge.

We grilled at the Pie Place every day in summer. However, if you don't have a grill or you don't want to go to the fuss, you can get a similar result by broiling in the oven or using a griddle on your stovetop.

Chef's note: Serving on rice helps the peppers to stand up, or you can do a thin slice across the bottom to help them stay upright evenly.

(photo by Mary Beams)

Breaking Bread

Life is best lived one moment at a time – a beautiful sunset over the lake, a chittering feathered friend demanding the daily ration of seeds, the laughter of a child, the smile on a friendly face and, one of my favorite joys, a warm slice of bread fresh out of the oven.

Paul Taubr definitely is a warm bread kind of guy. I first met him one spring afternoon when he came into the Pie Place on the hill for lunch. A quiet, introspective gentleman, Paul didn't say much, except that he would like a slice of French bread to go with his soup.

Was our bread homemade? he inquired. I assured him it was and that the French bread was my favorite.

Paul said that his partner, Karen Vogl, made their bread, and it was very good. He seemed less than confident that our bread would pass the test. I served up the simple meal, and though Paul didn't say a word about the bread, he asked for another slice. Comment enough.

Later I learned Paul and Karen were building a home in Lutsen, and Paul was in Grand Marais to meet with the builder.

Basically, though, Paul ate and left without much conversation. Soon, however, his visits became quite regular, and our conversations more animated. He described his love of food, the progress on their new home, his upcoming visit to a Buddhist retreat center and a meditation group he was attending. He and I had much in common.

Soon, too, I met Karen, an outgoing, energetic woman who approaches life head-on. An avid cyclist, she's also an accomplished cook and baker and enjoys surrounding herself with friends. They both love to entertain, preparing elaborate meals for friends and family.

Before long Paul and Karen became regulars at the Pie Place. We relished their visits.

Karen even brought gifts – homemade bread baked in the brick oven on their property, jars of cranberry sauce she had canned and Smartwool underwear, which kept me warm and toasty on many a winter's night.

Paul was right; Karen's bread was heavenly, and we savored the perfection of bread kneaded by hand with

Karen and Paul beside their outdoor oven. (photo by Kathy Rice)

love. We had found kindred spirits and as with so many others, these two customers became friends. One of life's great miracles is when people come together, souls connecting (or reconnecting), and friendship is born.

The more I learned about Paul and Karen, the more I learned about their bread making. Our family has wanted a brick bread oven for years and knowing they had one piqued my curiosity. Turns out they've created a cooperative bread-baking system.

Paul is in charge of building the fire and preparing the brick oven. With his analytical approach, he has every detail worked out to perfection. Karen works her magic in the kitchen, combining the ingredients then kneading the dough and letting it rise prior to sliding the shaped loaves into the oven on a wooden peel.

The end result of this joint creation is some of the best bread I have ever tasted.

Paul and Karen have invited me to their place for a bread baking experience. I think they need a quality control person, and I am definitely up to the task.

It's been years since Paul tasted that first slice of French bread at the Pie Place on the hill and then stuck with us when we moved to our restaurant on the harbor in downtown Grand Marais. Much changed over the years, but one thing remained the same – bread on the menu.

The love of bread brought us together, and one crumb at a time we followed the pathway to where we are now. Enough crumbs to make many loaves; enough moments to build a friendship.

"Just as someone starving can't eat a whole loaf of bread at once,
but must break off pieces and eat slowly,
so must the conscious heart live off small pieces of infinity
in order to digest what will nourish."
– Wayne Muller, *A Life of Being, Having and Doing Enough*

Pie Place French Bread

A loaf of warm, crusty French bread to serve with a savory fall stew – talk about comfort food. Homemade French bread is the base for so many of our sandwiches, we'd like to share our bread recipe with you. See if you don't just love it as much as Paul does.

Makes 3 large (24-ounce) loaves or 6 small ones

Amount	Ingredients
2 (0.25 ounce) packets	active dry yeast
1 Tablespoon	sugar
2 cups	warm water (110° to 115° F)
3 cups	bread flour
1 Tablespoon	salt
3 cups	all-purpose flour
For sprinkling	cornmeal

Glaze:

1	egg yolk
1 Tablespoon	heavy cream

Instructions

Preheat oven to 350° F.

Combine yeast and sugar, stir in warm water and let rise to a sponge (about 10 minutes).

Add salt to the bread flour, mixing thoroughly with hands, and stir 2 cups into the sponge when it is ready. Whisk until smooth, add the rest of the bread flour (1 cup) and mix, switching to a wooden spoon. Gradually add the all-purpose flour, 1/2 cup at a time. Stir as you like, moving from a wooden spoon to mixing with your hands until you are kneading the dough, working in the flour.

Turn dough out onto a lightly floured board and continue kneading until the dough is pliable and silky.

Place in a large mixing bowl oiled with olive oil, cover with a warm damp towel and set in a warm place, free of drafts, to rise. This can take 45 minutes to 1-1/2 hours.

Cover a baking sheet with parchment paper and sprinkle the paper with cornmeal. Punch down the risen dough, form into loaves, set onto a baking sheet.

Combine the egg yolk & heavy cream, whisking until smooth. Brush the glaze over the loaves. Cut slits in the loaves in whatever pattern you like.

Let loaves rise until doubled in size and until the dimple you poke with your finger remains and does not spring back.

Bake loaves in the 350° preheated oven for about 35 minutes, until crust is golden and the loaves sound hollow when thumped on the bottom.

Chef's note: If you have a bread brick, by all means use that in the making of this bread. Feel free to sprinkle the top of this French bread with poppy seeds or, as in this photo, sesame seeds.

(photo by Kathy Rice)

From Russia with Love

We've known Mike and Laurie Senty since we first bought the Pie Place on the hill. They own Senty Log Homes, a stone's throw from our first property on Highway 61.

The original log home business was started by Laurie. Small in stature, the power of this woman is tangible.

Finding family in Pskov, Russia, from left, Laurie, Hana, Alex, Mike (in back), Kostya, Archie, Natasha and Ilya. (photo courtesy the Sentys)

She excels in everything to which she puts her mind, whether it's building log cabins, running an ironman marathon or becoming a certified healer in Chinese methods and starting her own practice.

Mike and Laurie are resourceful folks who construct beautiful log homes in the true spirit of craftsmanship not often seen today.

Every Thanksgiving, Laurie would call the Pie Place to order pumpkin and apple pies, along with a couple dozen of our homemade dinner rolls, checking off a few things from her busy list for completion of a traditional turkey dinner.

Other times of the year, we liked to drive by the "log lot" to see another stunning home being erected in a manner reminiscent of the Lincoln Logs of our childhood, one notched log fitting snugly on another.

One summer our guys, Josh and Ben, peeled logs to make extra money. They soon found out just how much muscle it took to complete the task.

Several years later, Josh worked for Mike and learned the skills necessary to build one's own cabin. After some time with Mike, Josh concluded, "There are folks who can build log cabins, and then there are craftsmen. Mike and Laurie are craftsmen."

As one might expect, the Senty daughters, Hana, Kelly and Tess, are spirited young women, knowing their own minds. Mike joked that he sometimes felt outnumbered in his household of women.

But he wouldn't be the lone man for long.

In Grand Marais lives Natasha Kirk, a seamstress who owns a shop where she makes beautifully handcrafted polar fleece coats, hats and mittens.

A big-hearted woman, every penny Natasha made at the store she sent to Russia for her sister, who operates an orphanage. Natasha explained there is little provision in Russia for the care for homeless children.

Tess became friends with Natasha's son Ev and came home from school one day announcing that Russian children were awaiting adoption, and her parents should consider adopting one.

After a long, teary family discussion, Laurie and Mike decided they would indeed travel to Russia and bring back a child. In short order, Ilya and his twin brother, Alex, joined the Senty family. Soon Mike and Laurie returned to Russia to bring Kostya back to the family fold. While in Russia, though, daughter Hana met Losha, a sweet and sensitive 15-year-old. The Sentys had spent all the money they had for tickets and adoption expenses, but Hana insisted that they had room for one more brother. How can you

Laurie, Losha and Mike in a family pose by St. Basil's Cathedral in Moscow. (photo courtesy the Sentys)

say no to love? They found the means and Losha came along home.

Four young men, eager for a family, even one filled with sisters, found home at last.

Within a few short years, this family of five had sprouted to nine, requiring a much bigger house, which was the easy part for Mike and Laurie.

Once when I asked Laurie how many children that she and Mike intended to adopt, her reply was simple. "As many as need a home!"

As the boys grew older, Losha, Kostya and Ilya all worked at the Pie Place doing dishes. Like all young men, they were eager to earn money of their own.

Losha worked the longest with us and felt like our own family. Losha, an easygoing friendly fellow, quickly adjusted to life in the little village of Grand Marais as if he'd always lived here. He excelled in track and his outgoing personality won him many friends. He was crowned homecoming king by his fellow students.

Family comes in many forms. There can be the family into which we are born, but there can also be a family built child added to child, the family for which we are chosen. And the Senty family fits together as snugly as a well-built log home – one where their hearts live.

Mom's Parker House Rolls

When we came together as a restaurant family 20 years ago, we brought many of our mothers' recipes with us. We all remember those foods that it seems like only our mothers could make. These homemade dinner rolls became one of the traditions at the Pie Place, especially at holiday time.

Makes 20 rolls

Amount	Ingredients
1 (0.25-ounce) packet	active dry yeast
1/4 cup	lukewarm water
8 Tablespoons	butter, cut into pieces
2 teaspoons	salt
1/4 cup	sugar
1 cup	milk, scalded
2 large	eggs, beaten
4-1/4 cups	bread flour, sifted
4 to 6 Tablespoons	butter, melted

Instructions

Sprinkle yeast in warm water, stir and let stand until foamy, about 5 minutes.

Scald milk by heating in a saucepan on medium heat until milk begins to bubble around the edges of the pan.

Add scalded milk to butter. When butter is melted, stir together with yeast mixture, eggs, sugar and salt.

Add flour gradually, 1 cup at a time, stirring with a wooden spoon after each addition. Stir in enough flour to make a slightly sticky dough that forms into a ball.

Knead on floured board until smooth and elastic, about 10 minutes (or 5 minutes in a standing mixer on low speed). Knead in more flour if dough is too sticky.

Form dough into a ball and place in a lightly buttered bowl, turn to coat with butter. Cover dough ball with pastry cloth or plastic wrap. Let rise in a warm place for 1 hour or until doubled in size.

Roll out dough on floured surface with floured rolling pin to 1/4- to 1/2-inch thickness. Use biscuit cutter to cut out rolls. (If you don't have a biscuit cutter, a large water glass will do. That's what my mom used.)

Place cut pieces on lightly greased baking sheet (or use parchment paper on baking sheet, something our mothers didn't have!). With a butter knife, lightly score the center of each piece, folding one side over the other, creating a half circle.

Cover loosely with pastry cloth or plastic wrap and let rise an additional 45 to 60 minutes, or until doubled in size.

Preheat oven to 375° F.

Brush top of rolls with melted, slightly cooled butter before placing the baking sheet into the oven. Bake until golden brown, 20 to 25 minutes. Let cool on rack for 5 minutes and serve warm.

(photo by Mary Beams)

Yes, She Could!

These days people view politics as "tainted" or words much more volatile and much less kind. But having grown up in an era of political activism and social change, I'm filled with hope to see passionate people who care deeply about our country and community and who enthusiastically put their efforts where their good hearts lead them.

In the 2008 U.S. presidential election, many people were inspired by the impassioned rally of "Yes We Can!"

During my formative years of the 1960s and '70s, I watched in horror as those involved in the Civil Rights Movement were attacked by police with billy clubs, dogs and firehoses. I was frightened

Sandy receives her "Most Calls for Obama" award from Maryl. (photo by Denny Fitzpatrick)

for, though proud of, the black children who walked into newly integrated schools through a gauntlet of screaming angry people who apparently feared the skin color of these youngsters. The Freedom Riders, young people my age of all colors, chose to put their lives on the line for what they believed was right, in the belief that a more just world, where all were equal, would be created.

So in 2008, I could fully appreciate that the possibility of electing America's first African-American president brought out citizens who had never before been involved in politics. History was in the making, and many people across the nation wanted to be a part of it.

Even in our small village of Grand Marais, the fervor was noticeable. Local people delivered and put up signs, traveled to the national convention, attended rallies, marched in parades, helped register people to vote and supported candidates with contributions of money and time.

A retired couple, Al and Sandy Taenzer, longtime customers and friends at The Pie Place Café, split their time between Illinois and Grand Marais. Their Illinois home brought a special passion for their candidate, also an Illinois resident.

In 1998, Sandy first encountered the future president when as an educator and advocate for early childhood development, she testified before an Illinois Senate committee giving her findings about at-risk children. One young senator asked "exquisite, in-depth questions," and when she was interrupted by someone, he admonished, "No. I want to talk to her!"

After the hearings, Sandy asked someone in her group, "Who was that?"

"Senator Barack Obama" came the reply. Sandy knew then that this was a young man who would go far.

Al and Sandy are not just passionate about politics; they have a commitment to participating in their community.

Al is an active member of the Grand Marais Lions Club. Sandy, a lifelong advocate for early childhood programs, has worked to write grants for the local school system, implementing programs for special needs children, and works with children and families in the area offering her expertise, compassion and deep well of love.

During the 2008 presidential election, Sandy and Al found their own way of drumming up support. They opened their home to volunteers for making thousands of phone calls. Sandy hosted events to discuss the issues, the candidates and their particular positions. She cooked, canvassed and called in equal measure.

Jimmy Carter once said that true and lasting change must come from the people, and Sandy demonstrated people power.

As election day approached, I would talk with Sandy in The Pie Place Café, listening to her part in the unfolding of history. By November, she was weary but did not waver. She kept making phone calls and talking to anyone who would listen. She'd come in with a sometimes hoarse voice, but after a cup of tea, she would be off and dialing once again.

We know how the story ended. With their votes, the people of the United States broke a color barrier for the country's highest office and opened that opportunity for any political party going forward. Sandy and many others like her were part of an important moment in history.

One day when Sandy and Al came in for lunch, Denny Fitzpatrick and Maryl Skinner, two like-minded supporters, came into the restaurant with a gift for Sandy.

She pulled the red, white and blue tissue paper out of the gift bag, and her smile spread from ear to ear. There, nestled among the patriotic folds of tissue, was a brightly sequined phone, an objet d'art made especially for her by Maryl as an election keepsake.

Yes, Sandy heeded the call to become involved and then made the most phone calls in the process.

Hot Artichoke Dip

This appetizer is a favorite with our guests and appeared often in our Evening Repast. Perfect for a party, serve it to family and friends and get rave reviews.

Serves 6 to 8

Amount	Ingredients
2 (8.5-ounce) cans	artichoke hearts, drained and chopped
1/2 cup	Parmesan cheese, shredded
1/2 cup	cheddar cheese, shredded
2 cups	mozzarella cheese, shredded
1 cup	Hellmann's mayonnaise
1 teaspoon	garlic salt

Instructions
Preheat oven to 350° F.

Mix ingredients together in medium-sized bowl. Fold into an 8x8-inch baking dish. Bake 25 minutes until heated through. Serve with assorted crackers or on toast points using our French bread (recipe page 99), thinly sliced and toasted for five minutes in the oven.

For the Birds

Twice a year, in spring and fall, the North House Folk School hosts the Boreal Birding Festival. The event draws folks from far and wide, and we often spot the "birders" who make the migration to the North Shore every year and alight in our restaurant.

When the Boreal Birding Festival began years ago, I met Bob Janssen and his wife, Suzanne.

Bob, an avian expert, gave lectures at the North House and led expeditions along Lake Superior and into the boreal forest to catch a glimpse of the sometimes elusive feathered friends.

Suzanne, who loves the North Shore, would come along to enjoy some quiet time reading, knitting and shopping. She and I often found time for an enjoyable lunch together.

Bob's attraction to birds started young. He bought his first birding book at age 13. Fascinated by what he read, Bob pored through its pages, eager to learn all he could.

Bob has been birding on the Gunflint Trail since 1939. Back then, the Gunflint was a narrow gravel pathway to the boreal forest where he spent countless hours peering through binoculars.

Bob has co-authored *Birds in Minnesota*, first published in 1975 and revised in 1989, *Birds of Minnesota & Wisconsin* and *Birds of Minnesota State Parks,* just published in 2015. It's an impressive body of work.

Greg Wright, executive director of the North House Folk School, summed up Bob's birding style by saying, "He came to see … he came to listen."

One day, Bob and I talked about what would make the forays more appetizing. He suggested fresh scones available for the birders, and we were happy to comply. Soon we were making bag lunches, and I would meet Bob and his group in the early morning hours to see them off with their goodies.

Birding with Bob is no walk in the park, and anyone who has followed him as he clambers up Mt. Josephine can attest to his zeal.

Bob loves all the birds, but he admits to a preference for the turkey vulture, LeConte's sparrow and one that we find in our neck of the woods, spruce grouse.

The birding group often ended the day in The Pie Place Café for dinner, eager to converse about the day's sightings. I enjoyed hearing the stories of what each person had gone through to find the rare bird

Bob looking for birds and, facing page, with a bird in hand. (photos courtesy Bob Janssen)

needed to complete his or her bird list. I, too, delight in watching birds at our feeder in winter, so these more adventurous birding tales elicited my rapt attention.

Every year, Bob would depart saying, "Next year why don't you come with us?" Eager as I was, the duties of the restaurant called me. After all, who would get their lunches ready? However, I always await Bob and Suzanne's return with the same anticipation I feel for the return of the hummingbirds in spring.

Our long days in the restaurant were made easier, though, as we watched the antics of birds on the feeder hanging in the tree just a few feet from the kitchen window.

Our food-stained copy of *Birds of Minnesota Field Guide* served us well and nearly every day, we identified a new bird munching sunflower seeds (if birds do indeed munch). Anyway, our meager bird list, though small compared with Bob's, grew to 54. Once during a winter blizzard, a snowy owl came to rest and stayed a few days to wait out the storm. On another dark early winter morning outside, wings whooshed just above my head. Startled, I didn't solve the mystery until the sun came up. A huge great gray owl was perched on the fence of our bee yard.

One of our northern favorites is not rare. We enjoy the spunk and ever-happy demeanor of the chickadees.

Perhaps someday I will be able to attend Bob's birding excursion. Until then, I can delight in the birding festival that happens every day just outside our kitchen window.

"… Said the little bunny
"I will be a bird and fly away from you."
"If you become a bird and fly away from me," said his mother
"I will be a tree that you come home to!"

– Margaret Wise Brown, *The Runaway Bunny*

Brandied Fruit Pie

When preservation was a problem, the hearty folks here dried apples, plums and berries to store in the root cellar, giving the resourceful cook options during long winter months.

Serves 6

Amount	Ingredients
1 recipe	pie dough, page 23

Step One – dried fruits:

1 cup	pitted dried plums, coarsely chopped
1 cup	dried apricots, coarsely chopped
1/2 cup	golden raisins
1/4 cup	dried cherries
1/4 cup	dried apples, coarsely chopped

Step Two – spices & flavorings:

1/3 cup	sugar
1/4 cup	butter, melted
1/3 cup	real maple syrup (we use Wild Country Maple Syrup)
1/3 cup	applejack brandy (optional)
1-1/2 teaspoons	vanilla extract
1/4 teaspoon	ground cloves
1/2 teaspoon	ground ginger
1-1/2 teaspoons	ground cinnamon

Step Three – the finale:

1/4 cup	chopped walnuts
1 large	egg, beaten
For topping	heavy cream, fresh whipped

Instructions
Preheat oven to 375° F.

Roll out half the dough into an 11-inch round on a lightly floured surface, using a floured rolling pin, and line a 9-inch pie pan with bottom crust.

Combine the dried fruits in a medium saucepan, and cover with cold water. On medium-high heat, bring to a simmer for 10 minutes, stirring constantly. Drain well and return fruit to saucepan. Add spices and flavorings, stir well, set aside and cool to room temperature, stirring occasionally.

When you're ready to assemble the pie, stir in the chopped walnuts to the cooled fruit mixture. Pour filling into the prepared unbaked crust. Top with a rolled pastry crust. Vent, or if you're adventurous, a lattice top works well and looks fabulous. Brush top with 1 large beaten egg.

Bake about 50 minutes, until top is a deep golden brown. Cool and serve with fresh whipped cream.

Grandma Lillie's Apple Pie

How many of us hold memories of "the best pie in the world" made by our mothers, grandmothers or aunts? Most of us, I suspect.

I do because my Grandma Parr made the best raspberry pie ever (sorry if you thought it was your grandma!). Made with raspberries fresh from her berry patch and glistening with sugar atop the flaky pie crust – it was the best. Oh, and Grandma Strong's custard and mincemeat pies were sublime. The berry pie spoke of summer to me, while the others shouted "Thanksgiving!"

We all in our restaurant family have our own pie stories, which is probably not surprising when you consider that we operated a restaurant where the pie was as important as the meal.

We also love to hear other people's tales about the illustrious pie, and Steve and Penny Ortmann have a good one.

Grandma Lillie Teigland, hands always at work. Penny, with Steve, has fond memories of her grandmother's pie. (photos courtesy the Ortmanns)

Steve and Penny are longtime Pie Place Café guests. I got to know Steve better when we were co-chairs for the North House Folk School's Points North Auction a few years back. Our time together blossomed into a wonderful friendship.

A pragmatic, no-nonsense guy with a big heart and an imaginative sensibility, Steve is also prone to constant teasing. I'm fond of him despite that, though I must confess that I'm not always sure if he's kidding.

Steve and I both love eggs, which he isn't allowed to have at home. Penny has a severe allergy to eggs. So it's

not uncommon for Steve to email me with a breakfast invitation: "Want to meet me for eggs?" I always do.

At first, I wasn't aware of Steve's artistic side. It was hidden behind his several observations of "artistic temperament" in a not exactly flattering way. So imagine my surprise when I arrived at a photography exhibit at the Johnson Heritage Post Art Gallery to find his work front and center. My warning of "I'm on to you, Mister!" was met with a mischievous smile.

Penny, the love of Steve's life, is a fiber artist. Steve still gushes when he declares, "Penny is the nicest person I have ever known."

He still calls Penny his girlfriend, and, after 42 years of marriage and three children (two daughters and a son), that says a lot about their relationship.

The story of Grandma Lillie's pie came up one day while I was having lunch with Penny.

As a young woman who loved to make pies, Penny's grandma honed her baking skills and sold pies at a local café to help out the family. Penny remembers her grandmother's pies with a great deal of sentimentality and happy tastebuds. Penny unfolds the story of her family pie-baking this way:

"Grandma Lillie's Apple Pie. Somewhere I have a recipe card with those words at the top. Many years

ago, I made out the card because it was my favorite pie. Grandma Lillie said she was happy to share this with 'her favorite redhead,' as she often referred to me. However, it was difficult to write any of it down. There were no measurements, each ingredient was just flour, sugar, cinnamon, lard … and, of course, apples.

"Each Thanksgiving, Grandma would bake the pies. Apple and mincemeat are what I most remember, the mincemeat stored upon the shelves of her canning cupboard. The ingredients for that were a mystery to me, but I liked the spicy, meat-filled pie.

"I remember sitting on the floor by the bowl of apple peels as Grandma Lillie sat in her chair with (another) bowl in her lap filling with peeled and sliced apples. I began to spend time on my own at Grandma Lillie's house a few blocks away from our home. I loved to watch her make pies. To this day, apples and peels remind me of my grandma.

"Now I am a 'mormor,' the Norwegian equivalent of grandmother. I love making kringla with my grandchildren. Though a favorite in Norway at Christmastime, we love to make this sweet roll anytime. My youngest sister, Mary Jane, is now the official pie baker of the family. She uses my Mom's old recipes. Family traditions and pies for every occasion and time of day – can there be anything better than that?"

I understand completely. So often what we taste brings back pleasant memories.

Once a guest ordered a slice of chocolate cream pie that I brought to her table, returning later to ask if she liked her selection. Her dining companion looked at her and said, "Tell her."

I was taken aback; the woman's eyes brimmed with tears. Then, her voice choked, "This pie tastes exactly like my grandmother's chocolate cream pie! I haven't had a slice like this since she died many years ago. We were very close, and I have missed her so much. After tasting this pie, I feel her presence so strongly."

Oh, how like a pie; there's a memory hidden in every bite.

(*our secret recipe*)

Northwoods Apple Pie
We have a special pie that calls to us when the leaves turn brilliant red and gold and frost coats the pumpkins. I'm pleased to share our Northwoods Apple Pie and the memories it holds of fall harvest.

Serves 6

Amount	Ingredients
1 recipe	pie dough, page 23 (the easiest is to prepare a full recipe, but use only 3/4 of the dough to make a "rustic" crust, as shown here, or measure 12 ounces of dough if you have a kitchen scale)
1/3 cup	walnuts, coarsely chopped
1 teaspoon	cinnamon
1/4 teaspoon	nutmeg
1/4 teaspoon	ground ginger
1/4 teaspoon	cardamom
2 Tablespoons	cornstarch
3/4 cup	brown sugar
4-1/2 cups	apples (your choice, but we like Honey Crisp)
1/4 cup	currants
2 Tablespoons	brandy (optional)
2 Tablespoons	butter
For brushing	half-and-half
For sprinkling	sugar and extra nutmeg

Crumb top (optional):
Mix together

1/2 cup	all-purpose flour
1/3 cup	light brown sugar
1/2 teaspoon	salt
2 Tablespoons	butter, melted

Instructions
Preheat oven to 375° F.

In a large bowl, mix all the dry ingredients. In a separate bowl, toss the apples and currants in brandy. Then combine both.

To assemble the pie, roll the dough into a 13-inch round on a lightly floured surface, using a floured rolling pin. For a rustic crust, you want the dough round much larger than the rim of the 9-inch pie pan. Drape the crust in pan (dough round will hang over the rim of the pan).

Fill with apple mixture and dot generously with butter. Fold the crust gently up and over the fruit. Brush with half-and-half and sprinkle with sugar and nutmeg

Bake in oven for 1 to 1-1/2 hours, checking at intervals after 1 hour until crust is golden, apples are tender, and the juices are thick, bubbly and clear.

Chef's note: Sometimes in the restaurant we toss a bit of crumb topping over the exposed fruit in the center of the pie. It's not necessary, but adds crunch and protects the exposed fruit from over-baking.

Chef's bonus note: If you make the full pie dough recipe, you can use the leftover for cookies with cinnamon and sugar sprinkles.

(photo by Mary Beams)

Winter Warmers

A snowy forest near Grand Marais. (photo by SteveOrtmann.com)

Second Chances

Everyone deserves a second chance, and I've seen some breathtaking examples of that during my 65 years. (It's OK to say my age; I don't pay attention to those kinds of things.)

You might say my friends Ed and Marcy Nelson, both substance abuse counselors, specialize in second chances. I met them 15 years ago when they came into the Pie Place on the hill for breakfast, one of their (and my) favorite meals of the day. Marcy discovered she loves our French toast or waffles with the locally harvested maple syrup we serve.

That day they were here for their anniversary getaway, a trip up north that they relish each year. We chatted about spirituality, their work, their children and home schooling and about other things of the heart. The connection came instantly; we loved each other immediately. From that day, I eagerly anticipated their annual anniversary visit. They always dropped in for breakfast.

One year they brought their lovely family. After our usual greetings, their son Caleb exclaimed, "Wow! You were right! They really do hug you when you walk through the door." While waiting on the family, it was clear that these articulate and joyful children had been loved and parented well.

Ed and Marcy are the first to admit that they had their share of trials as young people. They faced many of the challenges their clients have, including struggles with addiction. Yet as is often the case, our trials make us stronger and give us the tools, in turn, to help others.

Hence Ed and Marcy have guided many young people, couples and families through the painful experiences of substance abuse and its effects. They bring to those around them hope, love, humor and the wisdom of having been challenged themselves. When they say they understand, they really do.

Then about two years ago, they came to Grand Marais and The Pie Place Café "just because."

It turned out Ed, who was suffering from liver failure, was in need of a transplant.

Ed and Marcy appreciate and enjoy all of their second chances.
(photo by Sherry Clyde)

I think they wanted to find some of the energy that is this place we call home to give them the spiritual fuel to face the coming trials.

I could tell as I sat at the table holding their hands, talking and looking through the windows at Lake Superior, that Ed was in desperate need of the transplant surgery that would come in the following months.

Ever the optimists, and with a faith that sustains them, their talk turned to their 25th wedding anniversary the following November and the party they wanted at The Pie Place Café.

They discussed what food to serve and where they would stay. It needed to be someplace big enough for all the children and grandchildren.

As they were about to leave, I hugged Ed and whispered into his ear, "You stay out of trouble now. You've got an anniversary party to attend."

With a weary, though still playful, smile on his face, he winked and slowly walked through the door.

Ed did receive a liver transplant, a difficult procedure, and in his case a successful one. Then a little over a year later, Ed found himself needing a kidney transplant, too. Marcy was a match, and today with her kidney, the love, prayers and commitment of a wonderful network of family and friends, plus the advances of modern medicine, Ed has yet another second chance at life.

Oh, and yes, they did celebrate their 25th anniversary here with all their clan in joyful attendance.

As I hold them in prayer on this day of second chances, I request for them any and all of the second chances they may need and plenty of anniversaries long into the future.

Gingerbread Waffles

These moist and spicy waffles make any breakfast a celebration. We love pairing them with Crème Fraîche, an easy, yet elegant, garnish drizzled on soups or over waffles. Or try Wild Country Maple Syrup.

Serves 4 to 6

Amount	Ingredients
2 large	eggs, room temperature and separated
1/2 cup	dark brown sugar, firmly packed
1/2 cup	molasses
1/4 cup	unsalted butter, melted and cooled
2 cups	all-purpose flour
2 teaspoons	ground ginger
1-1/2 teaspoons	baking powder
1 teaspoon	cinnamon
1/4 teaspoon	ground cloves
Pinch	salt
2/3 cup	milk
For brushing	vegetable oil for the waffle iron

(photo by Paul L. Hayden)

Instructions

Beat egg yolks and brown sugar until thick and pale, and then beat in the molasses and butter.

In a different bowl, sift flour, ginger, baking powder, cinnamon, cloves and a pinch of salt. Add the sifted mixture to molasses mixture, alternating with the milk.

In another bowl beat the egg whites until they hold soft peaks, then fold into batter.

> ### Crème Fraîche
> 1 cup heavy cream
> 1 teaspoon cultured buttermilk
> (or use apple cider vinegar)
> Combine heavy cream and buttermilk in saucepan, heating until kitchen thermometer reads 85° F. Let stand at room temperature until thickened (several hours). Stir gently and refrigerate until ready to use. It will keep about one week in the fridge.

Heat waffle iron, brush with vegetable oil and pour 1/4 to 1/2 cup of batter onto iron (amount depends on the size of your waffle iron). The batter is a bit stiff, so you may need to spread it evenly over waffle surface with a spatula. Cook until done.

Chef's note: This makes a moist waffle, so if you like crispier waffles, leave them in the iron longer.

Our Modern-Day Explorer

There are those who harken to the beat of a different drummer. They hear a distant pulsing that sparks a fire in their hearts and puts dreams in their head that few understand and that will not be extinguished. Some people, it seems, just have adventure in their blood.

That certainly seems to be the case for Lonnie Dupre, who is descended from Jacques Cartier, the French explorer who established Quebec. The need to explore might be genetic.

We live in a community where many people come to fulfill a dream – to become an artist, to build cabins, to live off the land, to start a restaurant. Lonnie takes that a little further (and farther).

Lonnie grew up on a farm in central Minnesota living close to the land. As a boy, he loved the cold, seemingly inhospitable winters. He went ice fishing, hunting and trapping with his father and friends. These early experiences left an indelible mark on the man, an inner thirst for something more. At an early age, Lonnie read voraciously about the Inuit people's winter camping and survival techniques.

Lonnie's smile stays the same at home or, facing page, in Greenland. (photos courtesy oneworldendeavors.com)

Lonnie also loves to work with his hands; he built beautiful log homes to make his way in life. He bought huskies, learned the skills of dogsledding and enjoyed the frozen north that had become his home.

He got involved in several Arctic expeditions, honing skills that would prepare him for bigger adventures.

In 1997, Lonnie and Australian adventurer John Hoelscher started work on their Greenland Expedition, a kayak and dogsled journey covering more than 6,000 miles. Their goal was to circumnavigate Greenland using traditional Inuit travel methods. The actual expedition, which spanned 22 months in Greenland, was completed in 2001; the pair used the trip to call attention to the effects of global warming. During the expedition, they lived among the Inuit people for a time, experiencing a simpler way of life.

After more than two decades, Lonnie has traveled across 15,000 miles throughout the Arctic regions of Russia, Lapland, Alaska, Canada and Greenland. He has led five major Arctic expeditions and participated in several others. Working with Greenpeace, National Geographic and other environmental organizations, he has tracked the effects of global warming and climate change on the planet.

Lonnie brought his message to the world through articles, books and his new documentary film, "Cold Love." He has written two books about his experiences and findings, *Life on Ice* and *Greenland: Where Ice is Born.*

He also founded One World Endeavors with a mission to create and lead pioneering expeditions in the coldest regions of the globe and to advocate for protection of these fragile environments.

Lonnie brings his commitment for a healthier world to his lifestyle. His lives in a small, energy-efficient home in Grand Marais, and it's not uncommon to see him walking or bicycling around town. Much of the equipment used on his expeditions he makes himself, using craftsman skills of an earlier time.

Lonnie teaches dovetail log cabin classes at the North House Folk School, demonstrating traditional construction techniques from the 1700s to complement modern-day lifestyle.

When Lonnie and Emmy Award-winning documentary filmmaker Deia Schlosberg were editing "Cold Love," they stayed at the Harbor Inn. It gave us, a family who believes in supporting each other's dreams, a chance to see one of Lonnie's dreams come into being.

Preparations for an expedition are vast, as one can imagine. There is the gathering, or making, of proper equipment and then there is the physical training. You can imagine the stamina needed to pull sledges through high snow with ropes around your waist, to check equipment in extreme weather, to care for your team of sled dogs and to prepare your body for the unknowns ahead.

Lonnie regularly visited The Pie Place Café, and we came to recognize the signs of an impending expedition by what he ordered. Like a bear bulking up for winter hibernation, Lonnie ate protein-laden breakfasts with gusto whenever a new journey was around the corner.

This Arctic explorer loves the Pie Place Maple Sausage Patties and consumed vast quantities before leaving for another adventure.

As Lonnie once admitted to me, "There were times when I was so cold, exhausted and weary of our rations of dehydrated food that my mouth watered for a maple sausage patty!"

We jokingly talked about creating dehydrated patties for One World Endeavors. But, of course, the secret recipe could not be shared with an unsuspecting polar bear on some arctic ice floe.

Living the life that is in his soul, Lonnie is an integral part of our northern community.

Just a few nights ago around our family dinner table, Mary spoke up and said, "I heard that Lonnie made it to the summit!" We all cheered for our friend, thankful that he had completed his ascent. He was safe, and would be returning home to Grand Marais soon.

On January 11, 2014, after three solo attempts, Lonnie made it to the top of Denali, North America's highest peak. His was the first solo summit during the hazardous month of January.

Who knows what new adventure awaits Lonnie. All we know for certain is that there will be another.

"You cannot start thinking about the finish line
on day one, two, three, because you'll never get there mentally if you do.
You need to make each day your life."
– Lonnie Dupre

(*our secret recipe*)

Pie Place Maple Sausage Patties

You've never tasted sausage patties until you try this Pie Place original. Cheryl created the recipe, and they have been handcrafted at the Pie Place since our beginnings. We are happy to share this legendary recipe now with you, so you and your loved ones can have them anytime your hearts desire.

Makes 22 to 24 patties

Amount	Ingredients
3 pounds	ground pork sausage (use one that is not too lean,but has a good fat content. We always liked John Morrell Sausage)
1-1/2 teaspoon	garlic salt
1/3 cup + 2/3 cup	real maple syrup (use only real maple syrup; pancake syrup will not work! We use the local Wild Country Maple Syrup). Besides mixing in 1/3 cup, use an additional 2/3 cup to pour on the patties as you fry them)

For a smaller batch (9 patties)

Amount	Ingredients
1 pound	ground pork sausage
1/2 teaspoon	garlic salt
1-1/2 Tablespoons +1/3 cup	real maple syrup, the extra 1/3 cup is for drizzling on patties in the fry pan

Instructions

Combine the ground sausage, garlic salt and maple syrup in a mixing bowl. Combine ingredients completely, but do not overwork. Form sausage mixture into patties uniform in size and thickness, about 2-1/2 inches in diameter. Place the patties in a large non-stick frying pan. Pour remaining maple syrup over patties, so the entire pan is covered with a thin layer of syrup (if you're frying them in two batches for the larger recipe, divide the extra syrup between the two batches). Turn heat to medium.

Here is the key to caramelizing the maple sausage patties:

1) Stay very close to the stove during the cooking process. The patties can go from golden brown perfection to burnt very quickly.

2) Watch for the syrup to foam and bubble; that's when the browning process begins. Do not flip or move the patties until you check one by lifting it gently with a spatula to see if sausage patty is browned.

3) With a non-stick spatula, flip the browned patty so that the cooked side is up. Let the other side brown, check as before and flip again so that its face is down in the syrup. Allow the patty to caramelize, and then flip it again. This is how the patties will have the satiny glaze on the outside. Check for a nice browned glaze before you flip each time. **Do not allow to burn**!

4) You have to work fast at this point because the syrup will not stay at the foamy stage long before the syrup and the pork fat separate.

5) Remove patties from pan when both sides are golden brown and caramelized. Place on a baking tray or serving dish and repeat the process to complete the remaining batch of ground sausage mixture.

Chef's note: We have included an ingredients list for a smaller family-sized batch of maple sausage patties, and one to accommodate a larger gathering. Any extra cooked maple sausage patties can be frozen for later use. Just place them in a flat sealed container with wax paper between patties.

Chef's note on cleanup: After years of making maple sausage patties, we recommend that you have an empty can available in which to pour the hot syrup from the frying pan. While the pan is still hot, very carefully wipe it clean with a paper towel. The caramelized maple syrup is extremely sticky and is more easily cleaned while the pan is still hot.

(photo by Paul L. Hayden)

Rainbow & Sigurd

Keith "Rainbow" Trout knows how to tell a story.

Some 12 years ago, Rainbow began coming into the restaurant for breakfast. He drives to Grand Marais every month from his home in southern Minnesota to host "Polka Time," followed by three hours of "Classic Country" on our local radio station WTIP. Keith brings the gift of his colorful personality and spirited music selections to his listeners.

At first glance Rainbow seems a rather shy fellow. Don't let first appearances fool you. Keith is a man full of stories, eager to tell them.

During the Depression, Keith and his younger brother, Duane, were separated from their parents. With no jobs and no money, the boys were cast adrift. As the older brother, Keith did what he could to provide for his younger sibling. Life was not easy in those desolate days, and Keith struggled to find a job. He reflects that this early life of hardship created within him a restlessness that has followed him all of his days.

Rainbow in his favorite hat and, below, as a young railroad worker. (photos courtesy of Keith Trout)

As the hard times came slowly to an end, Keith sought work at the Illinois Central Railroad. At first skeptical of hiring a "scrawny kid," a railroad boss decided to do just that. When he saw this young scrapper's work ethic, the boss told Keith he'd keep him on, but only if he'd take his first paycheck and go to school to become an electrician. Back then in the 1940s, cars were pulled with steam locomotives. The boss knew that steam engines would soon be replaced with diesel, requiring electrical knowledge. Keith took the man's advice and fondly remembers the stern but kindly boss who opened up to him the world of railroads and a steady paycheck. After obtaining his degree as an electrician, Keith next went to the Pennsylvania Railroad and worked in the roundhouse, maintaining and repairing those modern diesel engines.

Keith owns a sizable property not too far from Duluth, living in an old cabin tucked amidst the trees. But he has always been drawn to northern places such as Ely, Grand Marais and the Gunflint Trail. He spent his youth hunting, fishing and canoeing the inland boundary waters.

He also has volunteered to help create and maintain the Superior Hiking Trail, cutting trails into the dense forests and building bridges, steps and observation decks. In the boreal forest, doing the exhausting work of trail making, Keith found a balm for his restless spirit. We enjoy the majesty of the Superior National Forest today thanks to the hard work of Keith and many like him.

As a man who loves the forests and lakes, Keith discovered a kindred spirit in the works of Sigurd F. Olson from Ely. After reading everything that he could find, Keith wrote Sigurd a letter to tell the fellow environmentalist how his writing and work inspired him. That sparked a written correspondence that went on for years, culminating with Keith traveling to Ely to sit in Sigurd's writing cabin, where they discussed the concerns of the new Boundary Waters Canoe Area. Sigurd gave Keith copies of his books, signed with personal notes. In keeping with the generous spirit that is Keith, they all found their way into the hands of friends.

One summer day, when Keith arrived to visit his old friend, Sigurd's wife, Elizabeth, met him at the cabin door. The man Keith had grown to love and admire had passed on. Elizabeth invited Keith into the writing cabin and showed him Sigurd's final typed words, still in the typewriter on the old weathered desk. Keith well remembers them: "A new adventure is coming up, and I'm sure it will be a good one."

Elizabeth next picked up Sigurd's old pocket knife, explaining that it had seen many an adventure. She handed it to Keith. Sigurd would like a fellow adventurer to have it, she said. Though Keith is not one who covets material things, this cherished object meant a great deal to him. He kept it many years, and then, as is his way, Keith gifted the knife to Sam Cook, another adventurer and writer of wilderness stories.

Just this last summer, Keith called to tell me he'd be coming to Grand Marais to do his monthly radio show. I told him I was writing a story about him for my second cookbook and asked him to bring photographs. He came with old photos from his railroad years and all the stories that go with them.

We met for breakfast at The Pie Place Café, and, as you might guess, spent hours in conversation … or really hours with Keith telling stories and me absorbing them.

I doubt that Keith will ever run out of tales to tell, and I know for certain that I'll never quit listening.

"I have discovered that I am not alone in my listening;
that almost everyone is listening for something,
that the search for places where the singing may be heard goes on everywhere."
– Sigurd F. Olson, *The Singing Wilderness*

Pie Place New England Clam Chowder

We love clam chowder. I like mine without the bacon, so whenever we made it for the restaurant, someone would set aside a no-bacon bowl just for me. (How's that for love?)

Serves 8 to 10

Amount	Ingredients
12 medium	potatoes, peeled and cubed to 1/2 inch
1 teaspoon	dried thyme (or 2 to 3 fresh sprigs, remove stems and keep leaves)
2 (64-ounce) cans	chicken broth
6 (5-ounce) cans	clams, chopped (3 drained, 3 with juice; otherwise it tends to be too fishy tasting)
1-1/2 pounds	bacon, cooked until crisp and crumbled (reserve some crumbles for garnish)
5 Tablespoons	bacon grease (saved from cooking bacon)
4 cups	heavy cream
For garnish	parsley
To taste	salt and pepper

Instructions

Place cubed potatoes and the thyme into the chicken broth in a large pan. Simmer until potatoes are tender, but not mushy, and broth is slightly thick. Add clams, crumbled bacon and bacon grease. Continue to simmer for about 10 minutes. Turn off the heat, add the heavy cream, stir and serve. Garnish with parsley and crumbled bacon. Salt and pepper to taste (but do taste first as the bacon tends to make the broth salty). Makes at least 1 gallon of chowder, so invite lots of friends or reduce the recipe as appropriate.

A Yurt Sleepover

Seldom in the hectic life of a restaurateur can one manage a getaway to rest and restore. As a restaurant family, though, we learned the simple wisdom of having time to do just that.

Cheryl, creator of the wonderful meals served at The Pie Place Café, knew the value of play. She never ceased to create experiences for our family that helped us return to the restaurant super-charged and rarin' to go once again.

As first time "Northerners," we learned that to endure the long, dark cold winters, we must throw ourselves into the season with wild abandon. That's often hard to do, given the long hours that a restaurant requires and the short days winter offers.

Yet we found that if we were willing to don the requisite down coats, boots, long underwear (definitely not my color palette), mittens and hats, we could relish the great wintery outdoors. And enjoy we did.

Barbra and Ted after the blowdown. A Mongolian hot pot, in the center of the table below, provides a perfect yurt meal. (photos courtesy the Youngs)

We skied the lit cross-country trails at Pincushion Mountain after a day's work, snowshoed at George Washington Pines, part of the Superior National Forest, on our day away from the café and ice-skated in Harbor Park (thank you, Stephan Hoglund for flooding the rink) to our heart's content.

As lovers of the Gunflint Trail, we began to trek up to Poplar Creek Guesthouse B&B and the Banadad Ski Trail.

It was there that we met Ted and Barbra Young and found immediate friends. Hardy, amiable and outgoing folks, they made our trips to the Banadad memorable. Ted, a wild-haired woodsman, warmed us with stories and an energetic laugh. Barbra, an open-hearted hostess, invited us in after our day on the trails, serving steaming mugs of hot cocoa and showing me her collection of early Mongolian hot pots, sometimes called firepots. The cooking system reminds me of a doughnut-

shaped Bundt pan that sits atop a heating source such as coals (or sterno in these modern times). Ted prepared and served Mongolian Hot Pot dinners for guests staying in the yurts.

Ted was 14 when his family first vacationed on the Gunflint Trail. His parents eventually bought a 14-acre island on Poplar Lake, but soon after, in 1952, Ted's father passed away. Ted, his mother and siblings spent their summers at the lake, and Ted worked at Rockwood Lodge, where he began guiding.

In the mid-'70s, after college and a career in community organizing, Ted and Barbra moved full time to the island. They insulated the cabin and put in a large winter's supply of wood, but that first winter was cold and grueling. Living like true pioneers, they had no electricity or indoor plumbing, fetching water instead through a hole in Poplar Lake. Still, it became home.

The couple's son, Joey, was born there, and, just a few years later, he had learned to ski across the frozen lake in winter to attend school. Ted, Barbra and Joey lived on the island for three decades.

Ted became interested in sled dogs. He started with one dog and then added another, which led to the desired result – puppies. He wanted enough dogs to pull a sled, and his team grew to a sizable number, though not quite enough. He connected with local dogsled legend Arleigh Jorgenson, leasing dogs to fill out a team. He offered dogsled tours. Ted remembers times when he could drive his team right down the middle of the Gunflint Trail, as County Road 12 is known here. There was that much snow and that few people.

In 1984 Ted and Barbra put up their first yurt, adding two more soon after, and offered yurt-to-yurt skiing. Barbra, a fabulous cook and gracious hostess, along with "Chef Ted," served Mongolian Hot Pot dinners in the yurts.

Then in 2001, the Youngs moved to the mainland and opened a new inn, the Poplar Creek Guesthouse B&B. It was there that our paths crossed.

Our Pie Place family, especially Cheryl and I, had long dreamed of owning a yurt; I'd been searching out yurt options for years.

When we discovered that Ted and Barbra had yurt-to-yurt ski packages with overnight stays, we were in. What better way to know if we wanted a yurt than to spend a night in one?

Josh, Jeremy, Katherine and I made the trip up the Gunflint Trail in a blinding snowstorm. Three moose ran beside us before veering into the surrounding forest. We took that as a good omen of things to come, and we were right.

At Poplar Creek Guesthouse, with our skis and provisions packed onto a snowmobile, we piled on for our ride through the snowy forest. Awed by this beautiful winter wonderland, we thrilled when our yurt came into view as we rounded a gentle bend in the trail.

Our gear was quickly unloaded. We were shown how to light the gas lamps, where the extra firewood was and how to get our water from a hole in the frozen lake.

The yurt was already warm and toasty and a tiny steaming sauna awaited us. Way cool! Once our hosts left, we wasted little time peeling off our clothes and running through the snow to the sauna nestled among the pines. We spent a glorious hour letting the steam relax and warm our tired bodies, heaving a sigh of relief as a busy week seemed to melt away.

All day, we skied, took photos in the woods and curled up in front of the fire with glasses of wine and good books. That evening we did a Mongolian dinner in a hot pot I'd been given for my birthday. The beef, onions, mushrooms and root vegetables were skewered and cooked in hot broth much like fondue. I made some simple Mongolian sauces for dipping. After a day of skiing, fresh air and with a full belly, we quickly fell into our beds, serenaded by the howls of a nearby wolf pack as we drifted off to sleep. I can honestly say that night in the yurt was the best night's sleep I have ever had.

The next morning as Josh knelt at the hole to get water for our morning coffee, he saw the wolves crossing the frozen expanse across the lake.

Breakfast done, we awaited with a degree of melancholy the snowmobile that would take us "out of the bush." Our time at the yurt had been magical and unforgettable. It fueled our determination to have a yurt of our very own.

Back at the B&B, we thanked the Youngs for an incredible life-changing experience, assuring them that we would recommend it to our customers looking for a unique winter adventure.

Soon thereafter, we found the yurt of our dreams. The yurt, or ger in Mongolian, was made on the steppes of Mongolia and had felted wool walls, handpainted roof poles, door and crown, and braided yak hair ropes to tie on the felt and canvas sides. I called Ted and Barbra to let them know we'd ordered our yurt. They were excited, too, asking when it would be raised, so they could stop to see it when they were in town. It became one more shared experience.

The quietude of the forest is primordial; something mystical invades your senses along with the sound of stillness. When only nature surrounds you, perhaps that still small voice can be heard. In our own yurt, we tried to create a sacred space to hear it.

Ted and Barbra probably did not realize when they came to live on what has become Young's Island what an incredible life awaited them. We did not know, when our family came to make a life in Grand Marais, that our world would so naturally entwine with kindred spirits who also listen for the voices in the forest.

Roasted Garlic and Brie Soup

For those who love garlic, this is your soup. Garlic when roasted becomes sweet and buttery, with a robust, yet delicate flavor. This soup becomes the perfect meal served with warm, crusty French bread.

Serves 8

Amount	Ingredients
2 heads	garlic, skin on
6 Tablespoons	olive oil
1 medium	onion, finely diced
2 stalks	celery, finely diced
1 medium	carrot, finely diced
1/4 cup	all-purpose flour
6 cups	chicken broth
1 teaspoon	fresh oregano, chopped (or 1/2 teaspoon dry)
1/2 teaspoon	fresh thyme, chopped (or 1/4 teaspoon dry)
7 ounces	Brie, rind removed, cut into 1-inch cubes
To taste	ground white pepper and salt

(photo by Karin Holen)

Instructions
Preheat oven to 325°F.

Place garlic in a medium glass baking dish and drizzle with 2 Tablespoons olive oil. Cover the dish with foil and bake until garlic is golden and very tender, about 30 minutes. Transfer dish to rack and cool.

Heat remaining 4 Tablespoons oil in large, heavy saucepan over medium heat. Add onion and sauté until translucent, about 10 minutes. Add celery and carrot and sauté until vegetables are tender, about 10 minutes. Add flour and stir 3 minutes.

Gradually stir in broth, whisking out lumps. Bring to boil, stirring frequently. Reduce heat to medium-low and simmer until soup is slightly thickened, stirring occasionally, about 15 minutes. Peel garlic and transfer to food processor, add 1 cup soup and purée until smooth. Return mixture to saucepan. Stir in oregano and thyme. This can be prepared 1 day ahead, then covered and refrigerated.

Before serving, bring soup to simmer over medium-low heat; gradually add Brie, stirring until melted after each addition. Season soup to taste with white pepper and salt.

Footprints in the Snow

Our extended northwoods neighborhood is rich with multiple cultural influences.

People migrated to the North Shore from the Scandinavian countries and all of Europe, relocating in Grand Marais, on the Gunflint Trail and on Isle Royale. Each culture brought its utilitarian objects, used in everyday life, fashioned by hand and infused with the decorative motifs of their ancestral homes.

But one of the most distinctive and striking styles grew here long before immigrants arrived along these shores. The Ojibwe people, with the bright floral patterns traditional in their art for generations, have long infused everyday items with a vibrant life. Feathers, quills, shells and later brightly colored beads embellished workaday objects as well as ceremonial outfits.

Ojibwe women wove baskets of birchbark and cedar root for gathering, storage and cooking. Decorative rush mats served on floors and walls in birchbark lodges.

The animals of these forests – moose, deer and other furry creatures – gave themselves for clothing and footwear that protected against the harsh winters.

Once Europeans brought glass beads, beadwork developed as a natural outgrowth of traditional quillwork. It has been widely practiced at Grand Portage for generations, taught to children by grandmothers, mothers and aunts.

That is how Marcie McIntire, a traditional artist specializing in the floral designs of Ojibwe beadwork, learned her craft. Many of Marcie's relatives were bead workers, but she honed her art at an early age by watching her mother.

Marcie owns Ningii-OzhitoominOjibwe Art Gallery in Grand Portage, where she and her partner, Ernest Boyes, create and display native bead working

Ernest and Marcie wrapped in their fine work. Marcie's intricate beadwork below features the traditional Ojibwe style with colorful floral designs. (photos by Kathy Rice)

Marcie chose a turtle to decorate Mary's special moccasins. (photo by Kathy Rice)

in many forms. Marcie's images are inspired by the natural world around her, and it is these images that embellish deer and moosehide moccasins, bags, ceremonial armbands and jewelry.

Ernest, having learned moccasin making from his grandmother as a young boy, stitches the footwear in the old way, ready to receive Marcie's bead designs.

We frequent Marcie's gallery, always stopping by to say hello during Grand Portage Rendezvous Days and Powwow.

Ernest and Marcie attend the Farmers Market in Grand Marais on Saturdays selling their exquisite beadwork items. Regular customers at The Pie Place Café, they would come for breakfast or lunch while in town.

One day when we were at the gallery, Mary Lear was drawn to a pair of moccasins. Trimmed in beaver and embellished with brightly colored beads, she couldn't stop talking about how much she loved them.

Secretly I asked Marcie and Ernest if they would be willing to make a pair of moccasins for Mary as a Christmas gift from the family.

They agreed and set about making a pair. I trusted Marcie's expertise as an artist and asked her to choose whatever decorative image came to her as she was doing the beadwork.

A few days before Christmas, Marcie called. The moccasins were completed. Marcie, her mother and Ernest would be going to Duluth on Christmas Eve day, and they would drop them off at the Pie Place on their way.

Christmas Eve morning, in the midst of an unexpected blizzard and with a foot of snow in our driveway, a knock came on the door. Ernest stood holding out a box to me, a smile on his face.

He opened the lid to reveal an exquisite pair of moccasins nestled among folds of tissue paper. Turtle, that sacred being that holds Turtle Island, North America, on its back, graced the pair.

I threw my arms around Ernest, gushing a Merry Christmas wish. Then Ernest turned and trudged back through the snow, having fulfilled his duty as the bearer of a most precious gift.

That evening Mary couldn't believe her eyes when she unwrapped her present. Thrilled beyond belief, she put on the moccasins made just for her and has worn them almost every day since.

Marcie and Ernest have made other moccasins for our family since then, the most special, perhaps, being the tiny ones for Rosalee, the first baby in our family. I'm quite optimistic that, someday soon, another pair of tiny feet will arrive, needing to be warmed by moccasins crafted by our dear friends.

Whenever I think of that skillfully crafted gift for Mary, an indelible image comes into my mind. I see Ernest's footprints in the freshly fallen snow, to me a symbol of love on a snowy Christmas Eve morn.

Trail Walker Dip Sandwich

We know you'll be excited when you see this recipe. A Pie Place Café favorite, the caramelized onions, portobello mushrooms and delicate horseradish sauce make this sandwich worth hiking to get.

Serves 4

Amount	Ingredients
1 loaf	French bread, page 99, shaped in a long baguette
1-1/2 pounds	sliced roast beef, use deli cuts
4 to 6 Tablespoons	butter
1 small	onion, sliced
8 ounces	Swiss cheese, sliced
1 (8-ounce) carton	baby portobello mushrooms (or 3 large portobello mushroom caps, cut in 1/8-inch slices)
1 (12-ounce) can	beef consommé (or 1 (1-ounce) packet au jus seasoning)

Sauce:

1/4 cup	Hellmann's mayonnaise
1 teaspoon	horseradish (or get Hellmann's horseradish mayonnaise)

Instructions

Preheat oven to 350°F.

Sauté the sliced onion in 2 to 3 Tablespoons of butter until brown and caramelized, about 10 minutes. Set aside in a small bowl. Sauté sliced mushrooms in 2 to 3 Tablespoons butter until soft and slightly caramelized. Add to onions.

Cut the ends off the French baguette and cut the remaining bread into 4 equal portions. Slice each lengthwise down the middle (like a sub sandwich bread).

Do not use the ends. Lay bread pieces on the oven rack until warm.

Heat beef consommé in saucepan until hot but not boiling. Put sliced roast beef in the consommé to warm.

Remove bread from oven and slather with sauce. Layer the warmed meat, caramelized onion and mushrooms onto bread. Cut each sandwich in half for easy dipping.

Serve with small ramekins of consommé for dipping the sandwiches.

Round House

Fourteen years ago on a cold, wintery March evening, two weary women clad in flannel shirts arrived at the Pie Place greatly in need of a hot meal and a friendly face.

Adrienne Christiansen and Marilyn Hood had recently purchased property on Lone Cedar Road. On that particular night, they were feeling very alone indeed, having spent a hard-working weekend moving into the old cabin where they planned to stay while they built their new home.

I could see right away that some tender loving care was required and brought them steaming hot mugs of spiced cider while they awaited their dinner. Eagerly wrapping their frozen fingers around the mugs, they shared with me their dream of owning property in Grand Marais and building a "round house," a home for their eventual retirement.

I encouraged them, told them how brave and resourceful they were and set plates of food on the table before them. They had tears in their eyes, and a friendship was sealed on that night.

Over the course of the next several years, I came to know these women with pioneering spirits. Adrienne teaches at Macalester College, traveling extensively throughout the world. Marilyn works at Metro Transit and loves working with wood.

Adrienne & Marilyn at their wedding (photo by Bill Bradrick)
A very, very fine round house (photo by Adrienne Christiansen)

They brought their diverse skills to the construction of their home, doing some of the work themselves. They hired local craftsmen and learned from friends and neighbors, doing as much as they could.

Adrienne and Marilyn come to Grand Marais whenever they can get away from the demands of city life. Here they feel the most at home, in the quiet forest surrounding their property.

Last summer we received a call from the couple. They were planning to be married in Grand Marais, a small yet intimate affair that suited them well, with their children, family and a few close friends.

Marilyn asked if The Pie Place Café would be willing to do a simple breakfast, with pies served after the wedding ceremony.

The wedding would take place in their round house that years of sweat, tears, toil and love had built. The dream they had held in their hearts on that cold March night so many years ago was finally a reality. We were thrilled to be a part of the union of two women whom we have grown to love.

When Marilyn came into the restaurant to pick up the wedding pies, I happened to be there. We reminisced about the night we first met. Marilyn said that I was the first person she and Adrienne met in Grand Marais and the Pie Place was the first restaurant in which they'd dined.

"Because of that night," Marilyn said, "we knew we had come to the right place. Someday Grand Marais would be our home."

They've built a lot since that night so long ago – a beautiful round house nestled among the trees, friendship with many in their adopted town and an enduring, lasting marriage. When giving their wedding vows, Adrienne said, "I have traveled all over the world, but my life with Marilyn, buying our property and building the round house, and our marriage has been the greatest adventure of my life."

It's more than enough to build a life around.

Lamb and Winter Vegetable Stew

A perfect way to warm your tummy and soothe your soul after a day of hard winter work. Served with a warm, crusty French baguette, it's comfort food with style, one that will let family and friends feel the love.

Serves 4

Amount	Ingredients
1 pound	lamb stew meat, cut into 3/4-inch cubes (or buy a lamb shoulder roast, trim the fat and cut it into 3/4-inch pieces)
2 Tablespoons	olive oil
2 cups	beef consommé
1 cup	dry red wine (or additional beef broth)
2 cloves	garlic, minced
1 Tablespoon	fresh thyme leaves, snipped (or 1 teaspoon dried thyme, crushed)
1/4 teaspoon	salt
1/4 teaspoon	pepper
1	bay leaf
2 cups	butternut squash, peeled and cubed to 1/2-inch
1 cup	parsnips, peeled and cut into 1/2-inch slices
1 cup	sweet potatoes, peeled and cubed to 1/2-inch
1 cup	sliced celery
1 medium	onion, cut into thin wedges
1/2 cup	sour cream
3 Tablespoons	all-purpose flour

Instructions

In a large pot or Dutch oven, brown meat in two batches in hot oil, removing the meat each time with slotted spoon and setting it aside in a bowl. In the pot, place the beef consommé, wine, garlic, thyme, salt, pepper and bay leaf. Raise heat to high, stir and scrape the brown bits off the bottom – what Doe Chase called "the goodness" – until they dissolve into the liquid. Put the meat back in, and bring to a boil. Reduce heat and simmer, covered, for 1-1/2 hours.

Stir in squash, parsnips, sweet potatoes, celery and onion. Return to boiling. Reduce heat and simmer, covered, about 30 minutes more or until vegetables are tender. Discard the bay leaf.

In a small mixing bowl combine sour cream and flour. Stir 1/2 cup of the hot liquid from the Dutch oven into the sour cream mixture, making a roux. Pour the mixture into the Dutch oven, and cook and stir until thickened and bubbly. Then cook and stir for 1 minute more before serving.

Shopping at the General Store

When the Pie Place family moved to Grand Marais, we were thrilled with the "small town charm" of our new home.

Historic buildings were nestled here and there, reminders of an earlier time.

The small Christmas parade passed by our door, done in five minutes, but came back a second time when it circled the block. It delighted us to no end. This was what we'd been looking for in a home. The slow, easy pace and a place where everybody seemed to know and like each other.

Even the business establishments had a special appeal. At Leng's Soda Fountain back then, you could sit at the counter, perched atop vintage ice cream stools, and order a great burger and chocolate malt served in a frosty metal container.

And if a soda fountain wasn't enough nostalgia, you could, and still can, shop at Joynes Ben Franklin, a funky throwback to the five-and-dime stores of the '40s and '50s. Joynes has a twist, though, with some really excellent clothing fit for the north woods. We outfitted ourselves with flannel shirts, Woolrich vests, rabbit fur-lined hats, deerskin gloves, Sorel boots and ragg wool socks to protect against the biting winter winds that we soon encountered.

Rosemary and Howard started as college sweethearts and built a family and a business together.
(photo courtesy the Joynes family)

Years ago, my son, Josh, and I lived in Michigan's Copper Country of the Upper Peninsula. When I entered a small remote general store one day and couldn't find a can of Campbell's Cream of Mushroom soup, the store owner simply replied, "If we don't have it, you don't need it."

Now we were in another remote community, but this store seemed to have everything you could possibly want and then some. We'd never seen so many treasures tucked here and there among the shelves.

Tourists and summer people make their annual pilgrimage to "The Ben Franklin" to get a joyful experience that one just doesn't get when shopping at a mall. I can truly say that Joynes is one of the many reasons why people are drawn to our town. It's become one of the reasons why we love living here.

Joynes has a beautiful family history. The original store was built in 1914 by P.E. Alm. Old ledgers from Alm's time still exist today, along with the first cash register used in the store.

Howard and Rosemary Joynes purchased the store and opened their doors on the same day Pearl Harbor was bombed, Sunday, December 7, 1941.

Joynes is as vital to our community now as it was then. The store has been operated by three generations, son Dick picking up the reins when his father retired, and then two of the grandchildren taking over – Julie, along with her husband, Rodney Carlson, and Julie's brother Jim.

However, having worked hard his entire life, Howard didn't really understand the concept of "retirement."

He began working at the tender age of 8, feeling a deep responsibility to help the mother he so loved. Howard's life was shaped by those early childhood experiences. His granddaughter Julie related that her grandfather was actually an entrepreneur from the start. At age 8, Howard bought a little red wagon and stocked up on some sewing notions, going door to door to sell his wares. An enterprising little boy, he was trying to make some extra money to help his struggling mother.

The local neighborhood women soon realized what he was doing and bought things they really didn't need just to help the family.

So perhaps it wasn't surprising that even though his grandchildren had taken over the operation, Howard still worked at the store every day until a week before he passed away. He would take the bus from the Care Center to get there early to prepare for customers. As Howard's granddaughter said, "I really think that the store was the love of his life."

Well into his 80s, Howard would be out shoveling the sidewalk in front of the store in winter or inside making sure the shelves were stocked to overflowing. He always wore a friendly smile and had a warm greeting at the ready.

Howard's family crew in Joynes' store for his 90th birthday, standing, from left: Grandson Jim Joynes; great-grandchildren Ryan and Madi Joynes; Howard; great-grandson Aaron Carlson; daughter-in-law Skip Joynes; great-grandson Nate Carlson; granddaughter Julie and her husband, Rodney Carlson; and sitting are his sister Irma Toftey with her granddaughters Sarah Toftey (front) and Hannah Toftey (back) and his sister Donna Willett. (photo courtesy the Joynes family)

Rosemary had passed on before we came to Grand Marais, but Howard was a regular when the Pie Place opened at the edge of town, extremely regular. A creature of habit, he came into the restaurant every night at precisely 5 o'clock, sat at the same table and ordered the same types of foods. He liked simple, no-nonsense food, meals like his mother used to make.

As his nightly waitress, I developed a companionable relationship with him and got to hear his stories about his early days in Grand Marais.

After dinner, browsing through the local newspaper and a bit of a chat, off he'd go, returning to the store to "work on the ledgers" for the day.

One night he seemed tired. "Howard," I said, "why don't you just go home. You work hard all day and maybe it's time for a little rest."

He smiled wistfully. "My father died when I was a boy, and I had to start working to help my mother take care of my siblings and support the family. I guess I've been working for so long, I just don't know how to do anything else."

"Oh, Howard," I said and gave him a big hug.

He jumped up quickly and left, embarrassed perhaps at his admission. But I could tell that there was a soft spot in his heart for me after that. Talking came easier for him from then on, and he talked and talked, leaving his ledgers and the work of the day behind for at least a little while.

Howard is gone now, but his hardworking, friendly spirit lives on in his family and in the business that he built and loved.

History – the community's and this particular family's – is why we love Joynes Ben Franklin, and why we still shop there.

Cottage Pie

This rustic meat-and-potato pie is down-home comfort food, the type of food that Howard Joynes loved best. A savory pie that is simple to make and full of flavor, this is a perfect meal on a cold, wintery night. It's also a great way to use leftover mashed potatoes.

Serves 5 to 6

Amount	Ingredients
6 cups	potatoes, mashed (5 to 6 russet or Yukon golds)
1 cup	half-and-half, warmed
6 Tablespoons	butter, melted
3 pounds	hamburger
2 Tablespoons	butter
3 medium	carrots, peeled and sliced 1/4-inch
1/2 (8-ounce) package	mushrooms, sliced 1/4-inch
1/2 small	onion, sliced
1/4 teaspoon	ground marjoram
To taste	salt and pepper
For sprinkling	paprika
2 (14-ounce) cans	beef consommé (1 can for gravy)
6 to 8 Tablespoons	all-purpose flour

Instructions

Peel potatoes, cut in small pieces and place covered in boiling water in a medium saucepan for 20 to 30 minutes. Check the potatoes for doneness by poking with a fork. When soft, drain and place hot potatoes in a large mixing bowl. Mash potatoes with a mixer, adding the melted butter to the potatoes and then adding, incrementally, the warm half-and-half until any lumps disappeared. (You may not need to use all of the half-and-half). Set aside.

Brown the hamburger thoroughly in large skillet, separating meat as it browns. Drain fat well from meat and set aside.

Melt 2 Tablespoons of butter in skillet and sauté carrots, mushrooms and onions until the carrots and mushrooms are soft and the onions are translucent, about 10-15 minutes.

Place browned hamburger and marjoram into skillet with sautéed vegetables. Add 4 Tablespoons all-purpose flour and 1 can beef consume to mixture and cook on medium heat until thickened. If mixture is still too thin, add more flour, stirring to avoid lumps. Add salt and pepper to taste.

Preheat oven to 375° F.

Place thickened meat/vegetable mixture into a 9-inch pie dish or casserole (no pie crust required for this recipe). Top with the mashed potatoes and sprinkle with a bit of paprika for color. Place on a baking sheet and bake for 45 minutes or until bubbly and mashed potatoes are golden brown.

While Cottage Pie is baking, you have the option of making a simple gravy by putting 1 can beef consommé into a small sauce pan. Heat broth, add a dash of marjoram, salt and pepper to taste. Make a roux by whisking 2 Tablespoons all-purpose flour (or corn starch if you prefer) with 4 to 6 Tablespoons cold tap water until smooth. Whisk roux into hot broth and stir until thickened and smooth.

Remove pie from oven and let it rest for 15 minutes before serving. Cut into pie slices and serve with gravy.

(photo by Mary Beams)

Is There a Gretzky on the Ice?

If you live in Minnesota or Canada, as many of our Pie Place Café customers do, you probably have hockey in your blood.

As a retired "hockey mom," I can tell you that parents get caught up in the sport. It's just thrilling to see your son or daughter skate across an ice rink to score a winning goal, or actually any goal will do.

Trust me on this: You find yourself doing things you never thought possible.

My son, Josh, once said, "Mom, you yell so loud I can hear you out on the ice!" Quite the feat with a hockey rink surrounded by other zealous parents shouting at the top of their lungs, too.

The Kyrola family by their Lake Superior dream getaway and, below, at their Duluth home's hockey rink. (photo by Dawn Kyrola)

Hooked on hockey, you will travel to Canada to get the perfect skates, sit on a bench in a frigid arena until your bum is numb and spend countless days traveling to away games. Who would have guessed?

Many of our Pie Place Café friends either play on a hockey league or have children who love the sport.

Scott and Dawn Kyrola, who live in Duluth, came to the Pie Place every year for their anniversary, a little getaway from the hustle and bustle of jobs, children's activities and all the consuming things it takes to be a good parent.

We always tried to make their annual dinner a celebratory one.

Often in the summer, Scott and Dawn would bring their children, Ryleigh and Corbin, to the North Shore. As we came to know the younger members of this close-knit family, a wonderful story unfolded.

Scott, who played hockey in college, is now in a men's league in Duluth. It goes without saying that their son, Corbin, is a hockey player as well. Their family hockey stories brought back fond memories and much commiseration about the highs and lows of life on ice.

Given that the family lives in northern Minnesota, this hockey scenario may not seem like anything unusual. But this is where the story gets way cool.

One year, Scott flooded the family's rather large backyard, turning it into a hockey rink for the neighborhood kids. He strung lights for evening skating, placed benches for lacing skates onto wool-clad feet, and Dawn kept hot chocolate at the ready for rosy-cheeked Gretzkys in the making.

Before long word got out and the whole neighborhood began to show up for hours of skating practice, impromptu games and healthy fun. Parents joined in, bringing treats and watching their kids glide around the rink. Each night after everyone went home, Scott spent hours flooding the ice, an arduous task, and Dawn prepared goodies for the next day's festivities. Friendships were established; a true neighborhood was born.

I recall the camaraderie between families when Josh played hockey. It was one of the best parts of the sport.

When the Kyrola hockey rink became a neighborhood attraction, parents no longer wondered where their kids were and what they were doing. Now, years later, Corbin, 10, still loves hockey. Daughter Ryleigh, a seasoned hockey player at age 12, is a goalie. (You go, girl!)

A pint-sized face-off at the backyard rink. (photo by Dawn Kyrola)

And now there's a new twist to the story.

Last summer during Fisherman's Picnic in Grand Marais, I bumped into Scott, Dawn and the kids. They had exciting news: They'd just bought a cabin on Lake Superior. Now they'd be a part of our neighborhood.

If they come to the cabin in winter, they'll be able to skate at our local outdoor rink. We're hoping that someday there will be a return of the Harbor Park ice skating rink. We can build a bonfire on the shore, bring a Thermos of hot chocolate and skate the night away under the stars. I can't wait!

Pork Tenderloin with Bleu Cheese Applejack Gravy

You can never go wrong with a moist, juicy pork tenderloin. In this flavorful gravy, applejack brandy, distilled from fermented apple cider, gets paired with pungent bleu cheese for a flavor that is divine.

Serves 4

Amount	Ingredients
8 slices	bacon, chopped
2 large	onions, thinly sliced
2 large	Granny Smith apples, peeled, cored and each apple cut into 8 wedges
1 Tablespoon	sugar
2 Tablespoons	all purpose flour
1 cup	apple cider or juice
1 cup	chicken broth
1/2 cup	Applejack or other apple brandy (Calvados)
1 cup	crumbled bleu cheese
To taste	salt and pepper
1 to 1-1/2 pounds	pork tenderloin

Instructions

Preheat oven to 350° F.

Cook bacon in heavy large skillet over medium heat until crisp. Transfer to paper towels to drain and save for use as garnish later.

Spoon off 1 Tablespoon of bacon drippings from the skillet and reserve. Drain all but 2 Tablespoons of the remaining drippings from the skillet. Add onions and sauté until golden, about 15 minutes. Push onions to 1 side of skillet; add apples and sugar and sauté until apples are golden, about 20 minutes. Transfer mixture to a bowl.

Heat the 1 Tablespoon of reserved bacon drippings in same skillet. Add flour and stir 1 minute. Gradually whisk in juice, broth and applejack. Boil until gravy thickens, whisking frequently, about 4 minutes. Add cheese and whisk until melted. Season with salt and pepper. Add onion mixture to gravy and stir until heated through. Remove from heat. Cover and keep warm.

Season pork with salt and pepper. Heat large nonstick skillet over medium heat. Add pork tenderloin and sear on all sides, about 6 to 8 minutes per side. Transfer meat to baking dish or roasting pan and roast in oven until meat thermometer inserted in the center registers 135° F, about 20 to 25 minutes. Remove from oven and let the meat rest for 15 minutes; temperature should rise to the USDA recommended minimum of 145° F while resting.

Slice and pour warm sauce over the meat. Garnish with bacon and serve.

(photo by Mary Beams)

Friends

They are one of life's most precious gifts.

Friends bring laughter, support, encouragement, inspiration and advice. Friends lend a willing shoulder when we need to cry on it, and a listening ear when we need to talk. We, in turn, will do the same for them in the spirit of friendship.

Talking to a friend can clarify our thoughts and feelings. We can express our fears, review our failures and reveal our dreams and triumphs. A friend lifts us up when it seems we can't make it through another day.

Friends celebrate us and let us know that we matter. We play together, even as adults, forgetting our troubles if only for a few hours and returning to our work and lives refreshed. A friend tells us their stories … and we tell them ours. We comfortably share a companionable silence in front of a campfire or talk the night away after a delicious meal.

Yes, when you have dear friends, ones who happen to be named "Friend," it makes you think about what friendship means.

Stewart and Kathy Friend and their children, Coryander "Cory" and Alex, seemed to have walked into the Pie Place and into our lives almost from the day we opened our doors 20 years ago. A vital and fun-loving family, they're full of life and their visits bring conversation that flows as easily as water in a stream.

The Friends own an island on Saganaga Lake at the end of the Gunflint Trail.

Red Squirrel Island – a name the family inherited from the previous owners and likely based on the permanent chattering residents – features two cabins and a wood-burning hot tub. A little piece of the wilderness, it's no wonder they love returning season after season.

As friends often are, Stewart and Kathy proved to be my perfect sounding board for discussions about parenting. We also had shared our interests in art, and some of their cabin choices came from our gallery.

Friends, indeed – Kathy, Coryander, Alex, Stewart and pup Eily at Saganaga. (photo courtesy the Friend family)

Extremely generous, Stew once left an exceedingly large tip that I was sure was a mistake. When I hurried to the car to let him know he had accidentally overpaid, he said, "No I didn't. The food is great, and you're worth it!"

Every year in late spring, Stew and his "crew" of George Govas and Gary Ligocki come in advance of the family to open the cabin for another season. They put in the docks, make necessary repairs and continue the construction work there that has been going on without end for as long as I can remember.

Stewart, Gary, George and the late, great Norman the dog at the cabin. (photo courtesy the Friends)

George, ever the trickster, sports long, wild hair and a beard. Gary is quiet with gentle yet mischievous eyes. They are Stew's constant sidekicks (or perhaps he is theirs).

Whenever they made a trip up the Gunflint, the trio stopped at The Pie Place Café to have breakfast and pick up pot pies and gravy, bread, muffins and, of course, pies (very berry and apple). Provisions, after all, are essential on a trek into the forest.

One year just before our annual Mocha Moose Café poetry reading in October, Stew and the crew arrived unannounced. I was flitting about, lighting candles, checking the mic and putting out poetry books. An early guest suddenly alerted me with, "Kathy, there's a biker guy giving the peace sign through the window!"

I turned and there was George. I ran out and gave him a big hug, inviting him in for the readings. Alas, he confessed, poetry is not his thing. He declined with gentlemanly grace. The gang, he assured me, would be in for breakfast the following morning.

Once the cabin is opened for the season, the Friend family gets about the business of spending companionable days together fishing, sunbathing, reading and relaxing. Alex and Cory arrive from California, often with a cadre of friends. These young people, intelligent, energetic and now very cosmopolitan, still love their lake time.

It seems incredible sometimes to Stew and Kathy. "Can you believe it?" they tell me. "They still want to be with us!" What could make a parent happier?

When their family arrives, we get caught up on all that's happened while they were away. We pore over photos of Cory's latest set designs and get news of Alex's latest creative pursuits, like his NIUKA tea, a blend of healing tea leaves that make flavorful and medicinal brews. Then we fill their car with homemade food and wish them well as they leave with broad smiles and visions of Red Squirrel Island awaiting them.

Last summer Stew and Kathy invited us up to Saganaga for a day at the cabin. Someday soon we will do just that. I can't think of a more perfect way to spend a summer day than with Friends.

> "Then at last I was back, and as I paddled along and saw
> the old familiar reaches of blue, the islands riding at anchor in the distance,
> the gnarled old trees and lichen-covered cliffs, it seemed as though I had never been away …
> The loons were calling as they had always called in welcome to a voyageur."
> – Sigurd F. Olson, "Farewell to Saganaga" from *The Singing Wilderness*

Pie Place Chicken Pot Pie

We were The Pie Place Café, and our pies brought folks back again and again (and still do to the bakery). But not all pies are desserts. Our signature Chicken Pot Pie was a tradition for folks like Stewart and Kathy. Whenever our friends make a trip to their cabin on Saganaga Lake, they call ahead and order pot pies and plenty of gravy. It's their summer thing, but I feel a pot pie speaks of winter comfort food.

Serves 6

Amount	Ingredients
3 to 4 large	carrots, peeled and diced to 1/2 inch (save the peelings)
3 large	potatoes, peeled and diced to 1/2 inch (save the peelings)
4 to 6 Tablespoons	butter
1/2 large	onion, diced
2 medium stalks	celery (including leaves if they are nice)
1 (12-ounce) package	frozen corn
4 breasts	chicken, boneless and skinless
1 (64-ounce) can	chicken broth or stock
1 cup	carrot, onion and celery peelings (leftovers)
2	bay leaves
1 cube	chicken bouillon
3/4 cup	all-purpose flour
1 cup	cold water
8 to 10 sprigs	fresh thyme (or 1 teaspoon dried thyme), plus some for garnish
1/2 teaspoon	ground sage
1/3 to 1/2 cup	heavy cream
1 teaspoon	garlic salt
To taste	salt and pepper
1/4 cup	half-and-half
1 recipe	pie dough, page 23 (use 6 individual pot pie tins or a single 9-inch deep dish pie pan)

Instructions

Place diced carrots and potatoes into a small amount of salted water in a medium pan, bring to a boil and cook until tender, about 6 minutes. Drain and add to a large bowl. Set aside.

Melt 2 Tablespoons butter in a large skillet and sauté onions and celery until soft, then place them into the bowl with the other vegetables. Add the frozen corn and set aside.

Using the same skillet, melt 2 additional Tablespoons butter, salt and pepper the chicken breasts and sauté them until golden brown and thoroughly cooked. Rest 10 minutes then dice into 1/2-inch cubes, the same size as vegetables. Place cooked, diced chicken into the large bowl with the vegetables. Remove thyme leaves from stems and add thyme, sage, garlic salt and salt and pepper to taste to the mixture. Set mixture aside or refrigerate while you are making your pie dough.

Place 1 can of chicken broth or stock, 1 cup vegetable peelings, bouillon cube and bay leaves in a

large pot and bring to a boil. Simmer 30 minutes. Remove bay leaves and strain through colander to remove peelings.

Whisk together 3/4 cup of flour with 1 cup cold tap water to make a roux (thickening agent). It should be the consistency of tomato soup. If it appears too thin, add a bit more flour. Stir the roux gradually into the hot broth, whisking until smooth and gravy has thickened. Add up to 1/2 cup heavy cream to thickened gravy to reach medium consistency. Set gravy aside to cool.

Follow pie dough instructions on page 23. Divide dough into two balls, one slightly larger for top crust. Roll dough on a floured surface and place in a lightly greased (with a bit of Crisco) and floured (1 Tablespoon) 9-inch deep dish pie tin. If you want to make individual pot pies, which is a nice touch, make 12 small balls and use six 5-inch tins. Once you've placed the dough in the tins, you are ready to assemble the pie/pies.

Pour some of the gravy into the chicken/vegetable mixture and combine. Place the mixture into the pot pie crust. If you are making individual pot pies, put an equal amount of the mixture in each crust. If they seem to need more gravy, ladle some over the top of the filling.

Roll the additional dough ball and place over the filling to cover. Crimp, cut vent and brush with half-and-half. (Or you can do the rustic crust as shown below.)

Preheat oven to 350° F.

Place the pie tin(s) on a baking sheet, in case there is bubbling over, and bake for 45 minutes to 1 hour, until golden brown.

Any extra gravy can be used at serving time to ladle over the top of slices or on individual pies. Garnish with sprigs of fresh thyme.

(photo by Kathy Rice)

F. Scott & Good Company

I hope as I write this story that F. Scott Fitzgerald will afford me more than a bit of literary license, as I am, after all, in very good company.

I met Phil and Theresa Westine and Dick McDermott when we were at our Pie Place location on the crest of the hill just outside Grand Marais. Phil and Theresa winter in Texas and own property on the shore of Lake Superior. They came to the restaurant often. One time they brought along their dear friend Dick, whom I adored immediately.

Dick on the trail. (photo by Phil Westine)

I came to know Dick well when we catered a special dinner for his nephew, close family and friends. A local historic hand-hewn cabin was a great setting for the event that Dick wanted to orchestrate. Dick wanted everything to be perfect, and he and I went over and over each and every detail. Near the end, his daily calls seemed to be simply for reassurance that all would be as he wished for those he loved. I didn't mind the calls; I knew how much he wanted everything to be just so. I thought it very dear of him to care so much.

On the day of the event, he awoke to a plumbing problem. He called, understandably in a tizzy.

"Not to worry Dick," I reassured him. "Everything will be just fine. And even if it isn't, we have blackberry peach pie!"

A plumber was contacted, the problem fixed and food delivered all in good time. As Phil and Theresa, two of the guests, will attest, a good time was had by all. The pie was peachy.

As I grew to know Phil, Theresa and Dick better, a most wonderful story surfaced about their friendship and what their shared passion had accomplished.

In 1975, the St. Paul apartment building where F. Scott Fitzgerald was born and the building next door were purchased by Phil, Theresa, Dick and nine other people. The two three-story brick buildings on Laurel Avenue became the 12-unit "F. Scott Fitzgerald Condominium Association."

After renovation of the buildings, Dick took up residence in F. Scott's birthplace in 1976 and would live 36 years in the apartment where Fitzgerald was born and lived as a baby. Dick read every book the author wrote and took his job as the "resident" F. Scott Fitzgerald historian seriously, providing tours of the house and giving visitors insight into Fitzgerald's literary legacy.

It was not uncommon for a group of tourists from another country, eager to see the birthplace of this literary giant, to knock on the door of Dick's apartment, asking for a tour. Dick willingly shared the wealth of knowledge he'd gleaned through the years. Soon word got out and bus tours began to arrive outside the house. Dick gave uncountable tours of his apartment, never turning anyone away. Those Fitzgerald lectures became a special part of his life.

Unlike the city-loving Fitzgerald, though, Dick was as comfortable in the north woods as in the heart of the Twin Cities. Every spring and fall, Dick came up to the North Shore to help maintain a 5-mile segment of the Superior Hiking Trail. He and fellow trailmates Phil Westine, Sam Haroldson and Ken Wielinski would meet at the Pie Place for a hearty breakfast before heading out to the trail and then spend the day stabilizing wooden walkways, posting trail signage, clearing fallen trees off of the woodland paths and picking up litter. For nearly two decades, these friends rendezvoused twice a year to care for their segment of trail.

Then in 2012, Dick was diagnosed with lung cancer. He decided against aggressive treatment that might undermine the quality of his remaining time. He'd lived a good, full life, after all, and wished to remain in his home. Although weakened, Dick still entertained visitors with F. Scott stories, though now from his bed in the room where the famous author had been born. He generously funded the startup of "Fitzgerald in St. Paul," a nonprofit that continues to be devoted to celebrating the author and his work, especially in his hometown. Dick rallied to meet with the group's directors up to the last weeks of his life, participating in the planning of the emerging organization.

On September 2, 2012, our beloved friend passed away peacefully in the home that, in essence, he shared with the author whom he had championed.

A short time after Dick's passing, Phil, Sam and Ken returned to do fall trail maintenance and this time to hike in honor of a man who had loved the woods, and cared for it, as passionately as he had F. Scott's house.

They arrived at The Pie Place Café, our new location overlooking the harbor, to have their traditional breakfast. That year it was a sober, yet still celebratory affair. We shared a story or two remembering Dick and what he'd meant to each of us. He would have loved to join us, and perhaps he did.

The trail crew, Sam, Dick, Phil and Ken and below, Dick on the Grand Marais Harbor.
(photos by Phil Westine)

Before the hikers left, I gave them a piece of paper with a quotation from F. Scott Fitzgerald. I asked them to read it somewhere along the trail when they felt called to do so.

I know that Dick was waiting for them under the forest canopy, eager to hear F. Scott's words one last time.

"It isn't given to us to know those rare moments when people are wide open and the lightest touch can wither or heal.
A moment too late and we can never reach them any more in this world.
They will not be cured by our most efficacious drugs or slain with our sharpest sword."
– F. Scott Fitzgerald

Pie Place Raspberry Rhubarb Streusel Pie

New guests came in one day with the announcement that our pie had been in *The New York Times*, and they were here from New York to taste it. This pie will breathe new life into your family dining experience. A Pie Place customer favorite, we just can't seem to bake them fast enough. Now you can make one at home, and bring a taste of summer to winter by using frozen rhubarb and raspberries. Of course, fresh in summer is a great option.

Serves 6 to 7

Amount	Ingredients
1 recipe	pie dough, page 23

Filling:

4 cups	frozen or fresh rhubarb, diced
1-1/2 cups	frozen or fresh raspberries
1-1/4 cups	sugar
1/4 cup	all-purpose flour
2 Tablespoons	butter

Pie Place Crumb Top:

3 cups	all-purpose flour
1 cup	brown sugar, tightly packed
1/2 teaspoon	salt
1/2 cup	butter, melted

Instructions

Preheat oven to 375° F.

Place unbaked pie crust into 9-inch pie tin and crimp the edges.

Place rhubarb and raspberries in a bowl and then mix with sugar and flour. Put all of it into the unbaked crust. Dot with butter. Place on a baking sheet to catch juices.

To make the crumb top, toss all ingredients together thoroughly, rubbing out any lumps. Sprinkle crumb topping generously to cover all of the fruit. (Store any remaining crumb top in refrigerator up to two weeks for later use.)

Bake in a preheated oven for about 1 hour, checking to see if juices are thick, clear and bubbly and the fruit is soft.

When done, remove pie from oven and let set for at least 1 hour to cool before serving.

Chef's note: Baking times may vary depending upon many factors, such as weather, what else is in the oven, etc., so you might need up to an additional 20 to 30 minutes baking time.

Celebrations with Love

Cara and Michael Corey celebrate on Lake Superior. (photo by Joe Crimmings Photography)

The Girl in the Flannel Pajamas

I don't know about you, but sometimes a warm, sticky caramel roll with that first cup of coffee just calls to me.

In the early days of the Pie Place, Doe Chase, a family member, would rise early in the morning and bake a batch of caramel rolls. When she turned them out of the pan and onto a plate, our mouths would water to the point where we had to "step away from the table!"

Like a mother hen hovering over her chicks, Doe would guard the caramel rolls, wooden spoon in hand, as she carried them to the bakery case. She did, on occasion, make them on a Sunday morning as a treat for her hard-working family.

Word of the caramel rolls spread quickly throughout our small community. Doe, and later Katherine, baked them on Fridays. Soon people would crowd around the glass bakery case first thing Friday morning in eager anticipation. Dreaded were the words: "We just sold the last caramel roll. So sorry!"

Perhaps the biggest caramel roll fan was Carol Backlund and she showed up every week to get one. One Friday, Carol called to ask, "Is anyone in the restaurant right now? I'm still in my PJs, and I want to come up and get a caramel roll."

Are those PJ bottoms? Maybe, but the box definitely has caramel rolls. (photo by Jeremy Chase)

I assured her that the "coast was clear," so up the hill she came. By the time she got to the restaurant, though, folks had arrived for breakfast. Oops!

As she padded into the dining room, clad in slippers and flannel pajamas, she was greeted with smiles and waves. Anyone who'd tasted our caramel rolls understood.

Carol is our "mail lady" and keeps our letters coming and going from the mailbox at the end of our road. One day as we were talking about our recently installed mailbox, I mentioned that I wanted to write a story about her for our second cookbook.

She laughed heartily when I reminded her about the caramel roll pajama caper. Our conversation led to something I didn't know (as a newcomer to the community of only 20 years).

Carol's father, Carl Nunstedt, built the Harbor Inn, formerly called The Hub, in 1961. Carol's parents owned and operated the business for 15 years.

The Harbor Inn passed hands once before Carol and her husband, Ted, bought it. This second-generation couple owned the Inn and ran the restaurant for 18 years, cooking, cleaning rooms and doing all the things it takes to make a successful enterprise. Carol baked pies, too, just as we do.

Her story amazed me – I did not know of her family ties to what became our Harbor Inn and The Pie Place Café. (It seems there are very few degrees of separation between anyone

Before it was the Harbor Inn, it was The Hub. (postcard courtesy Carol Backlund)

in a small town, even if you don't know it.) Carol ended our conversation by saying, "I know what it takes to operate a restaurant, to keep the quality of food at a consistent and high level. I want you to know that I appreciate what you and your family have done to carry on this tradition. It means a lot to me."

From someone who's been there, who knows the joys and struggles of being a restaurant family, Carol's words mean the world to us.

Have we seen Carol in her PJs lately? Not since that morning years ago. But I can assure you, she's welcome at the Pie Place bakery for caramel rolls any time … even in her pajamas.

(*our secret recipe*)

Sticky Pecan Caramel Rolls

These caramel rolls are to live for – so good that Carol came in her PJs to make sure she got some. Served warm on a holiday morning, these sticky rolls create a festive mood.

Makes 12 to 16 large caramel rolls

Amount	Ingredients
Dough (prepare the night before):	
3 cups	lukewarm water
2 (0.25-ounce) packets	active dry yeast
1-1/2 Tablespoons	kosher salt
6-1/2 cups	unbleached, all-purpose flour
Caramel topping:	
6 Tablespoons	butter, softened
1/2 teaspoon	salt
1/2 cup	light brown sugar, packed
1/3 cup	chopped pecans
Filling:	
4 Tablespoons	butter
1/4 cup	sugar
1/4 cup	light brown sugar, packed
1/2 teaspoon	salt
1 teaspoon	cinnamon
1/4 teaspoon	nutmeg
1/2 cup	chopped pecans, toasted

Instructions

For the dough, combine all ingredients in the order listed, stirring with a wooden spoon as each ingredient is added. If necessary, add a small amount of additional water to incorporate all of the flour. Place into a container with a loosely fitted lid. Let rise 2 hours before placing it overnight in the refrigerator. Keep the lid loose.

For the topping, use a mixer to cream together the butter, salt and brown sugar until the butter is well combined. Mix in the pecans. Spread the topping evenly on the bottom of a 9-inch cake pan or a 9-inch springform pan. Set pan aside.

For the filling, place pecan pieces on a baking sheet and toast them for about 5 minutes in a 325° F oven. Set aside to cool. Cream together all of the filling ingredients until smooth except the pecans. Add the cooled pecans. Both the topping and filling can be made the night before and refrigerated overnight or done the day you bake the rolls. Do return both to room temperature before working with them.

The next day, to assemble the caramel rolls, lightly flour the top of the dough and separate in two batches. (You'll repeat the steps for both batches.)

With dough at room temperature, dust it with flour and shape it into a ball, tucking it evenly into the round form. Roll out the dough with a rolling pin, to a 1/8-inch thick rectangle about 16x8 inches.

Sprinkle the rolling surface lightly with flour to prevent the dough from sticking to the surface or to the rolling pin. If the dough is too stiff to roll out completely, let it rest for 5 minutes before continuing. Then complete rolling out the rectangle.

Spread the filling evenly over the rolled-out dough, leaving about 1/2 inch of dough uncovered along one of the long edges for sealing. Begin on the opposite long side to roll the dough into a log, pinching closed at the seam.

Cut the log into 6 to 8 equal pieces with a serrated knife; arrange the pieces cut side up in the pan. Cover loosely with plastic wrap and allow them to rise for one hour.

Preheat the oven to 350° F.

Place a baking sheet below the pan of rolls to catch any drips. Bake on a center rack in the oven for 40 to 45 minutes or until golden brown and well set in the center.

(photo by Mary Beams)

Immediately after removing the pan from the oven, run a knife around the inside edge to loosen the rolls. Place a large plate upside down on top of the pan, invert to turn the rolls out onto the plate.

The caramel will drip down and around the rolls and firm up as the rolls cool.

Chef's note: Do not allow the rolls to sit too long in the pan after taking it out of the oven, or they will stick and won't turn out.

If your family doesn't eat all of them, freeze the remaining rolls to pull out later for a special treat. Thaw them before reheating, wrap them in foil and heat for 20 minutes in a 350° F oven.

The Trading Post

In the early 1600s, French explorer Samuel de Champlain established a trading post near present-day Quebec. In 1670, the Hudson's Bay Company was founded, an important center for the fur trade.

Early trading posts became a lifeline to residents of remote communities. They carried blankets, guns and knives, cookware, cloth, necessities for northern life, as well as glass beads, clay pipes and tobacco and alcohol, amenities from "civilization." Fur traders often bought on credit, paying their bills at the end of the fur season.

Though hundreds of years have passed, and the fur trade is no more, an example of the early trading post at the Grand Portage National Monument and stockade draws thousands of visitors each year.

Grand Marais, though, has its own trading post. The Lake Superior Trading Post, established in 1971, is a modern version of the trading posts from the Hudson's Bay Company era. The shelves are stocked with far different items than those found in the early trading posts, but the concept of catering to all that one might need remains the same. It's a great resource in a remote town far from city shopping malls and department stores.

As a postcard of the Lake Superior Trading Post, circa 1980, proclaims, this is a unique store offering quality outdoor clothing, gifts, sporting goods and wilderness outfitting services. In the back, you can see Eddie Anderson's old fish house and Dockside Deli. No longer standing, their energy remains part of the shoreline landscape. A fire destroyed the buildings in 1988, but like a phoenix rising from the ashes, today's Lake Superior Trading Post emerged.

It no longer offers wilderness outfitting services (though you can bet the good folks there can help you find some). The Lake Superior Trading Post has anything you could want, as well as incredible finds you don't know you need until you see them.

A 1980s postcard and, below, the Lake Superior Trading Post family: Linda Zenk, Stephanie Anderson and Eric Humphrey. (photo by Kathy Rice)

Proprietors Linda Zenk and her son, Eric Humphrey, and daughter, Stephanie Anderson, have built a family business that continues to fill an important niche in Grand Marais.

When you walk into the Lake Superior Trading Post you are always greeted with a welcome smile. They are truly glad to see you and eager to help you find whatever you need.

There is a sense that you have walked into a trading post from the past as you climb the log staircase to the second floor. Wares, creatively displayed, beckon from every nook and cranny. You'll find practical wear for outdoor lifestyles – coats, hats, woolen socks – to fine quality gifts imported from Scandinavia. The store has a particularly thoughtful book section that fits its outdoorsy clientele.

Equally thoughtful are the community-minded and generous people who run the trading post. They are among the first to roll up their sleeves when help is needed.

When the area food bank needed donations for the Thanksgiving boxes, and a community Christmas toy and clothing drive was organized, they gave above and beyond – contributing money for abundant dinners and donating toys, children's books, games, puzzles and candy. It's the kind of people they are.

The Humphrey family, into which Linda married, has been in the dry goods business since the 1930s. The first store, started by Eric and Stephanie's grandfather and great-uncle, offered quality merchandise more than 90 years ago. Their savvy selections to this day provide goods here that we otherwise would have to travel hours to obtain – soaps and body care products, dishes, table linens, cookbooks, lamps, rugs, shoes, socks, specialty foods, outdoor clothing, blankets, baby items – the list goes on and on.

As a family who believes in shopping locally, we at the Pie Place know we're sure to find what we're looking for when we shop at the Lake Superior Trading Post. And likewise, Linda and her family often have had The Pie Place Café cater brunches for Sunday morning gatherings after church – the best time for a retail family to celebrate birthdays, christenings and other special occasions.

Our usual way to set up is at their home. We pop breakfast casseroles into the oven, put food in the fridge, and the family returns home to a warm, delicious brunch. Rusty, the official tail-wagging greeter, knows us by now and trusts that whatever we bring into his house, a tasty treat will await him.

Linda, always gracious and appreciative, makes what we do worthwhile. She is so effusive about how much her guests enjoy the food and how our work makes the occasion more festive.

The folks at the Lake Superior Trading Post often send customers down the street to the Pie Place, and we, in turn, send our guests to shop with them. In this remote community, we depend upon one another.

In many ways things haven't changed from the era of those first trading posts, and we wouldn't have it any other way.

Lingonberry Orange Scones

Scones are a perfect complement to an early morning breakfast or family brunch. When we're lucky enough to get handpicked wild lingonberries, our guests get a real treat. Warm flaky scones with a dollop of clotted cream make any day into a celebration.

Serves 6

Amount	Ingredients
Scones:	
3 cups + 1 cup	all-purpose flour, the extra cup for handling the dough
1/2 cup + 1/4 cup	sugar, plus 1/4 cup to sprinkle on top
4 teaspoons	baking powder
1/2 teaspoon	salt
1 cup	butter, very cold and cut into small pieces
1 medium	orange for zest (use whole orange)
1-1/3 cups	fresh or frozen lingonberries (or medium chopped cranberries)
1/2 cup	half-and-half
1 large	egg

Clotted Cream:

2 cups	heavy cream
1-1/3 cups	sour cream
1/3 cup	powdered sugar
1 teaspoon	vanilla

Instructions

For the scones, in a food processor or with a mixer, pulse the flour, sugar, baking powder, salt and butter until it is mixed to a grainy, pebbly state. Transfer to a medium-sized bowl.

Add the orange zest and the lingonberries, then toss all ingredients by hand to mix well. In a separate bowl, beat the egg into the half-and-half, then mix into the dry ingredients. Work quickly to form the dough, gently kneading it a few strokes. It may seem impossibly dry at first, but keep working with it, gently pressing it all together. Eventually it will cohere into a ball. If it resists coming together, you may add more half-and-half, a few drops at a time. If the lingonberries have burst and the dough becomes sticky, toss in a handful of flour.

On a generously floured surface, form a disc about 8 inches across and 2 inches thick. Sprinkle the top liberally with sugar, using at least 1/4 cup, then with a large knife, cut the disk into eight wedges. At this point, you can bake them right away or store the wedges in the freezer and bake as needed.

When you want to bake, place the scone wedges on parchment paper on baking trays. Lay the wedges in a row, alternating tips facing in toward the center or out to the edge of the tray with as much space between them as possible. You should put no more than 6 wedges to a flat baking tray, which will fit in most home ovens. The wedges tend to lean toward each other if they are too close together while they bake.

(photo by Mary Beams)

Bake for 18 minutes at 375° F, then check them for firmness and a golden brown color. Rotate the pan in the oven, bake for another 5 to 12 minutes, depending on whether they were frozen or fresh from the prep table. They should be golden brown and not soft when gently prodded. Serve warm, with clotted cream.

For the clotted cream, place all ingredients in a medium bowl and whip to stiff peaks with a mixer. We like our clotted cream less sweet. However, you can add more powdered sugar if desired.

The Christmas Mittens

Knitting has been an integral part of Scandinavian craft tradition for centuries. (Those fishermen need wool sweaters to ward off the icy winds of the sea, after all.)

Old photos show women knitting as they walked through a village on their way to the marketplace. Wooden needles clicked together industriously to make woolen socks, mittens, hats and sweaters to replace those worn and ragged from use.

Modern polar fleece and high-tech fibers have replaced many of the knitted garments of earlier times, but we still hold an appreciation of handmade things. And once you've owned a pair of beautiful homemade mittens, your polar fleece might pale in comparison.

Susan takes time from her knitting to sit among the flowers with her partner, Jim Tidwell.
(photo by Kathy Rice)

In Grand Marais, we certainly appreciate craftwork. There is a thriving Fiber Arts Guild here, complete with weavers, knitters, spinners and craftswomen.

On one of our forays to meet the community in the early days of our arrival, our family attended a Fiber Arts Guild exhibit at the Johnson Heritage Post Art Gallery. Women were spinning yarn, hand dying the twisted fibers into earth-toned hues. Intricate Jacquard coverlets hung on the log walls of the gallery, and beautiful sweaters, mittens and hats were displayed everywhere.

It was a visual feast for the eyes.

Since those early days, I've come to know Susan Wolff, a local fiber artist. She visited our Northern Impulses gallery to see if we'd like to carry her beautiful handmade greeting cards. They were a perfect addition to our gallery selection.

Susan came to the Pie Place often, meeting friends for breakfast or lunch. Never ones for idle hands, they sometimes brought bags filled with knitting needles and yarn and sat companionably throughout the morning knitting, chatting and drinking coffee.

They made their complicated craft seem so easy. Being a knit-purl kind of a girl myself, their creative expertise kept me in continual awe.

One year at the guild's Christmas Bazaar, I found a pair of mittens that I had to have. Hand-knit in a traditional Scandinavian design with gray and natural dyed yarns, they perfectly matched my winter coat. Best of all, Susan Wolff had made them. Still, I wasn't really in the market for new mittens, but Mary Lear was listening when I gushed about them at the bazaar. I found that perfect pair in my stocking on Christmas Eve. I must say, I adored them and wore them every day, all winter. My hands stayed warm and toasty.

One day, Jeremy's wife, Plami, noticed my mittens and exclaimed how much she loved them. So the hunt was on for another pair just like them. At the next Christmas Bazaar, we looked and looked for mittens to put in Plami's stocking. There were a dozen or more beautifully knitted pairs, but none seemed just right for her clothing palette. Then I had an inspiration.

On Christmas Eve, Plami unwrapped a box; among the tissue lay my mittens – the perfect match.

She jumped up, tears in her eyes, and gave me a big bear hug. I cried, too. If we didn't know it before, we certainly knew in that moment that gifts of the heart mean the most.

"You love those mittens," Plami said.

"Yes," I agreed. "I do, but so do you."

Now, lest you pity me with my bare hands, fear not. I found another pair of mittens knit by Susan. They appeared, quite magically, in my Christmas Eve stocking.

Chestnut Apple Soup

This soup is perfect for a festive holiday meal. The first time we made it we shelled whole chestnuts, an arduous task and hard on the fingers. Imagine our delight when we found that part of the process done for us!

Serves 6 to 8

Amount	Ingredients
1 large	leek
3 Tablespoons	butter, divided
2	apples, peeled and chopped (we prefer Macintosh or golden delicious)
2 stalks	celery, chopped
1 small	onion, thinly sliced
1	bay leaf
1 sprig	thyme
1 teaspoon	salt
1/8 teaspoon	nutmeg
2 (32-ounce) containers	chicken broth
1 (8-ounce) jar	whole chestnuts, vacuum-packed
1 cup	heavy cream or half-and-half
2 Tablespoons	all-purpose flour
To garnish	Crème Fraîche (recipe page 115) and freshly grated nutmeg

Instructions

Remove root, tough outer leaves and tops from leek, leaving 2 inches of dark leaves. Cut into quarters lengthwise. Thinly slice leek lengthwise; rinse well and drain.

Melt 1 Tablespoon of butter in a medium saucepan over medium heat. Add the leek, apples, celery and onion. Sauté 5 minutes. Add bay leaf, thyme sprig, salt and nutmeg; sauté 8 to 12 minutes or until apples and vegetables are tender.

Stir in chicken broth and chestnuts. Bring to a boil; reduce heat, and simmer 1 hour or until chestnuts are tender. Stir in cream. Discard bay leaf.

Process the mixture, in batches, in a food processor or blender until smooth. Return mixture to saucepan. Melt remaining 2 Tablespoons butter in a small skillet. Stir in flour until smooth; cook, stirring constantly, 2 to 3 minutes.

Add flour mixture to puréed mixture. Bring to a boil, then reduce heat and simmer 3 to 5 minutes or until thickened. Serve warm and garnish with a dollop of Crème Fraîche and nutmeg.

Over the River & to Our Woods

Our Pie Place family loves the holidays.

We always looked forward to preparing time-tested family recipes, adding touches that our guests came to expect. The most important ingredient at any holiday meal, though, is who sits around your table. Being together with those we love makes Thanksgiving one of my favorite times of the year.

For most folks, a traditional turkey dinner speaks to them. Through our decades as a restaurant family, we've tried many variations on that theme, always returning to what we and our guests love most – a traditional dinner with all the trimmings.

Family recipes, made with love by our mothers and grandmothers, take us back to when we would awake in the early hours of Thanksgiving morning to the aroma of roast turkey and stuffing wafting through the house. I can still smell it in my memory.

The old hand grinder came out of the pantry to make cranberry sauce. I loved the pop of the

cranberries as they were coarsely ground with apples, oranges and walnuts. Serve it all with mounds of fluffy mashed potatoes with rich savory gravy, squash casserole, pumpkin and mince pies, and we were happy!

Imagine piling into a horse-drawn cutter, a warm blanket thrown over your knees and the wind turning your cheeks rosy. Imagine voices raised in happy refrains of songs sung to while away the hours. Imagine arriving at grandmother's house eager for the warmth of a crackling fire and a mug of hot spiced wine.

Jeanne and Mike and Bruce and Julie — four good reasons for our thanks giving. (photo courtesy Jeanne, Mike, Bruce & Julie)

I've cherished that image since childhood, and my grandmother actually did travel that way. Today's modes of transportation, though, are warmer and far faster.

At The Pie Place Café, which was always open Thanksgiving, the excitement of the day drew many regular guests. Four guests-turned-friends were Bruce and Julie Browning and Mike and Jeanne Hatch.

Several years ago Jeanne's mother passed away a few days before Thanksgiving. Grieving for her mother, with whom she was so close, Jeanne told her friends, "Let's make a new Thanksgiving tradition." It would be a way to let the old tradition remain as part of her memories of her mother.

So the two couples decided to come to the North Shore and eat at the Pie Place. After that first year, our Thanksgiving wouldn't have been the same without their exuberance as they burst through the door in anticipation of the turkey dinner. We were grateful for their presence at our table.

Coming up each year from the Twin Cities became a Thanksgiving tradition for them.

Several years ago, Bruce called to make reservations for their annual pilgrimage (really, that pun just popped out of me), requesting their favorite table. The weather report sounded less than favorable, but he assured me they'd be here.

On Thanksgiving morning, it began to snow heavily. I suspected that the foursome might not be able to make the six-hour trip. Then Bruce called on his cell phone, sounding far away. "It's snowing here, but we're on the way. It may take longer than usual, but we'll be there!"

I assured him we'd be waiting.

Hours later, the weary and hungry travelers walked through our door, shaking snow off their coats and peeling off hats and mittens.

"Over the river and through the woods" went through my mind as I seated our friends for another Thanksgiving dinner.

Most of our guests had dined and gone by the time Bruce, Julie, Mike and Jeanne arrived, so they had the restaurant to themselves. There was still plenty of turkey, though, and all the fixings for our friends.

The important part was that they arrived safe and sound. That was the best blessing we could want at Thanksgiving … and to be with those we love.

Our north woods that they go "to" instead of "through."
(photo by Mike Hatch)

Our friends come to Grand Marais at other times of the year. Whenever they arrive, it's like old home week as we catch up on what's happening in their lives. We just seem to pick up where we left off last time, in that companionable way that good friends have.

No matter when they arrive, it is always a treat, and we always have reason for giving thanks.

(our secret recipe)

Cheryl's Thanksgiving Wild Rice Sausage Stuffing

Every family has a special stuffing for their Thanksgiving turkey. This is as much a part of the anticipated meal as mashed potatoes, turkey gravy and pumpkin pie. We'd like to share for the first time our family recipe, one that has become a popular Pie Place Café tradition.

Makes stuffing for an 18-pound turkey

Amount	Ingredients
6 cups	cooked wild rice
1 pound	Jimmy Dean spicy sausage (or use an artisan sausage)
2 pounds	Jimmy Dean original sausage (or use an artisan sausage)
16 Tablespoons	butter
3 (8-ounce) cartons	fresh white mushrooms, sliced
1 large	onion, diced
2 (12-ounce) bags	Pepperidge Farms herb seasoned cubed stuffing
6 cups	chicken broth
2/3 cup	chopped parsley
To taste	salt, pepper and garlic salt

Instructions

Cook wild rice per package instructions then measure out 6 cups.

Brown sausage, draining fat from meat after browning and placing in large mixing bowl. Set aside. Melt 3 to 4 Tablespoons butter in large skillet and sauté mushrooms and onions until soft (may need to do in flights depending upon skillet size).

Add mushroom/onion mixture to the sausage, along with stuffing mix, wild rice, the remaining butter (melted) and parsley. Combine all ingredients thoroughly, adding chicken broth incrementally to moisten. We like a moist stuffing, however, you may not need to include all chicken broth in mixture. Add salt, pepper and garlic salt to taste.

Stuff turkey loosely. Put bird in floured roasting bag. Place bagged turkey in roaster pan, and cook in oven per instructions on turkey wrapper. We like to use turkey roasting bags as it makes for a very moist bird. However, feel free to roast the turkey as your family tradition dictates.

Put additional stuffing in a buttered casserole, dot top with butter and warm in the oven during the last 1/2 hour of the roasting process.

Chef's note: Stuffing may be made 2 or 3 days ahead and refrigerated. It can also be made weeks in advance and frozen in zipper storage bags. Thaw the night before needed.

This recipe makes an abundant amount. Our family loves several days of leftovers after Thanksgiving. The recipe yields the equivalent of 35 to 40 side servings, so feel free to reduce it if it's too much for your family needs.

(photo by Mary Beams)

But I Have a Reservation

Grand Marais hugs the shore of Lake Superior and melts into the surrounding forests northeast to Grand Portage and the Canadian border. The Big Lake and the woods connect us with our friendly Canadian neighbors a mere hour away. They often visit in town and always seemed to find their way to The Pie Place Café.

It's with eager hearts that we welcome and reconnect with these old friends.

Jim Kelly and his partner, Aniela Sadowski (or Ann to us), are two of those regular guests who bring friendly banter, laughter and camaraderie.

As a reporter, Jim worked at the *Chronicle Journal* in Thunder Bay for 35 years. A rapid-fire reporter, he covered everything from court and crime to labor, education and health issues. He was greatly respected by his journalistic colleagues and retired eagerly looking forward to the adventures that lay ahead.

As a farewell article in the *Chronicle Journal* so aptly put it, Jim was a lover, fighter, gambler, golfer and reporter. I would add to that glowing list of descriptors the word "friend."

Jim and Ann are an energetic, fun-loving couple. Ever ready for their next adventure, they would come to Grand Marais to ski at Lutsen Mountains, stop to partake in a

Jim and Ann on the Ontario shore. (photo by Jim Kelly)

favorite pastime at the casino in Grand Portage, play golf at the Superior National Golf Course or head on to Duluth for anything and everything happening there.

Whatever their pleasure pursuit, the Pie Place remained a culinary destination for them, and they would come for breakfast, lunch or dinner (sometimes more than one meal in a day) on their way to and fro.

Often when they visited, they'd bring down or go home with DVD movies. As mutual movie enthusiasts, we kept a steady stream going over the border. I'd set aside my favorites for them and they'd share their favorites with me.

Perhaps because Jim was a reporter, they were up on American politics and shared their views. I, meanwhile, learned a lot about Canadian politics from them. Mainly we concluded that no matter where one lives, the issues remain strikingly similar.

In October we could expect a particular influx of visitors from the north; that is the month of Canadian Thanksgiving. Many families make the trip from Thunder Bay to The Pie Place Café to get their favored pies – traditional apple and pumpkin, as well as very berry (lovingly called by some "fruits of the forest") and coconut cream. I could tell by the pie orders hanging on the clip in the bakery which of our customers were coming for their Thanksgiving pies.

Some folks (including me) like Thanksgiving as much as Christmas. They just can't get enough of that succulent roast turkey, aromatic stuffing, cranberry sauce and pumpkin pie. If we could have more than one Thanksgiving dinner, that would be heaven.

That's why Jim is my kind of guy. Not only did he savor the Canadian Thanksgiving holiday in Thunder Bay, he always made reservations at the Pie Place for an American Thanksgiving dinner a month later.

Sometimes one or more of his many friends would join him. As one of the Pie Place's strongest advocates, he never seemed to have trouble finding someone to be his guest.

Jim came for so many Thanksgiving dinners at our restaurant that each year I would look at the reservation list and say, "Has Jim made a reservation yet?" He always did.

Then one Thanksgiving afternoon, Jim had not arrived.

"Has anyone talked to Jim in the last few days?" I asked, worry swirling in the pit of my stomach. No one had.

Something had happened; Jim hadn't missed a Thanksgiving dinner in years.

Thanksgiving evening arrived, and I was pulled into the hustle and bustle of stuffing and roasting turkeys, placing linen tablecloths, arranging fall-foliage centerpieces and lighting candles.

As I was seating some of our first guests of the evening, Josh came out to the dining room with a message. Jim was on the phone wanting to speak to me. I rushed to the phone and heard Jim's rather weakened, faraway voice apologizing for missing the dinner.

Jim had been rushed to the hospital the day before with acute symptoms of gall bladder attack and had undergone surgery. In his stable but weakened state, Jim had begged the doctor to remove his IV tubing and release him from the hospital pronto.

"Doc, you've got to release me. I have reservations for Thanksgiving dinner at the Pie Place!"

Neither Jim's doctor nor Ann could agree with his logic. He was staying in the hospital, and that was that. Not to worry, I told Jim, I'd fix him a plate, with extra stuffing and gravy, of course, and put it in the freezer.

"It will be waiting for you when you're able to get here. Get well, my friend … and, by the way, Happy Thanksgiving!"

Baked Sweet Potatoes with Maple-Jalapeño Sour Cream

Sweet potatoes are a wonderful addition to any Thanksgiving table. Over the years, we've served sweet potatoes in many creative ways, diverging from the more traditional approach. We offer some ideas here that are easy to prepare and full of unexpected flavor.

Serves 4

Amount	Ingredients
4 large	sweet potatoes
2 Tablespoons	extra virgin olive oil
2 teaspoons	coarse salt

Maple-Jalapeño Sour Cream Topping:

1/2 cup	sour cream
1 Tablespoon	pure maple syrup
2 teaspoons	jalapeño pepper, seeded and minced
1 teaspoon	fresh lime juice
To taste	salt and pepper

(photo by Karin Holen)

Garnish:

6 strips	bacon, cooked crispy and crumbled
6	scallions, sliced

Instructions

Preheat oven to 375° F with rack positioned in the center.

Scrub sweet potatoes, pat dry and rub with oil and salt. Bake directly on rack for 45 minutes to 1 hour, or until soft when pierced.

Combine all topping ingredients; chill until ready to serve.

Slice open potatoes and serve with Maple-Jalapeño Sour Cream, bacon crumbles and scallions.

Twice-baked Sweet Potatoes

May I suggest you try twice-baked for a special treat.

Serves 4

Amount	Ingredients
4 large	sweet potatoes
2 Tablepoons	extra virgin olive oil
2 teaspoons	coarse salt
2 to 3 Tablespoons	heavy cream
1 Tablespoon	pure maple syrup (Wild Country is our favorite)
1/4 cup	pecans, toasted
1/4 cup	pears, diced
1/4 cup	dried cranberries
For topping	aged white cheddar or Gruyère cheese, finely shredded

Instructions

Preheat oven to 375° F with rack positioned in the center.

Scrub sweet potatoes, pat dry and rub with oil and salt. Bake directly on rack for 45 minutes to 1 hour, or until soft when pierced. Switch oven setting to broil.

When potatoes are cool enough to handle, but still very warm, scoop out 2/3 of the cooked sweet potato and place in bowl. (Save the potato skins.) Mash it with the heavy cream until fairly smooth. Add the maple syrup, toasted pecans, diced pears and dried cranberries. Mix thoroughly.

Spoon mixture back into the potato skins. Top potatoes with finely shredded, aged white cheddar or Gruyère cheese.

Place potatoes on a baking sheet, broiling in the oven for 8 to 10 minutes until cheese is melted and golden brown.

Fishes & Loaves

Celebrations mark the passage of time in our lives … birthdays, retirement from a job long held and service long given, the wedding of a beloved child become adult, the births of grandchildren. There is a sad joy, too, in honoring the death of a loved one, held in tender hearts through a last farewell.

Time then weaves these changes into the fabric of our lives, forever altering and expanding the pattern.

We've been privileged to help celebrate many momentous occasions with our Pie Place friends, people like Jack and Linda Corey, whom we consider a part of our family. Jack and Linda live in Eau Claire, Wisconsin, and keep a cabin on the Arrowhead Trail in Hovland, Minnesota. They split their time between the two places, but they've thrown themselves into life here, taking classes at the North House Folk School, coming up for the John Beargrease Sled Dog Marathon, snowshoeing in the forest and, of course, eating at The Pie Place Café. They plan to retire here, and they're already integrated into the fabric of our community.

When Jack's family had a surprise birthday party for him, they came to the Pie Place. When he retired after 31 years in the Eau Claire Police Department, once again his sons Michael and Patrick and daughter-in-law Kate came to our restaurant to raise a celebratory glass to Jack for a job well done. Jack asked Jeremy, waiter, musician and Pie Place family member, to play the guitar and sing during the party.

When Jack and Linda called to ask if we'd host a rehearsal dinner for Michael and Cara, we were thrilled. We met with the bride and groom to plan the details: seating, flowers, candles, wine selection, menu choices. They chose the spicy beef tenderloin with mustard sauce and pecan-encrusted lake trout with an orange reduction. Wanting to focus on regional foods, lake trout was their heart's desire.

The meat was simple enough. Marlo, our local butcher, would easily fill the order. Fish was another matter. I called the Dockside Fish Market and told Harley Tofte, a local commercial fisherman, that we needed 17 servings of lake trout. He explained that lake trout had been hard to come by, with few in his nets.

"Well," I said with more certainty than I felt, "I'm sure we will have what we need when the time comes." I did call the eager couple, though, to consider an alternative. They agreed, but I heard the disappointment.

Even a small dinner party takes a lot of time and attention. As I typed the small menus to be framed with twigs at each place setting, I began to worry. Would Harley find enough lake trout in his nets?

I envisioned Harley's nets, the icy water cascading through the ropes and 17

Cara and Michael on their wedding day and Linda and Jack in their beloved north woods. (photo by Joe Crimmings Photography; photos by Jack and Linda, respectively)

silvery lake trout twisting and turning, awaiting the grand event. I was to call the fish market on the morning of the rehearsal dinner, but I wasn't holding the tension very well. I first called four days before the wedding. "Any lake trout today?" "No," came the grim reply. Each day, same call, same answer.

I called Michael to recommend that we switch to salmon. He reluctantly agreed.

On the morning of the event, I went early to the market … too early. Harley wasn't even off the lake. As soon as he got back to dock and had sorted the fish, he'd call, I was told. Three hours later, the phone rang.

"Kathy, you're not going to believe this! I pulled some lake trout this morning."

"How many?"

"Seventeen!"

Do I believe in the power of visualization? You bet! Do I believe we are co-creators with a Supreme Being called by many names? Yes, indeed. Do I believe that someone else also wanted Michael and Cara to have their very special day go exactly as they planned? Absolutely!

And with a little help from Harley, and Lake Superior, it did.

Spicy Beef Tenderloin

Sliced thinly, the tenderloin atop our Basmati and Wild Rice Salad, drizzled with hot sweet mustard, makes an elegant presentation, perfect for all special occasions. Serve it hot or at room temperature.

Serves 6

Amount	Ingredients
1 filet	beef tenderloin (about 3-1/2 pounds)
3 Tablespoons	paprika
2 teaspoons	cumin
1 Tablespoon	ground coriander
2 Tablespoons	pepper
1 teaspoon	nutmeg
1/4 teaspoon	Cayenne pepper
1 Tablespoon	salt
4 to 6 Tablespoons	butter
For serving	hot-sweet mustard (your favorite; we like Inglehoffer)

Instructions

Trim the filet of any visible fat and silverskin. (Ask your butcher to do this, or use a thin, sharp knife, inserting it under the silverskin to slice it from the meat.)

Mix the spices in a small bowl. Rub the mixture evenly over the beef. Place it in a large glass or plastic dish, cover and refrigerate for 4 days to marinate, but on the third day, sprinkle the meat with salt.

Preheat oven to 350° F.

Before cooking, let the meat sit at room temperature for about 1 hour. Preheat a stovetop griddle or a large cast-iron frying pan on medium-high, adding the butter. Sear the filet until brown on all sides, about 6 to 8 minutes per side. Transfer the meat to a roasting pan and roast in the oven until a meat thermometer in the center registers 120° F, about 10 to 15 minutes. Let the meat rest on a carving board (it will continue to cook), covered with aluminum foil, for 15 minutes. Slice thin. Serve with the hot-sweet mustard.

Basmati and Wild Rice Salad

This salad, full of flavor and color, pairs well with most meats. If your guests linger over wine and conversation before dinner, don't worry. It tastes great at room temperature.

Serves 6 to 8

Amount	Ingredients
For the rice:	
4 cups	cold water
4 teaspoons	salt
1/2 cup	wild rice
1-1/2 cups	basmati rice
1 (2-inch) piece	fresh ginger, peeled and sliced
For the vinaigrette:	
1/2 teaspoon	nutmeg
1/2 teaspoon	cumin
2 to 3 Tablespoons	fresh lemon juice
1/2 cup	olive or peanut oil
To taste	salt and pepper
To finish the salad:	
1/2 cup	green onions, chopped
1/2 cup	dried cranberries (soaked these in 1/2 cup of Marsala wine until soft, 15 to 20 minutes)
1/3 cup	slivered almonds, toasted

Instructions

To cook the wild rice, bring 1-1/2 cups of the water and 2 teaspoons of the salt to a boil in a medium saucepan. Add the wild rice, reduce heat to low, cover and simmer until the rice is tender, about 1 hour.

Combine the basmati rice and the remaining 2-1/2 cups water in a separate medium saucepan. Let sit for 1 hour, then bring to a boil and add the remaining 2 teaspoons salt and the ginger. Reduce heat to low, cover and simmer until the rice has absorbed all of the water and is tender, about 15 minutes. Discard the ginger.

To make the vinaigrette, combine the nutmeg and cumin in a small bowl and whisk in the lemon juice. Whisk the oil and season with salt and pepper.

To finish the salad, combine the wild rice and basmati rice while still warm in a large bowl. Toss the rice and vinaigrette, then stir in the green onions, dried cranberries and any remaining Marsala, and almonds. Adjust the seasoning, adding more vinaigrette to taste. Serve warm or at room temperature.

Pecan Crusted Trout with Orange Reduction Sauce

A simple way to prepare fresh trout, this crowd-pleasing recipe was featured in our first cookbook.

Amount	Ingredients
2 cups	pecans
1 cup, divided	all-purpose flour
2 large	trout, filleted without skin
A pinch	salt and pepper
3 large	egg whites, whisked lightly to mix

Sautéed vegetables:

3 Tablespoons	olive oil, divided
1 medium	carrot, peeled, cut into matchsticks
1	red bell pepper, thinly sliced
6 cups	Savoy cabbage, thinly sliced
2 Tablespoons	unsalted butter
For garnish	fresh chives, chopped

Harley Tofte with the day's catch.
(photo by Mary Knoble)

Instructions

Grind pecans and 1 Tablespoon of flour finely in food processor, then put on plate. Place remaining flour on another plate. Sprinkle filets with salt and pepper, coat in flour, shake off excess. Use pastry brush to coat each side with egg whites, then press each side onto ground pecans. Place on waxed paper-lined baking sheet. Chill.

After sauce is prepared and set aside, heat 2 Tablespoons oil in a heavy large pan over high heat. Add carrot and bell pepper, toss 2 minutes. Add cabbage, toss until it wilts, about 4 minutes. Season with salt and pepper. Remove from heat.

Melt 2 Tablespoons butter with 1 Tablespoon olive oil in heavy large skillet over medium-high heat. Place 2 filets into skillet. Cook until crust is gold and crisp, about 2 minutes. Using spatula, turn filets over. Cook until just opaque in center, about 2 minutes. Transfer to plate. Whisk sauce over low heat until warm. Divide vegetables among plates. Top with trout filets and spoon sauce over fish and vegetables. Garnish with chopped chives and serve.

Orange Reduction Sauce

1-1/2 cups orange juice
1 cup dry white wine
2/3 cup chopped shallots
1/4 cup white wine vinegar
8 sprigs parsley
1 sprig thyme
1-1/2 Tablespoons lemon juice
2 sprigs fresh rosemary
1/4 cup heavy cream
6 Tablespoons unsalted butter, cut into 12 pieces
To taste salt and pepper

Combine orange juice, wine, shallots, vinegar, parsley, thyme and lemon juice in saucepan. Boil 10 minutes, add rosemary. Boil until reduced to 1/2 cup, another 10 minutes. Strain into another saucepan. Add cream, bring to a gentle boil. Reduce heat to medium-low. Whisk in butter, 1 piece at a time (do not boil). Season with salt and pepper.

Building a New Life

A few generations back, people came from Sweden, Norway, Finland and other faraway places to make a new life on the rocky shores of Lake Superior. Tucked among the trees, their dwellings dotted the landscape, plumes of smoke curling from stone chimneys into the cold winter air.

These early settlers came with the hope of creating a new life for themselves and future generations. When I lived in Michigan's Upper Peninsula many years ago, I marveled at the craftsmanship and ingenuity of those early Finnish settlers who built their log homes, snug and warm against the bitter winds.

Friends of mine restored a Finnish homestead on their property. The cabin, barn and smoke sauna (a *savusauna* in Finnish; one without a chimney) were made of logs fashioned by hand. I learned later from some of my elderly Finnish friends that when a family arrived in the area, the barn and sauna were always built first. Shelter for the animals that would feed the family got the first priority. The house came later as time and supplies allowed. Most families, sometimes with as many as five children, spent their first winters living in the sauna.

Today folks still come to the Lake Superior shore in the hope of a new life.

Mike and Lesa Hofer began coming to Grand Marais together in the fall of 1999. Mike, director of operations at a medical device manufacturer, and Lesa, an elementary school resource manager, were looking for a simpler, less stressful way of life. In his free time, Mike is an avid hunter and fisherman. The couple also loved to hike and canoe in the Boundary Waters Canoe Area Wilderness.

The woods lured the couple north whenever their busy lives allowed it. Before long, they bought property near town and began to take the timber-frame class at the North House Folk School.

They planned to build a small timber-frame cabin on their property where they could stay on weekend visits. Their ultimate dream, though, was to leave their jobs in the Twin Cities, find work in the area and make Grand Marais their home.

Mike and Lesa came to the Pie Place for breakfast the morning before their first timber-frame class. Warm and friendly, they were eager to begin, and I could tell they would fit nicely into our community.

What's more romantic than a couple with chainsaws and a home plan? Family and friends, below, helped Mike and Lesa raise their home. (photos by Mike Hofer)

From that morning on, whenever Mike and Lesa came to work on the timbers that would one day build their cabin, they'd stop to have breakfast. All summer and into the fall they worked, often coming into the restaurant exhausted and covered with wood shavings, but happy at the progress they'd made.

They often brought exciting news.

"We got our windows in this weekend!" or "Our wood stove was installed!" Believe me, when the black flies are buzzing or the temperatures dropping, these are not small accomplishments.

After several years of back-breaking, but satisfying toil, Mike and Lesa's timber-frame home was completed. Now the couple could begin to build a life here.

Mike and Lesa were married in Grand Marais at the historic 4-H Building, a quaint log structure just off the Gunflint Trail. For the reception, it was festooned with tiny white lights, yards of white gauzy fabric, wildflowers from the forest and heart-shaped rocks gathered by the couple from the Lake Superior shores.

The effect was intimate and magical.

They asked The Pie Place Café to cater the wedding, and we were happy to help celebrate the union of two people who had become friends.

The evening buffet reflected our northwoods cuisine. Roasted Mahogany Glazed Cornish Game Hens, twice-baked sweet potatoes stuffed with nuts, apples, cranberries and wild rice, along with roasted Brussels sprouts, were laid out on linen-draped tables shimmering with candlelight. A maple-syrup wedding cake by Lola's Sweet Life Bakery completed the meal.

Recently, we saw Mike and Lesa at the Grand Marais Art Colony Art Fair. They were contentedly strolling through the tents that line Wisconsin Street overlooking the harbor. It was quite clear that they are settling into life in our little town.

Later in the day we saw them again at Sydney's Frozen Custard. Before leaving, they went to their car and came back with a jug of maple syrup for us that they had made. We talked awhile, and agreed to get together soon.

Mike and Lesa, building a life together, pose at Artists' Point after their wedding ceremony. (photos by Mark Dunlop)

Many years have passed since that first day when Mike put his draw knife to wood.

They've built a lot in the time they've been here. One of the best things, of course, has been a new life together.

Mahogany Glazed Cornish Game Hens

Cornish game hens seem naturally festive. A delicate glaze and frequent basting create an elegant lacquered look.

Serves 6

Amount	Ingredients
3	Cornish game hens (about 1-1/2 pounds each)
3 small	onions, cut into quarters
6 cloves	garlic, crushed
To sprinkle	salt and pepper
1 cup	orange juice
1 cup	red wine (we like Burgundy or Beaujolais)
1/4 cup	honey
2 Tablespoons	soy sauce
1 bunch	fresh rosemary leaves

Instructions

Preheat oven to 375° F.

Rinse and blot Cornish hens dry inside and out with a paper towel. Remove any excess fat.

Sprinkle the inside with salt and pepper. Place 4 quarters of onion, 2 garlic cloves and a sprig of fresh rosemary in each cavity. Tie the legs together with baking string and arrange the hens on a rack in a roasting pan, breast side up. If you don't have a roasting pan with a rack, simply put the hens on a baking sheet and proceed with baking instructions.

Combine orange juice, red wine, honey and soy sauce and brush some of the mixture over the hens.

Place roasting pan in the oven. Bake 15 minutes, then brush more of the mixture onto the hens. Continue roasting for another 45 minutes, basting the hens with additional glaze every 10 minutes, until skin is crisp and dark brown, and the juices run clear when thigh is pierced with a skewer. Though basting this often may seem fussy, it is the frequent basting that creates the lacquered look. About 1-1/2 cups of glaze will be left. Reserve it for sauce.

Remove hens from roasting pan and allow to cool for 10 minutes. Pour pan juices into a saucepan, along with remaining glaze. Bring to a boil and skim fat.

Cut each hen in half with poultry shears or knife, removing string, backbone, onions and garlic. Place hens skin-side up on a large serving platter covered with our wild rice salad (recipe page 162), and garnish with the remaining rosemary sprigs. Place the sauce in a gravy boat and serve on the side.

Chef's note: You can substitute quail or ruffed grouse for the Cornish hens if you have a hunter in the family. If smaller Cornish hens are available, a single hen for each person is a rather nice presentation. However, half of a larger hen is nice, too, offering plenty of meat when served with rice and other courses.

Grandpa Lyle

Since moving here, we have found that the community of Grand Marais opens its arms, inviting people in and, through Nature and the nature of its people, can bring healing.

A community, of course, is only as generous as the people who live in it and in the way they reach out to touch each other daily or in times of need. How a community responds in these cases can speak volumes about a place.

Lyle Gerard, fondly known as Grandpa Lyle, shows just what Grand Marais is made of. A gentle, scholarly man with a huge heart, Lyle demonstrates what it means to live an ordinary life in an extraordinary way.

At 91, Lyle remains energetic and active, traveling extensively and maintaining a wonderful circle of friends.

Lyle taught English at the University of Minnesota in the Reading and Study Skills Center in Minneapolis, and also taught English in Japan. As an educator, he is still passionate about learning, teaching and reading in equal measure.

Lyle, his beloved Joan and their beloved Lake Superior. (photo courtesy Lyle Gerard)

Grandpa Lyle has been reading to young people from preschool through fifth-grade for 31 years. For 10 years, he was a regular at the Care Center, a home for the elderly, where he read to the residents everything from the local newspaper to books.

When a mutual friend and voracious reader, Joan Drury (who owns Drury Lane Books), was ordered by her physician to have bed rest, Lyle read to Joan during her confinement.

Lyle's love of books and the written word comes as no surprise. At age 10, Lyle, a studious fifth-grader, announced to the librarian his intention to read every book ever written. I came to know Lyle when he and his wife, Joan, began visiting the Pie Place on the hill. Sadly, Joan was already advanced in her Alzheimer's disease. The couple was attempting to cope with the devastating changes it brought.

I was touched by Lyle's attentiveness, patience and love in the face of things unraveling all around him. He brought Joan in for dinner every Friday evening, always ordering the "evening repast," a festive, six-course meal. Sharing the one meal, since Joan seldom ate much, Lyle would carry on a lively, often one-sided conversation.

I could see a glimmer now and then of the woman with whom he'd fallen in love and spent his life. She would laugh gaily at something Lyle said, but too soon she was gone again, quiet and only mildly responsive. Lyle sometimes confessed to me that he wondered if his attempts made any difference. I assured him they did.

Determined that I should know Joan as she was, one night Lyle brought photographs of her when she was a beautiful young woman. "She fell in love with me, of all people!" Lyle said.

Joan stayed at home to care for their children while Lyle was busy with his career. She expressed her creative side through artistic weaving, creating vibrant rugs and table runners.

As Joan's condition deteriorated even further, Lyle had to make the difficult, yet necessary, decision to move his beloved wife to the Care Center. He continued to bring Joan to the Pie Place, now for shorter outings during the day for tea and scones.

Before too long, though, Joan was no longer able to leave the safety of her sheltered life.

Lyle continued to order the "evening repast" as a birthday or Valentine's gift to bring to Joan, or sometimes picked up scones for the occasional afternoon tea.

Throughout this difficult time, he read to his wife. Lyle read because, as Joan slipped away forever, it was all he could think of to do. He read because, as a lifelong teacher, words and books meant so much to him. It gave him comfort, too, after her passing.

A couple years ago, our community came together for a 90th birthday celebration for Grandpa Lyle at the North House Folk School. Several hundred people attended, eating birthday cake and sharing their stories about this wonderful man, such a vital part of Grand Marais.

Lyle has not used his new nonagenarian status to stop helping others. He continues his gift of reading to others; it's just one way that he touches, comforts and loves those around him.

Lyle knows that words can heal a troubled soul, and we have a few words meant just for him: "We love you, Grandpa Lyle. Thank you."

Baked Brie with Blueberry Chutney

The perfect way to create a festive mood for any meal is to set the stage. Light a candle, get out the cloth napkins, and serve an appetizer before dinner. Make every day a special day.

Serves 2

Amount	Ingredients
1 sheet	frozen puff pastry (one-half of a 17-1/2-ounce package), thawed
2 wedges	Brie cheese, each about 6-1/2 inches long by 1-1/2 inches wide at rind end; remove the rind
1 large	egg, beaten to blend (for glaze)

Instructions
Preheat oven to 400° F.

Roll out puff pastry sheet on lightly floured surface to form 12-inch square. Cut diagonally through pastry sheet to form 2 triangles.

Place 1 Brie wedge in center of each triangle, with tip of cheese wedge facing 90-degree angle of triangle. Pull up and fold puff pastry gently to seal. Press with fork to seal seams completely. Transfer pastry-wrapped Brie to baking sheet, seam side up. Brush pastry with egg glaze. (This can be prepared 6 hours ahead. Cover and refrigerate.)

Bake Brie until pastry is golden, about 18 minutes.

To serve Blueberry Chutney (next page) with the baked Brie, put the chutney in a tiny soufflé dish or ramekin on the side. Spoon over baked Brie when ready to eat, so pastry doesn't get soggy.

Blueberry Chutney

Nothing says North Shore quite as well as blueberries, and this versatile chutney will make appetizers something special. It's also great served with roasted meats. Be creative.

Serves 3 cups

Amount	Ingredients
3 cups	fresh blueberries
1/4 cup	onion, minced
1 Tablespoon	fresh ginger root, grated
1/3 cup	apple cider vinegar
1/2 cup	brown sugar, packed
2 Tablespoons	cornstarch
1 stick	cinnamon

Instructions

Combine all ingredients in a large pot, bring to boil over medium heat, stirring frequently. Boil 1 minute and remove cinnamon stick. Cool, cover well and refrigerate. It keeps for up to one week in the fridge.

Though this makes a large amount, it's great for many uses. Spread crackers with cream cheese and top with chutney. Simple and special. You can also freeze the chutney in small quantities.

(photo by Mary Beams)

A Time to Move On

In the course of a life, we are touched by those we meet, sometimes for a brief moment and sometimes for a lifetime. People teach us, inspire us, encourage us, serve us and love us, and, in turn, we do the same for them.

One of life's greatest gifts is to bear witness to those folks whose lives touch ours.

Since our last cookbook, some of our beloved Pie Place Café friends have moved on. Those whom we've loved, and who have loved us, are here no more.

Several years ago after having written the first Pie Place Café cookbook, I was looking for someone to publish our book. A dear friend and fellow writer, Jean Husby, encouraged me to continue to send out manuscripts in the face of several rejections and much disappointment.

Jean, a vital, creative woman of 80, had just had her first book published, and her publisher asked her to write a second volume.

"Never give up on your writing," she encouraged me. "If I can get my first book published at 80, you've still got time!"

Those words helped me to persevere.

In 2012, Lake Superior Port Cities Inc. agreed to publish our cookbook. Jean was among the first to congratulate me, now a fellow writer.

What I didn't realize then was that writing is a collaborative activity and revision is a necessary part of the crafting. On one particularly difficult day during the editing process, I experienced an emotional meltdown and called Jean sobbing. She helped put me back together, assuring me that this was part and parcel of the process. "Do you want to come over for tea?" she offered. "You will get through this and you'll learn a lot about yourself."

A wise and beautiful woman, Jean was right. I learned to let go, something not always easy for me to do. As always, Jean was there lending her love and support.

And Jean and her husband, Harold (affectionately called "Hoh" by Jean and all who love him) were at The Pie Place Café to celebrate the cookbook's completion at the book launch party in 2013.

In the fall of 2014, Jean was taken to the hospital, having suffered what appeared to be a stroke.

A few days later, I was visiting with a restaurant guest when a yellow finch flew through the front door. The delicate little creature landed on the window ledge by the table. I felt its little heart beating as I gently picked it up and carried it outside.

After I held it nestled in my hand for several minutes, it finally looked at me and flew away, free and happy on the sunny morning breeze.

That afternoon, Jean and Hoh's son Scott called with the sad news that his mother had passed away. Her partner in life and her family were there with her. Talking a bit more, I realized that Jean took her last breath about the same time that the yellow finch had flown through our front door. I knew then that Jean had come to say good-bye.

Our family brought Jean and Hoh's favorite pies to the memorial service. Jean's grandson performed music, and there were displays of bright flowers and wonderful photographs of Jean and her loved ones. Family and friends filled the room with laughter in memory, something which Jean would have loved.

I shared the story of the yellow finch with Scott and his wife, Tracey.

People come into our life, love us, and then go on, free as a bird in flight. It is the way of things.

This book was written to all those whom we have loved and who have loved us well.

May their spirits soar, the memories of each of them etched in our hearts forever.

In Loving Memory of our Friends

Kristi Downing
Maria W. Faust
Curt Horwitz Hort
Jean Husby
Donald Larmouth
Terry Martin
Dr. Walter McCarthy
Dick McDermott
Donald Oberdorfer
Marilyn Taus

The season of The Pie Place Café, too, has become a memory, though its new life as a bakery starts right here, where we last served guests in our restaurant. (photo by Jeremy Chase)

Seasons of Change for Our Family

"To everything there is a season . . .
and a time to every purpose under heaven"

So much has happened in The Pie Place Café family since the first cookbook was published in 2013; I'd like to share some of the changes with which we have been blessed.

Ben Zang, Josh Rice and Jeremy Chase met and married their perfect life partners, a welcome addition of daughters to our family. They are doing what most young couples do … purchasing their first homes, embarking on careers and beginning families.

Ben and Nadya Shkurdyuk are proud parents of the first baby in our family. Rosalee, now an energetic 2-year-old, has personality plus and keeps her parents hopping. They bought a house in Milwaukee. Ben continues to pursue restaurant consulting, and also has started a business called "Tastefull. Milwaukee's Personal Chef." Nadya has taken on the role of motherhood in a way that's beautiful to behold. She balances her career in marketing, assisting Ben with his new business and parenting with energy and passion.

Jeremy, CEO of the Pie Place and Harbor Inn, continues the momentous task of managing the daily activities of both. Though the café has become mainly a bakery, his vision and savvy assist the growth of both operations. Jeremy is not all business, of course; his photography graces the walls of the inn, adding warmth and character to the spaces. His wife, Plami Chase, a creative young woman, has taken over the bakery, making the beautiful pies and scones you enjoy. One of Plami's passions is baking cakes. After she created Josh and Anna's wedding cake, we knew there would be cakes in our future. (The Pie Place will be offering her delightfully crafted cakes, made to order for weddings and special occasions.)

Josh traded a culinary career as chef at the Pie Place for an apprenticeship in bronze casting and sculpture and is enthusiastically engaged in all things metal. Working under the tutelage of Tom Christiansen, owner-operator of Last Chance Fabricating, Josh comes home after a day at the studio with a broad smile on his face. He and Anna Brown, who teaches fifth- and sixth-graders at Great Expectations Charter School, are busy designing an addition for their cabin. Anna brings heart and an energetic spirit for her eager young students, and she is currently writing her second book. Many of you met Anna at the restaurant, where she took your order and served your meal during her "off time" in the summer.

Mary Beams, our family "Pie Lady," is also moving on to another creative pursuit. An animator at Harvard in a past life, and an artist in many mediums, her path seems to be rolling out before her. She has taught animation to Anna's fifth- and sixth-grade classes, helped to spearhead a community art project, Art 'Round Town, and assisted in the creation of a winter film series in conjunction with our local library. She is also renewing her interest in painting and graphic storytelling

Mary Lear, pastel artist and Pie Place catering director, plans to expand an already successful catering operation. She loves doing weddings and events, and you'll recognize her culinary talents and the ambiance and refinement at any of her catered affairs. Tapping her skills as an interior designer in her previous life, she and Plami collaborated to make a new look at the Harbor Inn. Mary also plans to delve again into pastel landscapes, capturing the magic of our lakeshores and woodlands.

Clare Shaw, who has played a pivotal role in human resources and advertising for us, is stepping into the day-to-day activities of the Harbor Inn – greeting, scheduling and making sure guests are well taken care of. She is an active member of the Grand Marais Art Colony, writing grants and assisting in the growth of a vital pillar of our community.

Katherine Goertz, another "Pie Lady" from our days on the hill, remains passionate about baking and all things chocolate. She has become a traveler, spending time in California with her son and family

and enjoying all that the West Coast has to offer. She frequents museums with newfound friends, gleaning inspiration for her next pursuit as a fiber artist.

As many of you know, I've moved into a life of writing cookbooks. As this is our second one, I can begin to say with confidence that I am, indeed, a writer. I'm more active in our community, too, specifically at the North House Folk School. I'm serving a second term on the board of directors and am on the Growth and Development Committee. The mission of the folk school is to enrich lives and build community by teaching traditional northern craft. I've taken many classes there and am inspired by the spirit of this organization. I'm proud to be part of its continued growth.

I continue with our family outreach work, supporting art programs in Minnesota correctional facilities with the non-profit we started: the HEART Foundation (Healing and Education Through Art).

So many changes and new seasons for our family. It's been our greatest joy to serve you. You've become part of our Pie Place family. That seasons change is a natural, ongoing part of life. As someone wise once said, the one thing we can be sure of is change; nothing, not even the seasons, stays exactly the same.

As we leave our roles in the restaurant to embark on new creative pursuits, our season as a restaurant family is coming to an end. The Pie Place itself is taking on a new form, returning to its pie-making roots, but still with a welcoming heart.

In the midst of this change, we know for sure that the memories we've created and shared at the Pie Place, the friendships we've built and our passion for homemade food prepared with love will endure.

You and we have touched each other's lives. Regardless of the season, that connection will remain.

Our family: Rosalee with her parents Ben and Nadya (top) and (bottom from left) Jeremy, Plami, Josh, Anna, Clare, Mary L, Kathy (me), Mary B. and Katherine. (top photo courtesy Ben and Nadya; bottom photo by Mark Tessier)

About the Author

When do you begin to call yourself an author?

We all are authors of our lives as we tell stories that shape, inspire, change and move us. Some stories come in writing, others through brushstrokes on canvas, shaped clay, woven baskets, intricate beaded works or sculptures of bronze, metal and wood.

My story begins in rural Charlotte, Michigan, where neighbors knew each other and happily showed up when needed to milk cows, plant and harvest crops and gardens, raise children and "put up" food.

When I was a child, stories swirled around me. I'd sit at the kitchen table of Hans and Mimi Langmaach, my grandparents' friends from Germany who, like Grandpa and Grandma Parr, were hardworking dairy farmers. Elbows resting on the flour-covered table, I watched Mimi make cookies and marveled at her stories of the old country. (No wonder I connect stories and food.) Meanwhile, my Grandma Strong's real tales of "the olden days" conjured vivid images of my family's own history and truly inspired my storytelling.

As a young adult, I earned a nursing degree and worked in general practice, orthopedics and oncology in Lansing. For two years, I worked for the director of a community mental health center outpatient clinic in Houghton and volunteered with Little Brothers, Friends of the Elderly. I returned to Lansing for a degree in interior design, which led to a job with Mary Lear's design firm and eventually to the larger adventure with our restaurant family in Minnesota.

In Grand Marais, we embraced writing – creating poems, short stories, even would-be novels. I found that a writer inside of me longed to be set free, but I never dreamed that I'd become a published author!

I've discovered my connection to those around me is like the air I breathe, essential to my life. Sharing our stories seems natural. Don't get me wrong, writing is scary. Often a voice in my head whispers that no one will read what I write. Luckily another voice, in a quote by Guillaume Apollinaire, drowns it out:

> Come to the edge, He said.
> They said, We are afraid.
> Come to the edge, He said.
> They came.
> He pushed them and ...
> They flew.

I think I'm finally getting the hang of jumping off the cliff. Thanks for joining me.

Index

Ingredients & Recipes

People, Places & Things

From Lake Superior Port Cities Inc.

Lake Superior Magazine
A bimonthly, regional publication covering the
shores along Michigan, Minnesota, Wisconsin
and Ontario

Lake Superior Travel Guide
An annually updated mile-by-mile guide

*Lake Superior, The Ultimate Guide
to the Region, Third Edition*
Softcover: ISBN 978-1-938229-17-6

Hugh E. Bishop:
The Night the Fitz Went Down
Softcover: ISBN 978-0-942235-37-1

*By Water and Rail:
A History of Lake County, Minnesota*
Hardcover: ISBN 978-0-942235-48-7
Softcover: ISBN 978-0-942235-42-5

Haunted Lake Superior
Softcover: ISBN 978-0-942235-55-5

Haunted Minnesota
Softcover: ISBN 978-0-942235-71-5

Beryl Singleton Bissell:
A View of the Lake
Softcover: ISBN 978-0-942235-74-6

Bonnie Dahl:
*Bonnie Dahl's Superior Way, Fourth Edition:
A Cruising Guide to Lake Superior*
Softcover: ISBN 978-0-942235-92-0

Joy Morgan Dey, Nikki Johnson:
Agate: What Good Is a Moose?
Hardcover: ISBN 978-0-942235-73-9

Daniel R. Fountain:
*Michigan Gold & Silver,
Mining in the Upper Peninsula*
Softcover: ISBN 978-1-938229-16-9

Chuck Frederick:
Spirit of the Lights
Softcover: ISBN 978-0-942235-11-1

Marvin G. Lamppa:
Minnesota's Iron Country
Softcover: ISBN 978-0-942235-56-2

Daniel Lenihan:
Shipwrecks of Isle Royale National Park
Softcover: ISBN 978-0-942235-18-0

Betty Lessard:
Betty's Pies Favorite Recipes, Second Edition
Softcover: ISBN 978-1-938229-18-3

Mike Link & Kate Crowley:
*Going Full Circle:
A 1,555-mile Walk Around
the World's Largest Lake*
Softcover: ISBN 978-0-942235-23-4

James R. Marshall:
Shipwrecks of Lake Superior, Second Edition
Softcover: ISBN 978-0-942235-67-8

Lake Superior Journal: Views from the Bridge
Softcover: ISBN 978-0-942235-40-1

Mark Phillips:
*The Old Rittenhouse Inn Cookbook:
Meals & Memories from the
Historic Bayfield B&B*
Softcover: ISBN 978-1-938229-19-0

Kathy Rice:
*The Pie Place Café Cookbook:
Food & Stories Seasoned by the North Shore*
Softcover: ISBN 978-1-938229-04-6

*Secrets of The Pie Place Café:
Recipes & Stories Through the Seasons*
Softcover: ISBN 978-1-938229-32-9

Howard Sivertson:
Driftwood: Stories Picked Up Along the Shore
Hardcover: ISBN 978-0-942235-91-3

*Schooners, Skiffs & Steamships:
Stories along Lake Superior's Water Trails*
Hardcover: ISBN 978-0-942235-51-7

Tales of the Old North Shore
Hardcover: ISBN 978-0-942235-29-6

The Illustrated Voyageur
Hardcover: ISBN 978-0-942235-43-2

*Once Upon an Isle:
The Story of Fishing Families on Isle Royale*
Hardcover: ISBN 978-0-962436-93-2

Frederick Stonehouse:
*The Last Laker: Finding the Deadliest Storm's
Lost Shipwreck*
Softcover: ISBN 978-1-938229-23-7

*Wreck Ashore: United States
Life-Saving Service,
Legendary Heroes of the Great Lakes*
Softcover: ISBN 978-0-942235-58-6

Shipwreck of the Mesquite
Softcover: ISBN 978-0-942235-10-4

Haunted Lakes (the original)
Softcover: ISBN 978-0-942235-30-2

Haunted Lakes II
Softcover: ISBN 978-0-942235-39-5

Haunted Lake Michigan
Softcover: ISBN 978-0-942235-72-2

Haunted Lake Huron
Softcover: ISBN 978-0-942235-79-1

Julius F. Wolff Jr.:
Julius F. Wolff Jr.'s Lake Superior Shipwrecks
Hardcover: ISBN 978-0-942235-02-9
Softcover: ISBN 978-0-942235-01-2

**Lake Superior
Port Cities Inc.**

www.LakeSuperior.com
1-888-BIG LAKE (888-244-5253)
Outlet Store: 310 E. Superior St., Duluth, MN 55802